The Man from Scottsboro

What flag will fly for me
When I die?
What flag of red and white and
blue,
Half-mast, against the sky?
I'm not the President,
Nor the Honorable So-and-So.
But only one of the
Scottsboro Boys
Doomed "by law" to go.
August 19th is the date.
Put it in your book.
The date that I must keep with
death.
Would you like to come and look?
You will see a black boy die.
Would you like to come and cry?
Maybe tears politely shed
Help the dead.
Or better still, they may help you—
for if you let the "law" kill me.
Are you free?
August 19th is the date.
Clarence Norris is my name...

—*Langston Hughes*
from "August 19th... A Poem for
Clarence Norris"

The Man from Scottsboro

Clarence Norris and the Infamous 1931 Alabama Rape Trial, in His Own Words

by

Kwando Mbiassi Kinshasa

with a foreword by

HAYWOOD BURNS

McFarland & Company, Inc., Publishers
Jefferson, North Carolina, and London

The author is grateful for permission to reprint the following material: Twenty-two lines from "August 19: A Poem for Clarence Norris" by Langston Hughes, ©1994 by the estate of Langston Hughes, reprinted by permission of Alfred A. Knopf, Inc., and Harold Ober Associates. *Hoboes: Wandering in America, 1870–1940*, ©1994 by Richard Wormser, reprinted by permission of Walker and Company, 435 Hudson Street, New York NY 10014, all rights reserved. "The Scottsboro Case," from *Felix Frankfurter on the Supreme Court: Extrajudicial Essays on the Court and the Constitution*, ed. by Philip B. Kurland, Cambridge, Mass.: Harvard University Press, ©1970 by the President and Fellows of Harvard College, reprinted by permission of the publishers. "Communism," from the *Bulletin of the University of Georgia*, Volume 35, no. 2 (November 1934), by Rollins Chambliss, reprinted by permission of the University of Georgia. "Report of Neuropsychiatric Examination of Clarence Norris," from the Allan Knight Chalmers Collection, reprinted by permission of Boston University Libraries, Special Collections. Articles from the *Chicago Defender* reprinted by permission of the *Chicago Daily Defender*. Articles from the *New York Times* ©1931, 1932, 1933 by the New York Times Company, reprinted by permission.

British Library Cataloguing-in-Publication data are available

Library of Congress Cataloguing-in-Publication Data

Kinshasa, Kwando Mbiassi.
The man from Scottsboro : Clarence Norris and the infamous 1931 Alabama rape trial, in his own words / by Kwando Mbiassi Kinshasa ; with a foreword by Haywood Burns.
p. cm.
Includes index.
ISBN 0-7864-0276-8 (library binding : 50# alkaline paper) ∞
1. Scottsboro Trial, Scottsboro, Ala., 1931. 2. Norris, Clarence — Trials, litigation, etc. I. Norris, Clarence. II. Title.
KF224.S34K56 1997
345.761'9502532 — dc21 96-45530
CIP

Manufactured in the United States of America

McFarland & Company, Inc., Publishers
Box 611, Jefferson, North Carolina 28640

In memory of Haywood Burns
who fought for justice, and to
those who still suffer injustices

Contents

Foreword

by Haywood Burns

The Scottsboro Case is an American story—at once tragic and gripping, ultimately, perhaps, ennobling. It is a window on a nation and a people at a point in time, with reflections forward and back of elements of national character that span all time, from the carving of European colonies out of a native wilderness down to the present moment. Dr. Kwando M. Kinshasa has done us all a great service in locating Clarence Norris, in 1980 the sole surviving "Scottsboro Boy," and through this volume bringing us Mr. Norris' story in his own voice. In so many ways, it is also our own story.

Scottsboro is the story of American justice at work—albeit the peculiar and perverse southern variety of justice in the 1930s and 1940s. It provides insights into the psychosexual social pathology that would seek to burn nine young black men (seven of whom were teenagers) either on the lynch mob's fiery pyre or in the state of Alabama's electric chair, basing its justification on the strength of two white women hoboes' unsubstantiated and unfounded claims of rape, even after one of these women recanted her testimony. Mr. Norris and Dr. Kinshasa worked together to provide an unusual and up-close, inside look at a case that drew worldwide attention and that formed the basis for an international movement calling for the freedom of the Scottsboro youths. This movement counted in its ranks hundreds of thousands of supporters from all walks of life, from unknown peasants in the far-flung corners of the globe to Thomas Mann, Theodore Dreiser, Albert Einstein, and other greats and near greats.

The Scottsboro Case is an important study in the role of mass movements operating in tandem with courtroom legal defenses to secure justice for the wrongly accused or convicted. In many ways, Scottsboro was one of the first United States race cases to mount this type of defense—with later echoes in the Angela Davis defense of the 1970s and the Mumia Abu-Jamal case of the 1990s. As such, it is something of a prototype for studying the way that support groups jockey for position in and control of a case. With Scottsboro, this principally involved the struggle between the International Labor Defense (ILD) and the National Association for the Advancement of Colored People (NAACP)—with the added element of the debate over the role of communists and communism in the defense effort and the charges and countercharges over the ILD's real motive for involvement (i.e., whether to free the Scottsboro boys or to use their persecution and deaths for the ILD's larger political agenda). Through Clarence Norris, we get to know what these issues looked like and felt like from the inside.

Scottsboro deserves our close scrutiny not only because of the social, political, and historical lessons to be learned but also because of the jurisprudential landmark associated with it. Unwittingly, unintentionally, the Scottsboro defendants made constitutional law. *Powell v. Alabama*, decided by the United States Supreme Court, not only broke new ground in the cases of the Scottsboro accused but became a major part of the foundation upon which rests the modern right to counsel for all criminally accused.

Tracing the Kafkaesque horror of the Scottsboro case through Mr. Norris' eyes, it is difficult not to be struck by the presence of unlikely heroes or unexpected common decencies: the white southern judge who paid more heed to the call for truth than to the clamor of the mob; the white hobo boys who would not participate in the railroad; the white organizers who, despite great personal jeopardy, went behind the "Cotton Curtain" to organize for the defense effort; and yes, even Ruby Bates, the initial accuser who had the strength to withdraw her story and defy all the pressure that was launched against her for doing so. Norris and Kinshasa make it clear that the rounded telling of this story does not allow for cardboard characters or snap judgments of those who lived it.

For all this book tells us about the Scottsboro Case, the authors have also given us great insights into the life and era of Clarence Norris himself. In this sense, what we have here is an important historical document. Through the first-person narrative, we are given a rich account of the life of a Deep South sharecropper—not just of the hardness of the life, though there is that, but also of the rituals and folkways of southern African Americans of that period. We travel with him to the labor camps, coal mines, and factories of the Depression and are introduced to a life of riding the rails, the life of so many American vagabonds who had no fixed home and no regular work. This book is an important oral history of life as Clarence Norris lived it—in a southern prison; in post–World War II Harlem; as a hustler in the underground economy; and as a fugitive from southern justice.

Dr. Kinshasa has enhanced an already rich narrative with informative, interspersed segments, original correspondence, and a valuable set of appendices. In the end, this volume goes far beyond the account of an infamous case as told by one of the principal participants. It is an odyssey of the human spirit. Clarence Norris, after overcoming injustice, racism, poverty, illiteracy, and so much more, looks back and shares his life's philosophies, opining on the "sophisticated lynching" that goes on today and holding forth on subjects as diverse as romance, family values, welfare, health care, and police corruption — not always in a manner that would garner the widest acceptance in progressive circles but in an honest, confident, engaging way that makes it clear that the "Scottsboro boy" emerged, through his life's saga, as nothing less than a man.

The late Haywood Burns was University Law Professor, City University of New York, and chair emeritus of the National Conference of Black Lawyers.

Preface and Acknowledgments

Clarence Norris stood at least six feet two inches. He towered over those who were even taller than himself. More significantly, he had the look of an individual steeled by life in those things one needed in order to survive with composure. His eyes betrayed a keen sense of observation, as well as a cold, dispassionate personality that could recognize any sign of threat, confusion, or weakness in a challenger. Anyone who has lived through the turmoil of war, death, or sharecropping during the depression of the 1930s would know this face, in which every single line of every single day had been etched by countless and often excruciating decisions. Yet, this was the face of a man who, while witnessing more than his share of life's tragedies, kept his own counsel.

I sat there, on the edge of the couch, not wanting to appear overconfident or too eager, yet knowing full well that this was going to be a significant and possibly demanding interview with a person whose life, to a large extent, personified the African American's experience with social racism and judicial bias. Norris sat back in an easy chair, smoking his ever-present cigar, seemingly comfortable in the knowledge that his own well-being depended solely on an ability to outthink, outfox, and outmaneuver others. In essence, he was a knowledgeable warrior, entangled by the realities of a society determined to limit those expressions of psychological and physical freedom that have historically disavowed any promise of genuine validation beyond that of mere social tolerance for him and others of his race. Accordingly, Norris' description of his life is replete with critical distinctions between the often convoluted notions of economic survival and judicial justice. Essentially, life had taught him that to survive in a hostile world fraught with backbreaking work and limited expressions of fulfillment, people must be decisive in their relationships with others while avoiding any excessive demonstrations of sentiment. Herein lies an intriguing irony in Clarence Norris' remembrances: his is an account of an African-American male who achieved manhood, public recognition, and celebrity status as a victim of racial oppression yet whose humanistic qualities of love, strength, pain, and determination were recognized only in a most simplistic, insulting manner by the outside world. His account is an excursion into the sensibilities of a man who, having no premeditated desire to confront the immoral baggage of a racist society, found himself immersed with others in the political intransigence known as American justice. In this respect, the following account is the recollection of a youth who was forced into manhood before his time, and at last became a man who *was* his time — a representative of a painful chapter of American history. He will always be a source of inspiration in understanding the African-American experience and the path we tread.

I salute Ms. Willie-Mae Lacy's foresight in attending a social gathering in New York where she met Clarence Norris. It was this chance meeting that set the stage for my introduction to Mr. Norris a few weeks later.

Though Mr. Norris is now deceased, my recollections of our subsequent nine-year friendship, and of my friendship with his companion and associate Ms. Mamie Dixon, are warmly felt and cherished.

Special thanks must be given to the staff at the Schomburg Center for Research in Black Culture, who in the early stages of this project allowed Mr. Norris and me to review their archival photo collections pertaining to the Scottsboro Case. As a result, we were able to place captions and dates on numerous photos that until then had been unidentifiable. Mr. Norris was extremely thankful that he could assist in this effort.

Special appreciation is expressed also to Jean Blackwell Hutson, Marie Yearwood, Jim Huffman, and James Murray. Their efforts in guiding me toward the indispensable NAACP and ILD papers were especially helpful.

I thank the staff at Howard University's Moorland-Springarn Research Center for their expertise and collegiality in granting me permission to view archival material pertaining to Langston Hughes and the Scottsboro Case.

Similarly, I wish to thank Ms. Carol Hunter, of the Birmingham Public Library in Alabama, and the Alabama Department of Archives and History.

I could not have completed this manuscript without the gracious assistance of academic institutions and media agencies such as the University of Georgia, Boston University, the Library of Congress, the National Archives, Harvard University Press, the *New York Times*, the *Chicago Defender*, the *People's Weekly World Newspaper*, and Bettmann Newsphotos.

I am also indebted to my wife, Imani Kinshasa, whose analytical abilities and patience helped me stay focused on the implications of Norris' thoughts, particularly his thoughts on the years he spent on death row. Her own discussions with Mamie Dixon added immensely to the overall perspective of this book.

Finally, I wish to recognize the importance of Clarence Norris' life, and the valuable lessons I derived from it. I will always be grateful for his tutelage.

K.M.K., Fall 1996

Introduction

In the summer of 1868, some three years after the end of America's Civil War, the Fourteenth Amendment was added to the American Constitution. This amendment in effect granted citizenship to over four million people of African descent and, in doing so, guaranteed these former slaves (freed by the Thirteenth Amendment) their constitutional right to due process of law. However, the vast majority of this populace lived throughout the southern states, where state constitutions were designed to abridge those rights that blacks might assume under the federal Constitution. In a sense, the defeated Confederacy was still in a state of judicial rebellion against federal prerogatives such as the Fourteenth Amendment.

For the next ten years, a period of Reconstruction was envisioned by many northerners for the former Confederate states, with the expectation that some equitable political relationship could be developed between former slaves and masters. By 1877, this experiment in social engineering had essentially been terminated and northern political and economic support for southern blacks diminished in the face of rising southern white resistance to the political and economic parity of the races. By 1896, African-American civil rights had been abridged by a number of judicial decisions such as *Plessy v. Ferguson* in Louisiana, which was soon to become a template for the legal separation of the races in every aspect of American life. African-American rights under the law was quickly replaced by mob justice and Jim Crow legislation.

Southern racism and terror campaigns against blacks in the first two decades of the twentieth century, as well as soil erosion and boll weevil plagues, pushed an increasing number of blacks away from sharecropping as a means for economic survival. Many blacks began to migrate either to southern urban centers or northern industrial areas. With the stock market crash of 1929, an ever-deepening economic crisis forced both poor blacks and poor whites to take to the roads and rails in search of employment. By 1930, 50 percent of southern blacks were already unemployed; having little or no money, they either starved or lived by their own wits. For those who chose the latter, traveling as a "hobo" was a way of finding work and consequently some food.

It was under these circumstances in March 1931 that Clarence Norris and eight other black youths found themselves on a freight train travelling from Georgia up into Tennessee and then down into northern Alabama. Somewhere between the towns of Scottsboro and Paint Rock, Alabama, a fight developed between a group of black hoboes and a group of white hoboes. When the train arrived in Paint Rock, the local sheriff and his deputies forcibly ejected nine black youths and two white women from the train. Fearing that they would be arrested as vagrants, the women charged that they had been raped by the nine black youths. Within a few days, all nine had been transported to Scottsboro, Alabama, convicted of rape, and sentenced to death. The plight and subsequent trials and convictions of these nine, now identified by the local and national newspapers as the "Scottsboro Boys," became an international cause célèbre.

Herein began a forty-five-year odyssey in which one of these black youths, Clarence Norris, experienced the pain of being a death-row prisoner for seven years, a fugitive from the law, a parole violator, and lived as a family man, while ceaselessly proclaiming his innocence. He witnessed the divisions, ideological confusion, pettiness, and eventual triumph of organizations such as the National Association for the Advancement of Colored People (NAACP), the International Labor Defense (ILD), the Communist Party, and notable public officials as they argued the Scottsboro Case both privately and publicly. He came to learn that central to the legal arguments surrounding his incarceration and eventual pardon some forty-five years later would be the time-honored question of the African American's relationship to the Fourteenth and Fifteenth amendments and, in particular, of how the Scottsboro case affected the debate.

Mr. Norris and I spent nearly a year together discussing and clarifying many aspects of his life which were touched by his years of imprisonment. Throughout this period he cried, yelled, and proclaimed hatred for the bestial acts perpetrated against him and the other Scottsboro defendants by southern racists. However, none of this seemed to have corrupted his inner core, which judged people by the content of their actions and not by their words. He looked each person deeply in the eye and made his own evaluation of that person's character and its importance to the moment. Though once one of the "Scottsboro Boys," he was now the "Man from Scottsboro."

Chapter 1

Sharecropper

On a cold, damp rainy morning in late March, forty-nine years to the day after his arrest in Paint Rock, Alabama, Clarence Norris sat comfortably in his favorite chair and awaited my avalanche of questions about his participation in the infamous Scottsboro, Alabama, rape case of March 1931. In a slow, self-assured manner, Norris began to reflect on a period of time most Americans would rather forget.

CLARENCE NORRIS: I'll tell you about my life, even though I'm sure some of the things I'm going to say might seem difficult to understand or appear downright silly. The truth of the matter, however, is that these events really happened, not only to me, but to countless others whose names you'll never know.

I was born in a little country town in Georgia called Warm Springs, on July 12, 1912. Back then Warm Springs wasn't very big; however, it received some notoriety as Franklin Roosevelt's summer home. I can remember that there was a large hotel in this town, as well as a public swimming pool and cabins for tourists all over the place. However, being country folk, we didn't travel to town too often, ... didn't really come into contact with other blacks living in town, ... and most certaintly never gave a moment of thought of staying at this hotel. In fact, the only time I came to town is when my parents took me in the wagon to buy supplies. Town was a foreign land with strange people in good clothes.

My family was about the average size for country folk, that is to say, I had seven sisters and four brothers, of which two brothers and a sister died when they were real small. But as families go, we had enough hands to do sharecropping, and that's the only kind of work I remember as a child. I chopped cotton, pulled leaves from corn, tied it up, dried it up, and picked it up to put in the barn, and of course I also fed the stock. All of this around the age of ten, or maybe even younger. That's how come I didn't get any schooling, I had to work all the time.

Most youngsters today don't know anything about real farmwork, not to mention sharecropping. For example, we raised cotton, corn, wheat, and oats,

Sharecropper and his children plowing a field in Georgia in the 1930s (photograph courtesy of the Library of Congress).

but our main crop was cotton and corn. The oats we fed to the stock, and the wheat we would harvest in the fall so that flour could be made out of it. But man, let me tell you, you ain't did nothing until you pick cotton with your hands. But before you could ever hope to get a good cotton boll, or what we called a "square," you had to make sure that back in March you planted it correctly and that was a task.

You see, cotton was planted in the South from March up until as late as May, depending on the ground. By June and July you should be working to rid the soil of grass and weeds from around the plant, because in or around September, this plant is just about ready to bloom into what we called a square. That of course is if the boll weevil hasn't eaten the plant away.

Now you plant cotton in rows. We used something called a "mule pull." A mule pull was a box tied up to a mule which drops seeds in the ground as it was pulled down the rows. This was still a lot of work, in fact you always had to figure out how much of the land could be worked ahead of time. Some people had what we called a one-horse farm, which was about twelve to fourteen acres of land. On this kind of farm you could raise cotton plus corn as cash crops and tomatoes, okra, and potatoes for yourself.

My daddy had a one-horse farm in Molina, Georgia, about twenty or thirty miles from Warm Springs and, yes, I was always working it. You've heard the statement "from sun up to sun down," well, that was us. If you didn't work, you didn't eat. It was as simple as that. Besides helping to plant cotton, corn, and wheat, me and my older brother had to take the corn to a "mealhouse" to have it grounded into flour. Back then if you lived on a farm, you wouldn't run down to the store to get cornmeal or flour, you simply took either wheat to the mill to be ground into flour, or corn to be ground into cornmeal.

While daddy had this one-horse farm, he didn't own the land, what I mean is that he was a sharecropper. When you're sharecropping like us, for every one bale of cotton you raised, the owner of the land got one bale ... at least that was the way it was done in some places. In fact, this system was called "farming on halves." Whatever you raised along with cotton was important, but not as important as cotton.

Some farmers wanted one-half of every damn thing you raised, whether it was cotton, corn, vegetables, or anything. But in the final comedown, the farm owner wanted one half of the *cotton* you raised. They could demand this because the land was theirs! Their deed to the land also allowed them to furnish us tenants with all of the needed tools for ploughing at a cost sufficiently high enough to convert the farmer into a creditor each year after harvest. You might come out financially ahead by some $50 to $100 based on the owner's figuring, but by the time you purchase next season's seeds and repair farming equipment, you'll find yourself right back in debt again to the farmer, who usually owned the supply stores in town.[1]

Furthermore, some of the younger "crackers" were very slick. They would let you have all of the wheat or all of the corn, because the real money was with cotton. Let me tell you something, they knew you had to sell your cotton right away because this was the only way you could get money to buy clothes and other items. So the big man who you are working for would put his share of the cotton harvested in a warehouse and let it sit there until the price of cotton increased. If it was 10¢ a pound, he ain't selling it until it goes up to 12¢, 13¢, or 15¢ a pound. That's how he would manipulate the market price and have an advantage over the little man, who had to sell his crop in order to eat. In fact, the farm owner would buy you out anyway. He would then put your cotton in his own warehouse until the price jumped up to, maybe, 20¢ or 25¢ a pound. One year cotton went up as high as 35¢ and 40¢ a pound!

I remember one year when I was a young fellow, my daddy made out pretty good with our crop, so he bought a new rubber-tire buggy and a horse. I was real small, but this is something you just don't forget. He paid as much for that horse in those days as you would for those early Model-T Fords. I think he paid something like $500, $600, or $700. Keep in mind, in them days, most folks had buggies before they bought cars. Of course, this was rare, and I think this was the only time my daddy ever profited as a sharecropper.

Nearly every season you wound up having to go to the owner to get seeds because now you're in debt to him. He then purchased seeds and furnished the fertilizer, so that whatever you raised and sold was used to pay for *your* part of the fertilizer.

Migrationist Henri Florette notes:

> As the price of cotton climbed from an average of $.0717 a pound between 1890 and 1902 to $.1062 between 1903 and 1915 and as high as $.2154 in the next decade, the efficient farm owner, beloved of Booker T. Washington, theoretically stood a chance of improving his condition and adding to his holdings. But, as Ray Standard Baker pointed out, in actuality most of the 552,400 black tenant farmers were very poor and rarely got an opportunity to better their situation; in fact, they almost never ended a year free of debt. Ignorant and illiterate, they signed (or X'd) contracts that they could not read or could not understand, and from which the law offered them no relief because, as Woodson says, "for them law is the will of the particular [planter] with whom they may be dealing." According to the usual arrangement, tenants had to buy their seed and supplies on credit from the plantation owner, paying him back with a quarter to a third of the crop they made. Exorbitant charges for purchases and interest usually ate up any remaining profit, and before the next crop the tenant was deeper in debt than the year before. Farmers kept their tenants in line more or less roughly; when Ray Standard Baker asked one landlord how he managed his tenants, the man picked up a hickory wagon-spoke and said, "When there's trouble I just go down with that and lay one or two of 'em out." Hopeless poverty and ill treatment did not encourage tenants to put down roots, or take an interest in school, church, co-operative ventures, and causes concerning the community or nation. Their tendency to move on from one place to another in search of a livable life for themselves and their children might, if they had been white, have been approved of as showing ambition; but when blacks moved along, they won the reputation of being natural migrants and drifters.[2]

CLARENCE NORRIS: Outside of cotton, your biggest cash crop were your vegetables. For example, you take your green vegetables, ... now that was something you could raise all over the farm. Even green corn, which we called "roast heads," was used. You could fry it or boil it just like what you see today in cans. We would give the hard corn to the stock to eat and take the other corn to the mill and have it ground into meal. But the largest amount had to be saved as feed for our stock such as the hogs, cows, mules, and horses.

For us, hogs were really important as a food source. We would usually kill a few during the winter. Once killed and cleaned out, we would salt them down then hang them up for a period of time. Eventually you'd wash the salt off and hang them to dry. Once dry, your final step was to "smoke them" in a place called a smokehouse by making a fire with hickory wood. If you let the wood burn slowly, the hickory smoke would help to preserve the meat. This is how every part of the hog, during my time in the country, was cured. We used the same process for sausages, ham, shoulders, pig feet, whatever. There's no part of the hog that you don't eat, except the hair and the hoof.[3] Even its guts are eaten. You know, chitterlings is eaten, especially around hog killing time, that's when they're fresh. You'd soak 'em, clean 'em, and cook 'em. Sometimes chitterlings were dried and then stuffed with all kinds of meat, something like a sausage. You would hang them up in the smokehouse and "cure 'em." One thing, however, was certain. Once the black sharecropper showed any level of success at making it as a tenant, trouble was close by.

For example, the owner of the farm we worked on would now and then come by our place, riding a horse like he was "massa," telling us to get the grass out of this area, mend the fences over there, get the weeds from around the corn, and so on. Sometimes his "inspecting" of the land was done in a somewhat friendly manner, other times it was a "must" attitude. This arrogant attitude was generally the basis for trouble. In fact, that's how come a whole lot of black and white farmers was murdered on each side. White folk, you know, "crackers," was always trying to tell you what you're going to do. Then they'll switch up and want things another way and eventually there would be an argument. If you can understand that, then just add the presence of my daddy riding around with a new buggy and a horse while being a sharecropper!

I remember a time when my dad went riding off someplace for two or three days, leaving the farm to us kids and my mother. The owner came by one day looking for my dad to do some work. When he realized that Dad wasn't there he became so angry that he drove the horses and cows, which were out in the pasture, toward a big creek where water was running pretty strong. He pulled my dad's horse over to the creek and shot it through the head. I know this is exactly what happened because my brother and I went looking in the large pasture area, the woods, bushes, in the pines, everywhere, but we couldn't find this horse. So we went home and when my dad returned, he and my uncle went out looking for this horse. They found him dead on the other side of the pasture near a stream of water. It had been shot through the head. They thought my brother and I simply pushed this horse in this ditch and killed it.

Well, he beat the hell out of me and my brother so much that it made me hate my dad the rest of my life. I never forgave him for that. Later, he came to find out that the horse was shot, but I never forgave him. It just goes to show you about people when they think they're right about something. I don't know why he would ask this cracker how the horse died and take his word over his own children. He was just that ignorant. However, I'm not surprised anymore by things of this sort. Look, right here in New York City you have black people who will take the white man's word before they'll take yours, in fact that's what's wrong with the courts today. You can go down to any courthouse and tell the absolute truth, looking them dead in the eye, and they will know you're telling the truth while the white man's lying, but they're going to take the white man's word before the black. Yeah, that's a fact.

Generally speaking, being black and male in the rural South during the early part of the 1900s, such as 1915 or 1920, was extremely difficult. If you were also trying to maintain a family, well this was nothing but a battle for survival. For example, once you became a teenager, like most young people your age, you want to put on nice things and start to like little girls and all that kind of stuff. However, you become aware very quickly that some people are more able than others to get things. Soon you see another boy, your same age, putting on a suit to go to church, while you're wearing overalls. They go to church dressed up in a suit, tie, and shirt, while all you got on is overalls. You feel embarrassed. You don't want to go to church, and you certainly don't want to go to Sunday school, but somehow your mother forces you to go. Man, it was painful. I recall going to church a few times with my mother and seeing white folks listening to our black preacher. For whatever reason, they always liked to hear black people preach and sing, just like they do today. The funny thing about this is that they would come to our church to hear our preacher preach and sing, but you couldn't go to their church! But of course, this kind of segregation existed throughout the entire South when I was coming along. Even in those typical little southern country churches with their log and board construction, capped off with a wooden steeple, the races would be separated. Nowadays these country churches are more than likely constructed out of brick and cement, but the message is still the same. And when it came to singing, our singers would rock the building, especially when they sang "by note." You see, in the South, all you had were Baptist and Methodist, and the Baptist church choir always rocked the building. You haven't heard singing until you hear singing in an old country Baptist church. Maybe it was the wooden floors, which responded with a beat when the congregation tapped their feet in unison. Even the walls of the church seemed to hold onto the singing, making everything hum with deep sounds. It was really something to hear. One thing is certain, that old country church was a refuge for black people. It was probably the only place we could be ourselves, and though I was little at the time, I just knew it was something important for us.

Even back then I sensed that the problems facing black men and women was somewhat different from what white folks had to contend with. For example, while being a black male in rural Georgia was difficult enough due to racism and poverty, black females generally had to face the same conditions and even more. First of all, girls such as my sisters had to work the farm just like the boys. They had to get out there and chop cotton with the best of them. And when that was done they were expected to help out in the house. In fact, this was a major reason why none of us could get an education. At a certain time of the year all of us had to stop school and harvest the crop, chop the cotton, and cut the grass out of the corn and cotton. So for us, regardless how smart we might have been, and for some reason the girls were expected to be a little smarter, there was no such thing as school when the harvest planting season was on. We were out there like everyone else. At the end of a day there was no time to do anything else like schoolwork. This had to hurt our parents. I know it hurt my mother because she also had to take care of us in the house. You know, in a natural sort of way, all mothers and most fathers wanted to give the best to their children. But being poor and not really having anything for themselves, yet owing almost everything at the end of the year to the white man, caused them, like others, to always feel threatened. They wanted their kids to look just as good as the white man's kids, the problem was we always owed part of everything we raised to the white man. And then quite naturally, most white males thought they could do just about anything they wanted with black women, especially if they were sharecropping on their land.

There was this particular day when my father was out working in the fields. Just me and my three older sisters were home. This old white man who my daddy was sharecropping with came by the house. I don't recall his name, but I know he was of the Barker family. Anyway, he came in, sat down, and started talking to my mother. Suddenly he got up and grabbed her, trying to kiss her and all that kind of stuff while pushing her into the bedroom. All of us started to yell and cry and made a commotion. He finally let her go and left the house.

When my daddy came home, my mother told him what happened. Now you see, my daddy and I are two different people, because all he did was tell this cracker: "Don't you never put your feet inside my house any more. And if you do, I'll blow your brains out." Now, if it were me, I would have blown them out anyway! But that's the difference between us. I often think about that incident and what my mother had to go through.

But I tell you what I did do to this white man. I must have been around twelve or thirteen years old. It was the fall season, and we was getting ready to harvest our own personal crops, which we would store away for the coming winter or sell for money. One day I came across a bunch of hogs owned by this same white man which he had turned loose in our garden area. They were eating the corn and everything in sight. I waited until these hogs wandered in to the woods, and then I shot five of them full of buckshot. The next day that old cracker came to the house and questioned my mother, "Does that boy of yours have a gun, and did he go hunting the other day?" She told him no. He said, "Where is he?" She said, "Well, he's not here." He went on to tell her that somebody shot five of his hogs and that he was plenty mad. My mother explained to him: "It was approaching hog killing time anyway, so what's the problem? Besides, my son doesn't have any gun." Now that was something I really enjoyed doing, ... but the point is, back then on these farms, the owners would do anything to try and stop you from getting more or even equal to what they got. We called it sharecropping, but they weren't sharing nothing with us, and in fact were trying to take it all.

We finished out that year, but my daddy decided it was time for us to move to another farm. Well, to be truthful, he would periodically leave home for about two months leaving us with our mother to bring in the crops. The farm owner, trying to get the most labor out of us, didn't want a bunch of children and their mother attempting to bring in the crop. When Dad returned this time, we simply packed up our belongings and traveled by wagon to Neal, Georgia, some twenty miles away. In those days, that was the primary way country folk traveled. In fact, there was more wagons, buggies, horses, and mules than anything. We didn't really get to know anything about cars until 1926 or 1927.

This new farm was actually a large old plantation. We worked this plantation for about a year, but of course the owner took everything at the end of the year. After about a year, we moved again to work for this same old cracker who tried to rape my mother. Now this is how it was. These old white farm owners weren't giving up on nothing, and black folk weren't getting even the time of day.

All of this came to a head when my dad died suddenly. His death was a traumatic blow to our family. You see, he was a man about six feet tall, brown-skinned, and who had straight jet-black hair. He was mixed with some Indian and used to wear his hair in a braid hanging down his damn back. For some reason or another, whenever white folks saw him they just got all fired up and upset. No question about it, he was rough.

I remember one day when I was working in the fields, I must have been sixteen at the time, he told me I wasn't working hard enough and I wasn't doing this correctly and so on. By this time I'm no longer a kid so I told him he couldn't just boss me around like this anymore. Well, he threatened to knock me down. So here we are, a father and a son, standing in the middle of some old plantation, yelling at each other. By now he just about had enough of me. He took a swing at me and missed, but I kept on mouthing him. He became so incensed that he charged me as I moved away and then began to run. The faster he ran after me, the faster I ran straight across this farm. Of course, he never caught me, but I swore then that I would never take another beating from him. Don't get me wrong, he loved my mama, but he was sure rough on us kids.

In any case, when he died, out of respect I had to go to the funeral. No matter how you fought or disliked a parent, during those days you went to their funeral along with family, friends, and lodge members. You know, for rural people and maybe for city folks also, it was at one's funeral that a person's status or importance in the community was recognized or even noticed. We took him to the graveyard with two mules and a wagon. This in itself indicated that he was in somewhat good financial standing with his Mason lodge. You had to pay so much money per month as dues to his lodge membership. If your lodge dues were all paid up, you could be sure that your burial was going to be decent. Depending on your status or position within the lodge you could also go to the cemetery in a hearse pulled by two horses. The only difference being that the hearse is covered and pulled by horses and the wagon isn't and is pulled by mules. Another aspect of the burial ceremony was that the deceased was laid out on what we called a "cooling board," which was actually a door placed between two straight-back chairs with a sheet over it. They called this a cooling board, but of course I knew it was simply the door from our house. They would lay you out on this board dressed with a coat, hat, a tie, for a few days before the casket was ready.

We got some "jack-legged" preacher to carry out the ceremony, paid him some money to say a few words at the grave, and that was it. Of course if you wanted a ceremony in a church, you either had to belong to that church or you paid the preacher to hold the ceremony in a church. Now that's how we buried our dead in the country back in those days. Of course today it's somewhat different. However, for me it doesn't make no difference about how you're buried, you're going right back to where you came from. Yes, one eventually has to deal with this question about heaven or hell, but I don't like to get too deep in this kind of talk because I have to deal with people who have all kinds of beliefs. So let the dead be dead, and that's it.

Since my oldest brother left earlier to work on a farm for wages, I was left with my mother, baby brother, and six sisters to carry on the sharecropping. Being the oldest son on the farm, I was supposed to be head of the house. It didn't take much time for me to see that sharecropping and dealing with a family was all about nothing. You didn't have anything at the end of it all, or anything in between. So I hired myself out to work for monthly wages on a nearby farm. They paid me $30 a month! I did that as long as I could because my baby brother was just about able to pull his weight doing sharecropping chores, and my wages would really help us to survive. But let me tell you something. You ain't worked until you sharecropped, I mean picking cotton and all that, just so you get a little change at the end of the year. I eventually quit that job and went back to help my mother and sisters bring the crop along until harvest, otherwise they would have never been able to do this by themselves. By now I was doing all the plowing, with my twelve-year-old brother helping out.

I'll never forget, one day I was out there in the field, and it just hit me. I just stopped working and started to wonder how long, how many years would I have to work this land in order to live a better life. The more I thought about it, the more I saw the hopelessness of working this farm as a sharecropper. Right there, I decided to stop working in these fields.

Later that evening I told Mother that I had to leave. I explained to her that it was useless for us to stay there, because at the end of the year we were not going to get a damn thing besides possibly some flour, some meat, or some little thing to live on. And even after that you're still going to end up with nothing once the farm owner does his figuring. This really hurt her, but I had to leave. I was seventeen going on eighteen years old, and man, I really didn't see this kind of lifestyle for myself. I told my mother this and then left home.

Chapter 2

Georgia Boy

White man was born with a veil over his face,
He seen the trouble 'fore it taken place;
Nigger was born with a rag in his ass
Never seen trouble till it done pass'd.
—*"The Dirty Dozens,"*
from Hard Travellin': The Hobo and His History, *by Kenneth Allsop*

CLARENCE NORRIS: When I left home around the age of seventeen, things were already pretty bad for black workers. This was just before the depression and the stock market collapse of 1929, when the entire country suddenly found itself in economic trouble. In Georgia, if you were a black teenager looking for work, the only place besides farms to find a job was with Public Works or in these old sawmills. And even then, if hired, you were expected to work some fifteen or sixteen hours a day plus forced overtime in order to receive, at the end of the week, $25 or $30. That wasn't any real money.

My first job was at a sawmill factory in West Point, Georgia, where lumber was "dressed" or cut to specific sizes. I worked there for a short period of time and then went to work for an old white man who was building a highway through Alabama. This job was part of Alabama's Public Works Program, and as such, all the workers had to live in what they called a "labor camp." Everybody stayed in this camp. They had a section where single men stayed and another section for married couples or those fellows who had girlfriends. They also had tents with cots in them and a general store.

Most of the work on this highway was done by hand. You picked up gravel, water, mud, or whatever and moved it from one area to the next basically by hand. This is where I became familiar with a device we called the "georgia buggy." The georgia buggy was a big thing that sat on two wheels. You could use it to carry cement, bricks, anything. Once you filled it up, you got to keep it rolling to where you're going to dump it. This thing was of course different from a wheelbarrow, which had two handles and a wheel. With the buggy, you just rode it, in fact by riding it in a certain way, one person could make it go faster and faster. We also had something called a "slip team," which was a large board that was hooked up with two or three mules, We would lower it so that when the mules pulled it, dirt would be forced on to this board. When it was full, you would untie it, push it or roll it to a certain area, and dump it by hand. So one could say that we built them highways with georgia buggies, slip teams, and wheelbarrows. But man, I had to leave this job due to the hard work and low pay, and even this wasn't easy. During that time, if they caught you just walking off the job, you would be beaten senseless. You had to sneak off, and that's exactly what I did. But it wasn't easy.

Usually when you slipped off one of these public work sites, they would send these "goons" out looking for you, figuring that you were close by. The week that I planned to leave this work site, I made the mistake of telling someone I found another job at a nearby coal mine. So when I slipped away, they sent two goons to the mine to bring me back. But at the last moment I changed my mind and headed towards Camden, Georgia, in the opposite direction. Somehow and unfortunately, I ran into these individuals and they carried me back. When we arrived, I was told to wait in a tent area until they found the white boss. Instead of waiting around, I went to the camp kitchen to get something to eat. One of the kitchen women said, "Look here Georgia boy, the best thing you can do is try to leave now, and go on about your business, cause if you stay here tonight, the man is going to damn near kill you." Man, I left there so fast it wasn't funny. I headed straight for the railway. You see, them crackers were damn near crazy. They would beat you with any damn thing. A stick, a pole, any damn thing. And in the South, back in them days, a Negro hardly ever did try to fight back. If you did hit a white man, you'd be dead. So, if you got the best of one of them, you best beat the hell out of him or kill him because they saw it as the same thing. In them days they'd hang you for hitting a white man. You'd be dead by nightfall, that's right. That's why in the South so many black people were scared of white folk. You'd go home and they would come and get you. If they didn't kill you, you'd wish you were.

This is true, and ain't nothing ever been done about it. In the 1920s and 1930s, working for the white man on these work sites and plantations was similar to working on a chain gang. First of all, they knew you didn't have any money, and even if you did have $25, $50, or $60, they knew you had to work for them in order to get it. They also knew that if you had more than $100, you probably got it from working with someone else, so they would beat you for doing that! Now that's the way it was. Furthermore, all of these sites were nothing but segregated labor camps. The only whites there were damn farmers and those who supervised the work site. The way I figure it, they were probably related to each other somehow. That means whites controlled the commissary where we bought our overalls, shirts, and other items, all of which came out of the little wages we were paid. Yeah, it was just like back in slavery.

Prison chain gang camp in Pitt County, North Carolina, 1910. The inmates were assigned to road work. They were quartered in the wagons shown, which were equipped with bunks. The wagons were moved from place to place where the convict labor was utilized. At each place where the wagons stopped, a camp was set up. Cooking for the inmates and maintenance of the camps were carried out by trusties. The central figure in the picture is Mr. J.Z. MoLawhorn, who was, at that time, county superintendent of chain gangs. Other white persons in the picture are the sheriff of Pitt County and guards of this particular chain gang. The dogs shown in the picture are bloodhounds which were used for running down any escapes from the chain gang (photograph courtesy of the Library of Congress).

The first time I heard folks talking about this I said to myself, no way was I going to be beaten, so I slipped off one day and traveled to a little place in Alabama called Mount Crescent. Mount Crescent was a coal-mining town for the Bradford Coal Company. When I arrived they assigned me to somebody who was going to show me what had to be done. One morning, I was standing by the mine entrance and I saw these people putting on these dirty old caps getting ready to go down into this tunnel in the ground with these nasty-looking mules. I realized at that moment, I wouldn't be working there. No way was I going to go underground if I could help it. So again, I simply slipped off and made my way to a little town called Gadsen, Alabama.

At this time in Gadsen, they were building something like five hundred houses for workers at a rubber plant. I remember the year I went there, 1928, because this was the same year the government reduced the size of the dollar bill. Up to this time, a dollar bill was as big as your hand. Anyway, I worked here for about two or three months doing construction work alongside of carpenters, unloading freight cars loaded with lumber, pushing wheelbarrows, rolling georgia buggies full of cement, and putting in a lot of overtime to bring in $30 or $40. This was hard work for $40, but for a black teenager it wasn't bad.

I soon got tired of this backbreaking work and went on over to Atlanta, Georgia. While there, I met this pretty little girl named Anna Pearl Brown. She was staying with her mother and aunt, but once I started dating her and we started to get real close, quite naturally we decided to get engaged and marry. However her folks nearly had a fit. They had plans for her to go on to college and probably marry somehow in that class. Anyway, we simply found an apartment, furnished it with everything, and basically lived together for two years. Of course, finding a job was a big problem, and I tried everything to find some money. Nothing was going well for us, so I just stepped off.

Most folks I've spoken with often ask, "If you knew conditions were terrible on Public Works sites in the South, why didn't you look for work in the larger towns and cities?" Now I can understand their somewhat disbelief that us black folk were somehow simply locked into a bad situation, but during this time, in the cities, towns, and rural areas, all labor was cheap. And black labor competing for jobs with white labor was explosive and in most cases down right impossible.

Look, I used to do construction work for 25¢ to 30¢ an hour back in the late twenties. If you don't believe it, ask some of the old-timers who survived that period. They know what I'm talking about. In fact, when I was coming up I used to hear a lot of talk about how better it was in New York. However, in 1944, when I first broke parole from Alabama and stayed briefly in New York City, I saw that New York itself was nothing but a damn slave town. And again when I returned in 1953—granted, many things had changed with the war being over and all of that—New York was supposed to be the city where everybody could make a decent living. Man, it was hell getting a job, say nothing about it being a decent one. The biggest thing going on at that time was the system's playing off Puerto Ricans against blacks for jobs. I've seen Puerto Ricans back then, right out of the country, just off the boat, couldn't speak a word of English, getting jobs for $1.25, $1.20, or $1.10 an hour when everyone else was demanding $2.00 and $2.50 per hour!

I had a job over in Brooklyn, on Sanford Street in a foundry in which we ground metal and handled hot molten metals all day long. This was dangerous work, and they were paying us only $1.00 an hour. However, they eventually hired some Puerto Ricans who didn't know what a time card was when it was right in front of them and in fact had to have these time cards tied around their neck so it wouldn't get lost. They paid them 90¢ and 75¢ an hour! Now I don't have anything against them, I'm simply saying that racism was and is very strong here in New York. Strong enough for them crackers to play off one group of immigrants against my folks.

Now you think this a joke, ... it's no joke man. The first time I came to New York back in 1944, you didn't see nar' black man on a garbage truck. All the garbage men were white. They was driving them, picking up garbage, doing everything. Of course today it's different, but during the time I'm talking about, nothing was happening for us or, at the least, very little. So when folks back in Georgia or wherever would tell me about New York, I'd tell them, man, don't be telling me anything about New York, I've been there too.

You see, in the South, while we was catching hell, there were some of us in these here little towns who had some money. In fact, they even had their own land with large frame houses on it. If they had enough land, they would rent parts of it out, similar to the regular sharecropping system, though generally they had enough kids to work the land and pick the cotton all for themselves. A few even prospered enough to purchase a car. You know, back then it was the old Model-T. Now the problem was if you had land, working land, and a nice frame house on it, you were certainly going to get white folks upset. It made no difference to them if you weren't poor like us or rich. If you were black, you had to be mighty smooth to keep your land, because they would take it away from you. Many a black man lost his land, house, everything by force because the white man was jealous. That was all there was to it.

I knew a man in Molena, Georgia, who had a bunch of kids, some of whom were grown. They had a big farm on which they raised corn, cotton, and all that stuff. He had enough money to build a brand-new house right in the middle of town. You know, the white folks let him build his house but wouldn't let him live there! That's right. He had to sell it for what they wanted to pay him for it and then get out of town. Now that's the goddamn truth. I remember when the house was going up. I used to hear my daddy and other people talk about it. These whites didn't want no black, no "nigger" as they said, living that close to whites. Now I really don't know what was going on in this man's mind when he decided to build this house, but I guess he figured that the white folks would see him differently. Well, he had to sell this house, and I imagine he got a little money for it but nowhere what he put into it. He couldn't even force the issue in a court of law like you can today. Back then they would have laughed him out of court and then beat the hell out of him.

But most black folks in Georgia in the 1920s and 1930s didn't have any money to build a large frame house. They were too busy trying to survive. For example, right after the stock market crash of 1929, times were so hard that if you found a job paying 25¢ or 20¢ an hour to roll a georgia buggy full of cement, you were lucky. Right before I got on this train to leave Atlanta in 1931,

I went to this construction site to find work. What I found was a line of men about a hundred or so yards long, waiting for work at this site. They would stand there all day long, waiting for somebody to get fired so that they could start to earn 25¢ an hour digging a building foundation with picks and shovels. I wanted a job, so I got in line.

A man would come down the line, inspecting everyone, picking out the "heavies," the big healthy men, saying, "You, come on," ... "You're OK," etc., right on down the line. Once chosen, you went directly into this large hole in the ground that other laborers were digging. There was this other white man telling you, "Every time the man next to you brings up a shovelful, you bring up one." If you missed bringing up a shovelful of dirt with the man next to you, you were fired on the spot and someone else from the waiting line above the pit was brought down! This went on day after day. Anyway, I was still a very small teenager standing in line with men twice my size, but this man pulls me out of the line and sends me into the pit. I was on the job for fifteen maybe twenty minutes and this foreman yells at me, "Hey, you bring up a shovelful each time this man brings up a shovelful." I said, "Shit, I'm going to leave here." I just threw the shovel down, climbed out of that pit, and walked away from there and went about my damn business.

You see, at this time, they didn't use any steam shovels to dig building foundations. If they could hire laborers, especially black laborers for 25¢ or even 15¢ an hour, they did. Everything was dug by hand, and by me being not really that big, this wasn't going to work at all as far as I was concerned.

They even had black and white chain gangs doing some of this kind of work all over the South. I remember seeing them as far back as when I was a kid. They'd have these black-and-white striped suits on, looking like a polecat, building highways and things like that. Folks used to also talk about this here farm near Atlanta which supposedly had hundreds of blacks imprisoned to do farm labor. I never saw it, but I understand they would bring these fool blacks from all over the country to work this plantation, promising them all kinds of money. Once they tricked them there, they would force them to do all kinds of work and have other blacks to watch over them. I think eventually the federal government looked into it and broke it up. But this happened back then during and before the depression if you was black.

This is why I ended up on that freight train going through Alabama. There was no decent work anywhere, or at least I couldn't find any. People were traveling from city to city on these trains trying to find work, and I was doing the same. Thousands of people in this country were doing this. For some reason we were called "hoboes."[1]

The thought of southern blacks migrating around the countryside has always had a destabilizing impact on southern society's notion of "the Negro." The conveyed image was of a rootless mass of people, lacking in family and

Armed guard watching farm labor convicts working a field. Similar scenes were replicated at the Kilby prison farm and Angola prison farm in southern Alabama (photograph courtesy of the Library of Congress).

emotional ties to any community. They in fact represented a danger that many associated with the mid-nineteenth-century Reconstruction era after the Civil War. At the center of this exigency for whites lay the fear of economic competition from blacks, while at the periphery lay the fear of being socially associated with an outcast race.

Closer examination, however, reveals quite the opposite in terms of demographic realities. A 1964 U.S. Department of Commerce report noted, "Negroes on the whole seem to have stronger emotional and family ties to their current places of residence than the white population." It added that there was "twice as much movement by white family heads between labor market areas as among Negroes."[2]

Although many reasons might explain this discrepancy, one clear rationale may be that white heads of family surely had more opportunities to find potential work, not being laden with the chains of race. Second, the specter of social mobility for whites was not generally tainted with the odor of criminality or its threat, which was associated with black male mobility. Consequently, the 700,000 blacks who left the South from 1920 to 1930 did so with much reluctance and anxiety, for the word passed quickly that to leave was no assurance of a job up north. However, to stay was no assurance of survival.

CLARENCE NORRIS: We were like a traveling labor force going from city to city. Practically every city had a place where we could sleep and fix whatever food we could get our hands on. In fact in most railroad yards, you would find groups of people living there, passing on information, the latest news on what was going on in another city, or whatever. As hoboes, we was like anyone else looking for work, except we chose to travel by train from city to city by stealing a ride. I personally rode all kinds of trains. Some were passenger types, others were either coal-burning, mail, or freight trains. Traveling this way you could cover eighty or one hundred miles in a fairly short period of time, and it sure beats walking. I'll tell you something else, you'd see just as many whites out there hoboing as there were blacks. You'd see us riding underneath the cars, on top, on in those gondola cars which were large open railroad cars used to carry coal or bard rocks called chert.

Survival on the road as migrants or hoboes was always more problematic for blacks than for their white counterparts. And though distinctions between the two groups were always fraught with exceptions, both were disposed to exclaim:

> Long lonesome roads I have been down, ...
> Hobo always havin' hard time ... Sometime I goes
> as a road hustler, from job to job, doing 'most
> anything. I am just a man gottins over the world...
>
> I'm a natural born ram'ler an it
> ain't no lie
> ...my foot in my han'.
> I'm do out-derndest travellen of a man..."[3]

Yet distinctions clearly existed. The history of southern black migration in the latter part of the nineteenth and early twentieth centuries, documented by scores of sociologists who followed "the trace of wandering Blues singers," indicates a cultural beat uniquely adaptative for survival.[4] One observer, Frederick Ramsey, noted that transcentury lifestyles of many rural blacks had not changed substantially: "scattered hamlets, sharecroppers' strips and canebrake shacks where the home-made entertainment was religious chants, reels and jump-ups for dancing, country brass bands playing tunes remembered from traveling 'coon' and tent shows of a century before, and the most rudimentary blues — all the rapidly dying tributaries that had confluxed into the formation of Jazz and the blues as they know today."[5]

For example, Tom Huff, who was born in the Oakmulgee district in 1871, recalled a once popular call-and-response song that, though pertaining to the last Holy City pilgrimage, was also indicative of closer migration:

... That's when — a we walk, walk this milky white
road...
I'm goin' to meet my livin' mother...
Tell her how I made it over my highway...[6]

Southern blacks isolated in rural, cornered-off villages often viewed the distant highway, the blacktop, as a symbol, a barrier that, once reached and even breached, cleared the way for escape to another lifestyle, environment, and in many cases, universe. No doubt much of this feeling of "crossing over" was steeped in not only religious symbolism but also the rejuvenating experience of escaping the deadening confines of plantation slavery. However, in a society caught up in the 1930s depression, any promise of substantive growth by blacks was stymied or ruthlessly crucified. The "highway" was now an apparition, a symbol of the irresponsible black drifter, as blacks desperately sought employment all throughout the South.

"Their hopelessness," wrote Ramsey, "began at home, when they tired of cotton-chopping and plowing, day after day, from sunup to sundown. So they left and went to work along the rails with the gaudy crews, in sawmills gangs, in backwater levee camps with mule skinners, and mud sand movers. Pay was low, and the hours were long ... they lived on beans and rice. They took it for a while, then moved on. Between camps they stole and begged. If they had met God, they would have asked Him for a bone ... the road, which offered adventure, was better than their homes, which offered nothing. Some left with regret, but they left just the same."[7]

Clarence Norris: Funny thing, at one time they were arresting people for being hoboes and jailing them for thirty days or something like that. After a while there was just too many of us and they realized that feeding all these people was just too much, so they just stopped bothering us.

When you traveled from city to city, the first thing you would want to know was were the police harassing the hoboes and which part of town was safe to stay overnight in for a few days. Sometimes you'd find us living in train tunnels, other times underneath the railroad bridges or highways overheads. If there were woods nearby, you might find yourself a nice spot, make a fire from some coal or whatever, and then lay down on the goddamn ground and sleep. When you got hungry, you would go out and beg. It was as simple as that. If you got a lot of food, you would often divide it up with your traveling partners. Some people stayed two or three days in these "hobo jungles" until they rested. During this time, clothes were washed in a nearby creek or river, dried, and put back on. After a while we'd catch a train and be off to another town. That was hoboing in them days. It was the only thing you could do. You didn't have any money to rent a room and you certainly wasn't going to get it for nothing. As sure as I'm telling you this, you weren't going to get up in the morning saying, "well, I guess I'll go out and find a job," because there was no such thing as that. And for some of us, it's damn near getting to that same point right now!

Look at our people today. They would work if they could find decent work but they can't, and that's just the half of it. You got working people out here right now stealing and highway robbing in all of these big cities. They wouldn't be out there doing these things if their money was right. It comes down to this, if you don't get some decent money to pay your rent, the landlord is going to put you outdoors. It's just as simple as that. You ain't got nowhere special to go, so now you're a bum, or that's what people call you. Yet, what happened in the twenties and thirties was worse than today, but people reacted differently.

For example, back then in Atlanta I would go up to a white person's house, go to the back door, and beg for food and think nothing about it because you'd be so damn weak you couldn't do any work for them even if they wanted you to cut wood or something like that. You did this or else you stole to eat. Now any man if he's hungry enough is going to steal to live. That's for sure. I know many a time I would go into a bakery shop and as soon as I walked in they would know I hadn't eaten for a while so they might give me some cakes or pies to eat. But most times you'd have to steal milk, juices, meat, everything. I used to lay and wait for the milkman to drop off bottles of milk and cream in front of stores early in the morning. You'd have to stand back about two or three blocks and watch the milkman deposit these small wooden crates full of bottled milk, cakes, and donuts in front of these grocery stores. Once he left I'd run up, grab a damn box of donuts and a damn quart of milk, and then hightail it. Other times you got so hungry, especially in 1930 and 1931, that you'd cook anything you got your hands on, and you stole everything you needed. Your clothes were about to fall off, your shoe soles would be worn away, and there was no money. It was terrible. Many a day I went by these stores where they used to put all their stuff out front sitting on the sidewalk, and "sized" up my size. Just before the store closed in the evening, I'd go by and snatch a pair of shoes and go on about my business.

I experienced all of this when I was still a youngster, but I wasn't alone. Thousands of people were doing the same thing. If there ain't no work, no money, but you got to eat and you want somewhere to sleep, you got to steal.

Now we didn't take, but we stole, and there's the big difference with today. We didn't kill and take, we simply stole to survive. I went through all of this, but didn't have to kill anyone. Today it's different. People are so fed up they don't care anymore. If you get in their way, it's you or them. I think everybody can understand that. And then some people have kids and no job. No kind of income. If they go up to these center where you're supposed to get some sort of assistance, they get questioned by people who generally appear to be hostile or angry at them. They want to know their age, how long they lived in the city, have you looked for work, and so on, and then keep you waiting for weeks until they tell you anything. What the hell do they think you're going to live on in the meantime? You got to steal something to survive. That's the way it is. If they do find some work, they take money out of your check before you get it and then ask you, "Why can't you save some money?" How in the hell do they expect you to make a living?

I look at this shit going on everyday and say, "Isn't this a damn shame." In this country we got people burned out of their houses, living in a rat hole and still surviving. It's not because they want to live like this, they just can't do any better. I'm not holding up [standing up for, supporting] for no rogue or man who just makes it a habit of ripping off people, however for some, the only way they can eat and keep a roof over their family's head is to steal. It's either live or die ... just as simple as that.

But you know what, other folks who got a little something will holler a bunch of nonsense about the poor not doing this or that while not really knowing what the hell they're talking about. The truth is, they don't give a damn. Poor people didn't put this world in the shape it's in today; the rich did it, and they're the ones that's going to have to reap what they sowed. They rob and take from the poor man even while we sleep. They're always calculating and analyzing on how to get you caught up in some big debt. They run interest on you, compound it, and have you wishing you were someone else.

Let me tell you one thing. As I stated before, when I first came to New York there weren't too many jobs around, yet I was lucky. I was just out of the penitentiary and only knew how to make a living by gambling. Yeah, that's right, I learned how to gamble and cheat in prison, and you know what, many a day I sent my kids to school and bought their clothes off of gambling money because that was the only way. I had to go to these gambling joints and sit up and scheme and cheat all night and all day just so my kids had shoes and clothes. Yes, right here in New York City. Why not? They weren't paying a laboring man no money, I mean only $40 or $50 a week! But when Uncle Sam got through with it, you didn't have a damn thing anyway. Like today, you had to know how to stretch it, especially since you paid $80 or $90 a month for rent, which was the hardest thing of all to get together. You got to eat, you got to sleep, you got to get them kids something to wear to school. Yeah, I know what it's all about. I didn't go out there and rob and kick in anyone's crib [an apartment] when I came to New York, but man, my kids could not have survived unless I went out there and used my brain. Yes, I had to hustle and I was good. I used the gift which I had.

There was one time when my daughter had to have a winter coat. I had no money to buy it with, so I had to get out there and hustle me $100, $200, or $300. I wasn't home in weeks, not because I was stealing, but I was sure hustling. If you can't do that, man, you're in big trouble. You're as helpless as a child. You got to know more than simply being able to "catch" a job. The fact is some people just got more willpower than others. They're stronger while others just give up completely. Now that's sad because they're in a hell of a shape.

I had a woman right down the street from here near 123rd Street who owned this nice brownstone building. She was separated from her husband, so it was no problem in me living there and setting up shop. Once we were really tight I started running illegal gambling games, cutting games, serving whiskey, while living like a champ. I wasn't out there looking for anybody with a pistol to stick up. I was simply doing my thing. Sometimes, of course, I would be picked up by the police, but it was only for a fine. Once paid, I was turned loose to go back doing the same thing. I wish I had them dollars right now which I paid these flatfoot cops because they was as hungry as I was. That's right, I paid off many a cop on the beat, one behind the other. I'd give one of them $2, $3, maybe $5. He'd go tell his buddies and in a few hours here comes another, looking for money. Now there ain't anything wrong with gambling, people just want to have some fun. And if you can make a honest living this way helping them, well that's OK too. I just had a talent for gambling. Everybody has a talent, they just got to use it in the right manner. It's all about survival, man, that's all.

Even as a youngster I knew about that. For instance, back in Georgia during the early 1920s when I was about twelve years old, me and several more youngsters used to go off a few miles to Warm Springs. We didn't realize it at the time, but this is where Franklin Roosevelt would make his summer home before he became governor of New York in 1928. Anyway, we went there to get a job, any kind of work. We found some work at this large resort area with all these rich sons of bitches who would be relaxing and partying all the time. Now our job was to cut the grass, water the lawn, and clean the swimming pool. The grass cutting was done in the early evening with hand mowers, after which the sprinkler was turned on. After this was completed, every night we then had to drain all the water from the pool, scrub the walls of the swimming pool, and rake the sand around the edges of the pool. We'd be there some six or seven damn hours and get $3 or $4 for our efforts. And even then, we didn't get paid but every two weeks. You know, it would come out to be something like $30 a week.

It didn't take us long to realize that these folks had what they called a caddie clubhouse where all kinds of things were kept. This might have been the first time I really stole anything to survive. Anyway, we knew that a window was broken and that all one had to do was to stick their hand through this broken window pane, flip the latch, and just climb on in. One night we did exactly that. We found golf balls, ice cream, cigars, candies, everything in there. We took a little of this and a little of that, but most important some golf balls, you know them real expensive kind. I think they were called "Blue Dots" or something like that. The next day we would meet these golfers out on the golf course and sell them these same golf balls at half the price! Today, people would laugh at this and think it's a joke, but man, it wasn't a joke. If you're poor you're going to do something wrong sooner or later to survive. But you don't have to go out there and kill for a dollar or two just to eat because you can eat without doing that. Yeah, now I know what I'm talking about, 'cause I lived it.

By 1931, right there in Atlanta, Georgia, I saw something at that age I thought I would never see. I mean poverty was kicking everyone in the rear so much that whites and blacks were doing things that in another city or in another part of the country would get someone killed. White women would be selling their bodies to black men and vice versa. these women would be coming in from farms and the suburbs doing anything to survive. It didn't make a difference what color you were. If you had the money, they'd be catching you as you came by, though they were careful not to go downtown as far as I could tell.

In any case, one night a friend and I were out walking in the suburbs of Atlanta when we passed these two white women who were sitting in a car. One of them called out as we passed by: "Hey, come here. You want to do some trading?" I looked at my friend, then glanced back at the car, figuring well maybe they had some goods or something for trade, like food, clothing, or whatever. When we walked back to the car, I asked them, "what do you have to sell?" because we really didn't know what was happening. Well, it didn't take long for us to figure out that they was selling their bodies. Man, we cut out of there so fast it wasn't funny. This was the first time I had seen this, and really man, I wasn't too pleased about being near them.

Now in Atlanta itself, downtown on Butler and Peter's Street there was a little place that had black women "fronting" for a white woman, asking, "You want to see some girls?" These black and colored women would sit on a porch in front of this frame house trying to "catch" men. Black men or white men, it didn't matter as long as you had some money. If someone was interested, and this woman "turned a trick," it cost about $2 or $3. You also have to keep in mind that $2 or $3 wasn't a hell of a lot of money, but back then, for $3 you could stay with them all night long. Furthermore, since money was hard to come by, you had to realize that this same $3 could buy you a lot of food, so this was a serious choice. Then of course you had a lot of white men out there simply looking for black rather than white women, but that's always been that way. It's that way right now.

The way I see it, the police must have been receiving some kind of payoff. No way would they allow this to go on without getting their cut of the money. You can see it right here in Harlem on 125th Street and 8th Avenue. There was a time when you couldn't come out of that subway without some woman propositioning you. It's been that way for a long time. In any case, this is what was going on up until I got on that there train leaving from Chattanooga, Tennessee. I figured the best thing for me was to try and earn some money along the way as I traveled. You know, a little job here and there, trying to make something of myself.

Chapter 3

The Meeting Place

By March 1931, Norris was "hoboing it," along with thousands of other Americans. Driven by a sense of adventure, low pay, and continual abuse by white foremen, Norris decided that the only way out from this vicious cycle would be to obtain some level of education. This meant learning the basics of writing his name, being able to read a newspaper, and having more of a sense of control about his life, none of which Norris could claim. However, money—which was hard to come—to feed oneself had to take precedence over any desire for self-development. To think about learning how to read and to write one's name, some would argue, was a luxury he could ill afford. In any case, these thoughts began to filter through Norris' mind, much as they have for countless other southern blacks trapped by the ignorance and brutality of a political system in distress.

CLARENCE NORRIS: When I heard about this freight train which was heading westward from Chattanooga, Tennessee, down into Alabama, then into a little corner of Mississippi, and back up into Memphis, Tennessee, I figured that this was for me. I figured that if lucky, I might be able to get some money further west in another state and even possibly pay someone or go to a school and learn how to read or least write my damn name. Man, it's a shame when you can't even do that.

Somewhere around the 24th of March 1931 in Chattanooga, I boarded this old coal-burning freight train that worked its way along the Tennessee Valley floor going into Alabama. During this time, these coal burners would reach about fifty miles per hour, but this one was traveling kind of slow-like as we passed through little whistle-stop towns such as Bridgeport, Stevenson, Hollywood, and Scottsboro, Alabama. This particular train had about forty cars, some of which carried coal, some rocks called chert and all kinds of other stuff. If I remember correctly, it was cold, not snowing or anything, just chilly that morning when I jumped aboard this train. I was huddled up in this car, somewhere in the middle cars with eight other fellows who were also hoboing for one reason or another. Though we were all in this car, we really didn't know each other that much. In fact, only a few of us were from Georgia; the others were "home" boys out of Chattanooga.

Now, there was some white boys on this train. They must have seen us getting into this gondola car. In any case, one of them stuck his head over the edge of the car, and when he saw us laying about, he called back to some others, "There's some niggers on the train, let's get them off." This wasn't surprising, that's what they used to do anyway. If a white man saw you enjoying anything he thought ought to be his, he'd get his buddies and then start jumping up to beat up some Negroes. Anyway, this time it was going to be different.

I know these boys thought for sure they was going to have some fun beating on us. So when this white boy returned with a whole bunch of friends and began jumping over into this gondola car, man it was like jumping into a goddamn wolf's nest. We beat the hell out of them. They was hollering, "Please don't kill me, please don't kill me." Some was yelling, "Don't throw me off." But we unloaded them. Others jumped rather than be knocked off. Now I figure, the biggest of them must have been really messed up because this train was moving right along, maybe at thirty miles per hour or so. If they weren't ready when they hit the side of these tracks, there were going to be some banged-up crackers.

Later on, during my first trial, a white farmer claimed that he saw us fighting on this train as it passed by his home. There was some confusion about the truth of his claim, but one thing is certain, there was a fight, the white boys lost, and they were thrown off the train with the exception of one who we felt sorry for due to the train's speed. We learned later that those who were thrown off went back to a little town called Stevenson and told a railroad worker that some "niggers" had beaten them up. By the time the train got to a little flag station in Alabama called Paint Rock, white townsfolk had been wired that some Negroes on this freight train had "bloodied up" some whites. So as the train pulled into this flag station to take on water and coal, a mob of white farmer-types were there to more or less "even the score."

Keep in mind, we're talking about a small rural railroad flag station in Alabama at the height of the depression in the early 1930s. For this economically depressed area, anything that could relieve whites of a sense of frustration and helplessness while offering them a scapegoat for their social predicament was seized upon. What better offering could they have but some "black niggers" who had the audacity to strike a white person, no less beat up a bunch of white males! When the train arrived, it was immediately surrounded by a mob. I mean, man, there was nothing but white people with sticks, guns, pitchforks, and every damn thing you could think of. They searched every part of this train, and every black man on this train was taken off. Folks were hollering, "Let's take them niggers off of there and put them to a tree and hang 'em." All of us thought for sure we would be lynched right there, with no questions asked.

Norris' anxiety about lynching was based in a social reality shared by both blacks and whites in and out of the American South. Northern newspapers such as the *Chicago Defender* periodically published articles describing, as well as alerting blacks to, the latest lynchings throughout the South, thereby providing a warning as well as a "travel advisory" for blacks living or traveling in the vicinity. For example, an article entitled "White Commission Declare Mob Lynch Innocent Men" was published in the *Chicago Defender.*

For black Chicagoans, especially those recently arrived from the South, this title was neither shocking nor amazing. The lynching of innocent blacks was part of the southern milieu. It was what made the South, as many blacks stated, "a good place to be from!" The South was a land noted for implicit assumptions about an existing European-American gentility, defending the gates of civilization while allowing the mob to satisfy those psychic desires saturated with the pain and agony of its own failures. Southern mobs ruled the South during the depression with such a vengeance against blacks that their exploits in terror were becoming dangerously acceptable as being the norm for the South.

This particular article reported the findings of a southern commission on lynching, which found, to its "startling" amazement, that "two of the twenty-one persons lynched in 1930 were certainly innocent and that eleven other victims of mob violence were possibly so." The article quoted the commission chairman, George Fort Milton, editor and president of the *Chattanooga [Tenn.] News*: "There is real doubt of guilt of at least half the victims of mob violence." He added, "Fewer than one fourth of the persons lynched since 1890 have been accused of assaults upon white women." Attacking white southern claims that "mob" rule was necessary when a judicial system became stagnated by procedural and northern liberal ineptitude, the commission noted, "Mob leaders can be identified without difficulty, although Grand Jury indictments seldom are brought." Judicial procedures were thus unlikely in lynchings, due to their occurrence in "sparsely settled areas" and to a "direct relationship between lack of education, low economic status and lynching danger."[1]

Violence between blacks and whites occurred on many levels throughout the South during this period. One could, for example, note that the living conditions for southern blacks were themselves a testament to a system's planned violence against blacks. Notions of direct and indirect violence no longer had any meaning, for they meshed into a socializing, symbiotic catharsis of pain, self-doubt, self-consciousness, fear, and more pain.

Cecil York, a twenty-seven-year-old husband and a father of two children living in the small Tennessee town of Smartts Station, had the "audacity" to address a white store owner, Jack Eagle, whom he knew over a period of years by saying, "Good morning, Mr. Jack." Whereupon the store owner replied, "Where did you get that Jack from, ... I'll teach you to call a white man by his first name." Jack reached for a revolver, and shot York to death as he tried to leave the store.[2]

CLARENCE NORRIS: At this point, two men came forward acting as though they were sheriff deputies or whatever. They didn't have any uniforms, but their jackets had some old gold-looking buttons. It's really hard to remember exactly who seemed to be in charge, but these two guys stepped forward and seemed to take command of this mob. One of them said, "We're going to take these fellows and put them in jail." When the crowd heard this, they got worse. All you could hear around us was, "Let's take these goddamn niggers and put 'em to a tree." These two individuals kind of pushed us through these yelling and cursing whites to a truck which really looked like a schoolbus. Once in the truck they put handcuffs on us and then ran a rope through the cuffs so that we were all tied together.

A newspaper report of this incident stated, "A mob at once formed at Paint Rock and would have lynched the boys there had not Sheriff Calvin Rousseau placed them in a barn and protected them until troops arrived."[3]

CLARENCE NORRIS: With ugly-looking "rednecks" trying to stop this bus, they drove us about thirty miles to a town called Scottsboro and placed us immediately in the town's small jail.

By the time evening arrived, we could hear an increasing commotion of cars and trucks coming into town. These people were coming in by the carloads and truckloads. You would have thought the president was making a speech. No sooner had they arrived when they too picked up the chant: "Bring them damn niggers out. If you don't bring them out, goddamnit we'll come in after them."

That's all you could hear, over and over again. Now the high sheriff had only three deputies, and supposedly they were to protect all nine of us who were locked up in a fifteen-square-foot cell! As he began to realize that the situation was getting dangerously out of hand, the idea of moving us became a point of contention between him and his deputies. The problem was, how do you move nine black youths through a hostile white mob, determined and fired up to see a mass lynching?

One of the deputies suggested that they divide up the "niggers," with each of the deputies taking three and the sheriff three! Well, the sheriff knew better than to go along with that scheme because these so-called deputies were down with the mob. He told them: "We can do nothing with that crowd of people out there. I'm not gonna take 'em out. If they get 'em, they gonna have to come and get 'em, cause I'm not gonna take 'em outta here."

You see, this was like some little game for these deputies, and man, they knew there wasn't any way they were going to bring us out of there and through that mob alive, no kind of way. Now some of the folks outside who were yelling for our necks were ready to storm the jail. This was really weird. You could first just hear a change in the mob's attitude without even seeing them, and then you could actually sense they were ready to try it. You knew they were coming. Everybody in the cell knew things were getting tight. In the middle of this, the high sheriff stepped outside on the front porch of this jail, showed his pistol, and said: "If you come any further, I'll blow your damn brains out. You boys understand me, there ain't nobody coming in here. If you try, if you put your feet in this door, I'm gonna blow your goddamn brains out." But the truth of the matter is that these deputies were in with the mob and I believe the sheriff knew it.

Throughout the rest of the evening and into the night, we could hear those suckers raising hell. Now, the way I figure it, the high sheriff must've eased out somehow or another and called the governor, who was Benjamin Meeks Miller at that time. He must have told him what was happening, because late that night the National Guard was coming in by truckloads and driving that crowd from in front of the jail. You can believe they were knocking some heads too, because this place was full of nothing but crackers who wanted to have a lynching that night.

The *New York Times*, however, reported "the attack" in Scottsboro in a somewhat biased manner:

> Fearing a mob outbreak at Scottsboro, county seat of Jackson County, following the arrest of nine Negroes charged with attacking two white girls, a detachment of militia was ordered to the Jackson County jail tonight.
>
> Sheriff Waun at Scottsboro asked for troops when a crowd which had gathered about the jail became threatening. The Sheriff wired to Montgomery that the crowd numbered 300. Later, however, the sheriff reported that the mob was dispersing, as the night was cold, and danger seemed adverted. The girls who gave their names as Ruby Bates, 23, and Victoria Price, 18, were in a box car with seven white men when the Negro tramps got in at a point between Stevenson and Scottsboro. They threw six of the white men off the train. The seventh and the girls are said to have fought desperately until the white man was knocked unconscious.
>
> The men who had been thrown out of the car telegraphed ahead to Paint Rock. When the train arrived there a Sheriff's posse surrounded the car and captured the Negroes after a short fight.
>
> The Negro prisoners and their white accusers were taken to Scottsboro where the Negroes were formally charged with criminal assault on a woman, a capital offense in Alabama. The white men who had been in the box car were held as material witnesses."[4]

Clarence Norris: The next morning some of the National Guard, with the high sheriff and his deputies, brought two women into the jailhouse. Later we found out that their names were Ruby Bates and Victoria Price, but at this point we didn't know who or why they were there. They lined us up in a little room, with Victoria Price and Ruby Bates standing off to the side, and asked them, "Now, which one had you?" Victoria answered first. She walked down the line, just as if she was inspecting us, and said "this one, this one," and so on until she pointed out five of us boys. Now they asked Ruby Bates which one had her. Ruby simply stared. She never did say a damn word. The deputy sheriff said, "No use ask'in her noth'in, the other four must've had Miss Bates ... yes sir, the other ones musta' had her." Seeing all of this happening, I told Victoria, "Woman, you're telling a lie, you ain't never seen me before." That's when one of these nasty guards struck me with a bayonet right across my right hand.

Now you know, back then, no black man was supposed to call any white person, woman or not, a liar! I did, and got a deep slash from that bayonet across my hand. You can still see the scar from it to this day. They then pushed us back into our cages, locked us up, and we was accused of rape. That's the way that happened. Just as simple as that.

We didn't know anything about the rape charge until this time. All of this was a frame-up. In fact, later, during one of our sham trials, the doctors who examined these two women said that neither of them had been touched by these Negroes in a gravel car. They even stated that not only were there no scratches on their backs, as was claimed by their attorney, but the semen found in their vaginas had been there for days! The fact is, they were just going up and down the road screwing these southern white boys, that's what they were doing. And for this, they was trying to give us the death chair! But you know what, if we hadn't been accused of raping these women, but simply beating up these white boys, we never would have gone to the Scottsboro jail. They would have killed us right there on the nearest tree. That's how strange things were, and in a strange way we were lucky. It was bad enough that we beat up some white boys, but then to be charged with rape! To this day, I don't know why these two individuals with brass buttons on their jackets was insistent that we be locked up rather than lynched on the spot. I don't know if they were policemen or firemen or what because I didn't see any blackjacks or gun on them, but they sure stopped us from getting killed.

In any case, that sheriff was very keen because if he wasn't the way he was, that mob would have come right on in. That's right, he's the only man that kept us from getting lynched. But you know, his life wasn't worth much. I heard later that this same sheriff went out into a mob of drunks who were demonstrating against us a few weeks later and somehow was killed, and nobody knew who did it. Yes sir, the same sheriff that saved our lives got himself killed.

This was serious business. When I think back to those times, I get scared all over. You see, I knew we was going to get killed! Now that's a bad feeling, especially when you know what them people would do to you before they killed you.

The next day we were transferred from Scottsboro, Alabama, to a little place called Gadsen, awaiting our trial. They put us in a jail guarded outside by the National Guard to make sure none of those crackers got to us. We traveled back and forth from Gadsen to Scottsboro with the Guard protecting the bridges on the highway to see if anyone placed bombs underneath them. I mean this was really something else. When we got to the courthouse in Scottsboro they placed five National Guardsmen between each of us. I never seen so many crackers at one place before in my life. They seemed to be just like hounddogs waiting to get a piece of fresh meat. The same thing happened when we were transferred to Decatur, Alabama. White folks just seemed to be crazy trying to get to us.

Newspaper accounts from both the black and the white communities of the country differed dramatically in their projection and perception of the "Scottsboro Rape Case." For example, the *Chicago Defender*, commenting on southern whites' response to the unfolding events, reported:

> For a week this little town of 2,000 inhabitants has been an armed camp while the "Alabama" brand of justice was being meted out to a group of youths who are accused of attacking two white women. Nine boys are charged with the crime and two have already been sentenced to die in the electric chair.
>
> The crime for which the nine youths are facing death happened several weeks ago. The boys, according to "facts" presented at the trial, were hoboing their way north in search of work when the freight car in which they were riding was entered by seven white boys and two white girls. A fight is said to have ensued between the two parties, which resulted in the white youths being ejected from the train.
>
> Later the two girls showed up in Scottsboro with the story that they had been attacked by the nine boys who won the fight. Police at once busied themselves in searching for the group, and aided by the white youths, arrested the nine, seven of whom are under 17 years of age. They were charged with rape and the trial started.
>
> So much space was devoted to the case in newspapers that all this section of Alabama was aroused. Men, women and children from miles around poured into Scottsboro and talk of lynching was heard on all sides. Saturday night Gov. Bibb Graves, who boasted that he has had no lynching in his administration, ordered state troops to the scene.
>
> The trial of the first two boys, Clarence Norris, 19, and Charlie Weems, 20, was begun Monday. Tuesday it ended, and both boys were sentenced to die in the electric chair. The only witnesses against them were the girls who made the original charge. The only evidence presented in their defense was their testimony, which was that they fought with the boys in the car, but did not attack the girls. The jury was out a little over an hour before it returned its verdict.
>
> Judge Hawkins, who presided over the trial, announced that he had received a telegram from Huntsville in which it was stated that the boys were being "framed" and that they should be given a change of venue. He declared that he had instructed Secret Service operatives to trace the message and try to locate the persons who sent it.
>
> Immediately upon conviction and sentencing of Weems and Norris the court proceeded with the trial of the third member of the party, Haywood Paterson, 16. It is freely predicted that he also will be sent to the chair."[5]

CLARENCE NORRIS: When we finally went to trial on, I believe, April 6, 1931, none of us knew what was really going on. The first lawyer we had in Scottsboro was some little white guy out of Tennessee. I believe his name was Stephen Roddy. We had never seen him until the day we were supposed to go on trial. He got us all in a side room in the courthouse and told us that some little group in Tennessee sent him down to Alabama to defend us. He added, "It was possible to save some of your lives if you plead guilty to all the charges!" Now, what kind of damn lawyer is that? We told him we wasn't going to plead guilty to anything which we didn't do.

In any case, all of us were tried in one damn day. Now you tell me how you're going to try nine fu_king men in one damn day. And look here, every time those twelve crackers went into that damn jury room, they would turn right around and come out saying, "We find them guilty!" That alone goes to show you if they had the least idea that we could get any kind of help, they never would have acted this way. They were just treating black people the way they wanted to, and that was that. All of this, knowing full well that "guilty" meant death.

One account of this day described the proceedings in the following manner:

> On April 6 1931 the trial begins.
>
> The jury sits waving to friends and comrades from the jury box. The judge, E.A. Hawkins, raps impatiently for a little order and some speed. Singly [and] in groups the "boys" are herded into the court room, while being shouted at.
>
> They hear Victoria Price relate a marvelous tale: From the top of a box car right next to the Gondola she and Ruby were in — a horde of black fiends leaped down upon them brandishing weapons. In graphic language she describes how she was ravished by six of the boys. "That one — the black thing" she spits from the witness stand pointing, while a knife was held to her throat and while the other three attacked Ruby Bates.
>
> Ruby is put on the stand. She tries to remember what Victoria said — she doesn't get it quite straight — the prosecutor comes to her assistance with leading questions to which she nods her head or says yes.
>
> Dr. Bridges [physician who examined both Victoria and Ruby when they were taken off the train for evidence of rape or sexual activity] is not called to testify. Not one of the men who worked on the train is called. None of the white boys who jumped off the train, nor Gilley — the alleged eye witness. They are kept safely locked in the jail house.
>
> The "Negro" boys were then placed on the stand. One after the other they swear they never touched the girls. Andy Wright, tall, slim, clear eyed, says "I'll stand on a whole stack of bibles and swear I never saw them girls till we was taken off the train." Olen Montgomery whispers, "Even if I had seen them I couldn't tell whether they was men or girls. I can't see."
>
> By late afternoon of April 6 — the jury has been charged, sent out and returns with a verdict of guilty. Applause fills the court house. Word is passed to the great crowds outside — held back by state troopers rushed from Gadsen by Gov. Miller when the papers started screaming the cry of "rape." In fact the

> boys had even been carried to Gadsen under armed escort until the opening of the trial for safe keeping from the lynch mad mob that kept growing larger in the big square outside the Scottsboro courthouse. April 6 was also horse swapping day in Scottsboro, Alabama and the crowds were thick and breathless. "Let the law take its course," counseled the newspapers—"Let the law take the lives of these Black fiends—let's show the world we're willing to let the law lynch them—no matter how our own feelings are outraged." That night, a parade is started through the streets of Scottsboro, a parade that circles the little jail house and makes itself heard right inside the cells with a brass band braying: "there'll be a hot time in the old town tonight."[6]

CLARENCE NORRIS: I can remember sitting there in this hot little courtroom, knowing that I'd never see my mother or sisters or anybody who I care about again. We all were thinking like this, and yes, things were getting desperate. One night we figured we had nothing to lose, so why not attempt to escape rather than simply submit to execution? On this particular night, they put us in a cage with six or seven other prisoners who weren't connected with our case.

Around midnight we started to raise hell, trying to make the guards open the cell door. We figured they would try to beat some heads, and in the scuffle, we'd take advantage of the confusion, overpower them, and escape. Well, they were smart enough not to open the cell door and come in there. Furthermore, we didn't realize that the National Guard was still outside guarding the jail against crackers who might want to get to us. When the guards heard the commotion, they came inside with their rifles, and we knew we done stirred up hell. Them crackers beat hell out of us, yes sir, they sure worked on us that night.

First they separated us from the six or seven prisoners who weren't connected with our case. We were then handcuffed and beaten. There was nothing we could do. They beat us with rifle butts and anything they could put their hands on while we was handcuffed together. We stayed like this all night and throughout the next day.

> GADSDEN, Ala., April 10 (AP).—
> Protesting against their sentences, eight Negroes condemned to death at Scottsboro yesterday for attacking two white girls rioted in the Etawah County Jail today, but were subdued by guards, who placed them in irons.
>
> The Negroes, who were returned here under military escort after being sentenced for attacking the girls traveling as hoboes, aboard a freight train, shouted demands for special food, beat on the cell bars and tore up the bedding.
>
> Their shouts were heard some distance from the jail and Sheriff T. L. Griffin, who occupies an apartment on the lower floor of the jail, removed his family.
>
> Sheriff Griffin appealed to military authorities for aid, and Colonel W. M. Thompson and Captain C. C. Whitehead went to the jail.
>
> With sufficient guards to prevent an attempted break, the "bull pen" in which the Negroes were confined was opened and guards handcuffed the prisoners in pairs.[7]

CLARENCE NORRIS: The following night, a Greyhound bus arrived, and chained like animals, we were transported to Birmingham, Alabama. We stayed there about three weeks before being sent to Alabama's infamous death house, Kilby Prison.

While we were there in Birmingham, not knowing whether there was support of any kind for our situation, a black preacher somehow got permission to see us. None of us had anything to say to this preacher, but it didn't seem to bother him. Every day he'd come by our cell and would go on and on about the charges against us and the evil in the world. Eventually when it was apparent his efforts to get us to communicate with him were not working, he simply said, "You all come and tell the truth, because some of you had these women!" That's why to this very day, I hate a damn black preacher. They always seem ready to either believe anything whites have to say, or they are trying to get you to not protect your rights. We even refused to tell him "go to hell!"

A few days later, attorneys Allan Taub and Joseph Brodsky came to visit us. At first, we didn't know who they were due to their farmers' clothing, ragged pants, and muddy shoes. By dressing this way, the assistant warden, thinking they were two lawyers out of Tuscaloosa, Alabama, let them in to speak with us. Taub and Brodsky no doubt probably told the assistant warden that this was going to be a quick trial and they was simply going to make some fast money. This was believable because everyone knew no lawyer in Alabama was going to do a damn thing to help us.

While these two lawyers were beginning to talk with us, you know, first asking what were our names, birthplaces, etc., this old warden and his assistant kept moving closer and closer, trying to hear every single word being said. One of the lawyers turns around, staring right in the face of this cracker, and says, "Could I have a little privacy with my clients, just a minute or so?" The warden and his assistant were so stunned by this request, they just backed up. In just that instant, Brodsky told us: "Don't worry, we're not out of Tuscaloosa, but from New York City. We've come to help you. Don't worry about going to the Penitentiary." Well, man, none of us knew anything about New York City, and if the warden would have suspected anything, these two white boys might have had some trouble getting out of Birmingham in one piece. In any case, this was the best news we heard since this whole thing began. We heard later on that the very next day, the Birmingham newspapers were lit up, saying that the ILD [International Legal Defense] was taking the case.

Not too long after these lawyers visited us they transferred us to Kilby prison, also known as "the death house." Assuming we were going to be executed, they placed us on death row, which was full of nothing but blacks. During this same week, William L. Patterson, Ben Davis, and some other folks came down to Kilby Prison and informed us that July 10 was set for our execution, but don't worry about it because our case was being appealed and going to a higher court. It wasn't too long after these ILD folks visited us that Walter White and Roy Wilkins and some others from the NAACP [National Association for the

Advancement of Colored People] came down to visit us at the death house. We explained to them that all of us had agreed to let the ILD represent us and that they were already fighting to save our lives from going to the chair on July 10. The problem was, these NAACP folks didn't want to hear this. They were telling us that the ILD was going to get us killed and there was no way the state was going to allow Communists to save us, and that everybody knew that they were out there only to use us for their own political purposes.

This went on a long time. However, most of us refused to accept the NAACP because they weren't there for us in the beginning of this case. In fact they refused to represent those of us who did want them as their attorney, because the rest of us wanted the ILD. Furthermore, several basic organizational differences made it difficult for these two groups to work together for our benefit. First of all, they had a different ideological orientation. During this time the ILD was a strong Communist organization, but because they were Communist, the government and many black organizations feared them. It was as simple as that. Secondly, their leadership was being harassed so continuously by government agencies that they were always trying to bail one of their clients out of jail, and in those days that meant putting up a cash bond, while at the same time trying to keep their own leadership out of jail. The NAACP argued that it could not afford to get itself involved in a political situation where it was perceived as an anti-American organization simply because it was associated with the ILD in a legal case. And finally, while the ILD was willing to take on a case in the southern states like ours, and fight the crackers "tit for tat," the NAACP was concerned about the legal cost of such a strategy, the constant harassment this would surely invoke for its membership to say nothing about the dangers it felt existed in being associated with national and international Communist and socialist entities.

> Events in 1931 surrounding the Scottsboro case tended to underscore Norris' sense of the legal and political predicament he and the other youths now found themselves in. For example, opinions as to their guilt or innocence became the focal point for debate and violence on both a national and international level as Communist and non-Communist organizations struggled for what they perceived as the proper and just manner of confronting the likelihood of a mass "legal" lynching of the Scottsboro defendants. In this war for judicial prerogative, newspapers and periodicals became a major weapon in a war of words. (See Appendix B.)
>
> For example, as early as mid-April, William Pickens, field secretary of the NAACP, was praising the efforts of the ILD in the defense of the Scottsboro youths. Asserting that "this is one occasion for every Negro who has intelligence enough to read, to send aid to you [the **Daily Worker**] and to the ILD," Pickers created the impression that these organizations with vastly different philosophical alignments might find a common agenda.[8]

The same day that Pickens' letter appeared in the press, the **New York Times** "reported that the Scottsboro boys did not want Communist help. The eight who were sentenced to die issued a statement to Stephen Roddy, two Negro ministers, and a former truant officer, all of Chattanooga. The youngsters, some of whom were illiterate, condemned the ILD and urged the Communists 'to lay off.'"[9]

The following day it was again reported in the **Daily Worker** that three of the parents of the Scottsboro defendants, Mrs. Mamie Williams, Ada Wright and Claude Patterson, actually petitioned the ILD and had never been consulted about having Roddy as the defense counsel for their children. They further denounced the ministers for sending Roddy to entice their children into attacking the ILD. One day later, the Scottsboro defendants reversed their position in favor of the ILD.[10] Interestingly enough, the NAACP maintained that *it* was the first major organization to respond to the defense of the Scottsboro youth. According to Walter White, secretary of the organization, "a group of Negro ministers and members of the National Association for the Advancement of Colored People had been stirred to action by the impending danger to the youthful defendants and by the far from groundless fear that their constitutional rights would be gravely endangered in such an atmosphere when charged with such an offense. These Chattanooga Negro leaders had raised about a hundred dollars to employ a lawyer. Knowing it would have been useless if not suicidal for a Negro lawyer to have appeared at Scottsboro, they retained Stephen R. Roddy, the only white lawyer in Chattanooga who, so far as they knew, dared face the hostile mob."[11]

From this perspective, the NAACP could clearly take credit in coming first to the aid of the Scottsboro youths. However, if so, they must also bear the burden of this legal counsel's apparent indifference to his clients' legal rights, his possible collusion with the prosecutor and a seemingly general incompetence as an attorney. All of which was confirmed by the United States Supreme Court's decision to suspend the youths' execution in 1932, when it was noted:

> (1) they were not given a fair, impartial and deliberate trial; (2) they were denied the right of counsel, with the accustomed incidents of consultation and opportunity of preparation for trial; and (3) they were tried before juries from which qualified members of their own race were systematically excluded... The only one of the assignments which we shall consider is the second, in respect of the denial of counsel....[12] (See Appendix C.)

Within this charged atmosphere newspapers provided a national and global survey of public opinion and reaction to the Scottsboro case, and in doing so clearly became an instrument for social and political influence. Examples of newspaper coverage follow.

> NEW YORK, MAY 1.—Using their night sticks freely and threatening to throw tear gas bombs if necessary, 20 police broke up a communist demonstration in Harlem Saturday afternoon.

The reds staged the protest demonstration against the sentencing to die of nine youths in Scottsboro, Ala. for alleged attacks upon two white girls.

Five of the 400 communists are recovering from battered heads, while four others are being detained in jail on charges of felonious assault on two patrolmen who were hurt in the riot.

The patrolmen were hissed and booed for the manner in which they swung their "democratic" clubs. Men and women reds were knocked down from the blows of the clubs, their placards jerked from their hands and a speakers stand at 140th St. and Lenox Ave. wrecked by police of the W. 136th St. station.

A police official explained that the patrolmen had used their nightstick because the reds had defied a police order and paraded down Lenox Ave. without a permit. This, he said, was violation of the law.

The battle, which lasted for more than an hour and a half raged from Lenox Ave. and 140th St. to Lenox Ave. and 135th St. The trouble began when the reds assembled at Lenox Ave. and 140th St. in a meeting protesting against the "railroading" of the nine youths recently convicted of criminal assault in Scottsboro.

The meeting began quietly with two women as the principle speakers. Mrs. Doretta Thornton was the first to mount the platform. She introduced Mrs. Janie Patterson [from] Chattanooga, Tenn., mother of Heywood [sic] Patterson, 17 years of age, one of the youths condemned to die in Scottsboro.

Mrs. Patterson, who had come here at the request of the communist, told her listeners how her boy and the eight others had been "framed" and were about to die for a crime they were not guilty of. Her listeners were urged to flood the governor of Alabama with telegrams and letters asking for a new trial for the boys.[13]

NEW YORK, MAY 6.—In spite of the attacks the Ku Klux Klan and other organizations made on the International Labor Defense, the organization having complete charge of the case of the nine boys sentenced to die in Scottsboro, Ala., the worker's defense has completed its final plans for the demands for a new trial and the four attorneys retained by the I.L.D. are about to present their legal briefs.

The second letter received by the International Labor Defense from the K.K.K. addressed to George Maurer, assistant secretary of the organization, reads in part:

"Whoever accounted to you for anything? Listen, boy, just come on down to Tennessee, Alabama, Mississippi or any other southern state and ask some white man to account to you, why a rapist is under conviction and to be electrocuted, and see the accounting you'll get. A necktie of hemp and your rotten carcass decorating a telephone pole or tree."[14]

CHICAGO, June 20.—Chicago's South side got a sample of Communism Sunday when several persons said to be members of the International Labor Defense unsuccessfully tried to interfere with a mass meeting of the local chapter of the National Association for the Advancement of Colored People at Wendell Phillips High School.

The meeting had been called to aid the convicted youths in Scottsboro, Ala.

These persons, who were distributed through the vast audience, heckled Congressman Depriest and Dean William Pickens, field secretary of the N.A.A.C.P. who had come direct from Scottsboro, where he had an interview with the condemned youths.

Although the program had been fully arranged in advance, those claiming to belong to the International Labor Defense practically demanded the right to speak. Dr. Herbert Turner, chairman of the meeting and president of the local branch of the NAACP, tried to reason with some of the agitators, but to no avail. Some one threatened DePriest and others kept bobbing up here and there in the audience, demanding that they be allowed to speak. It is believed that the communists were scattered through the audience for the express purpose of having the public believe the disorder was in general. The members of the NAACP here are firm in their belief that the communists had everything prearranged.

After a half hour's effort to reason with the agitators, who were being egged on by their white comrades, a policeman on duty at the school called for help. Two squad cars responded and six men and two women were taken to the police station.[15]

BIRMINGHAM, Ala., June 18. "Scottsboro," according to an Alabama editorial last Monday, "is significant of the whole task which lies before the south today; the task of preserving itself against the passions and misemployments of others, even as it cleanses itself of its own."

Alabamians in general feel that a prejudice as strong as any of which they themselves may have been guilty in the past has actuated some of the committees and individuals from outside the State who have concentrated funds and legal talent at Scottsboro in efforts to undo the death sentence passed upon eight Negroes convicted of criminal attack upon two white girls.

The crime charged against these Negroes is one which Southern law punishes with death and which southern opinion holds the most serious in all the categories. The accused men were subjected to regular process of law and found guilty. Local opinion has considered the trial a fair one. That this opinion is not confined to a so-called "professional" Southern element, but is held by many persons who do not hesitate at times to take issue with their fellow-Southerners on matters involving their deepest feelings is evidenced in the attitude of Grover Hall, editor of The Montgomery Advertiser, and winner of a Pulitzer prize a few years ago for his editorial war upon the Ku Klux Klan. "There was no intimidation of the court and the jury from Jackson County people," he declared in an editorial last week. "The only attempt at intimidation came from New York, where Dreiser's idiotic committee sent threatening telegrams to the judge. It was a fair and orderly procedure from beginning to end, and under the laws of this State, the decision is just."[16]

CHATTANOOGA, Tenn., May 23 (AP).—The city Interdenominational Ministers' Alliance of Negro Divines today broadcast a denunciation of the International Labor Defense for its activity on behalf of eight Negro youths under death sentence for purported attack on two white girl hoboes aboard a freight train near Scottsboro, Ala.

The statement of the ministers said the labor defense interest is "mainly for the purpose of drawing Negroes of the south into the Communist organization, and if the movement is successful it will tear the South asunder and destroy the peace and harmony existing for many years."[17]

The political antagonism between the ILD and the NAACP underlined America's social and economic cleavages as well as its deeply entrenched racism. In an address to a NAACP conference in Pittsburgh, field secretary

William Pickens underscored "the lawlessness of southern justice" by noting that the conviction and sentencing to death of eight youth in Alabama "ought to call the world's attention to the fact that, in spite of the fourteenth and fifteenth amendments, there are still black laws in the southern states." Pickens further noted that "in some respects the issue confronting us from Scottsboro is worse than the massacre at East St. Louis or the Burning at Tulsa. East St. Louis and Tulsa were manifestly in the hands of mobs, while the case in Scottsboro, while really of the mob, is technically of the state of Alabama."[18]

Pickens and other like-minded black leaders and spokesmen were only too aware of the developing political radicalization of the case, both nationally and internationally, and its implications for the "Negro" community as a whole. As a result they found themselves continually attempting to parley the direct attack from political radicals, Communist and non–Communist, who favored direct action against southern racism. A typical example of anti–Communist Negro sentiment was published in *The Birmingham Post* when P. Colfax Ramean, a follower of Booker T. Washington, wrote:

> For more than 25 years I have given my life and training to Negro welfare, social uplift service throughout Alabama, but for more than two years I have been dealing with the most hell-born menace to our industrial, social and domestic relations I have met in all my work.
>
> This city, county and state is flooded with communists and the NAACP. These outsiders have a line of propaganda that means death to our best racial interest.
>
> The great masses of Negroes living and working in homes and industries in Alabama and the south must be taught that Red Communists and the NAACP cannot be of social, political or industrial benefit to us because of their methods and policies.
>
> Race distinction is by no means race discrimination. The south is our natural home and the southern leading white people are our best friends. All that we are and all we hope to be must come from the south and the leading whites. Some 300 years ago we were brought to this land. Our fathers were heathens without a written language, and notwithstanding the chattel slavery we were given civilization, Christianity and a foundation of social and industrial manhood. We have through the proximity of the cultured Anglo Saxon, made more moral, Christian, social and industrial progress than any other race of people on the face of the earth.
>
> The Ku Klux Klan, irrespective of its southern enthusiasm, through its politics and methods, cannot rid the state of these Red Communists or these other outside interferences in our domestic and industrial, political life, but trained Christian Negro leaders can place the entire race in a position of rare distinction until the Red Communist, NAACP, the International Labor Defense, and all other outside trouble makers will be forced to take up their bed and walk.
>
> All that we ask is the moral and financial cooperation of the white people and the work will be done 100 per cent. As a separate and distinct race we must work out our own salvation. The laws of racial development are not along the

> lines of social equality, but in the adhering to the doctrine preached and taught by our beloved leader, Booker T. Washington. His preaching, and teaching is the solution for all our ills and racial evil that might poke up their sinister heads.
>
> "In all things that are purely racial we are separate as the fingers, yet one as the hand in all things essential to mutual progress."[19]

These liberal black leaders were also mindful of a growing intensity of international pressure by radical groups who were responding to the Scottsboro case in street demonstrations which, as in the United States, often turned violent. In Germany, for example, demonstrators allegedly belonging to the Communist party marched and eventually attacked the American consulates in Dresden, Leipzig, and Berlin. Similarly, Communist newspapers appealing to their political supporters urged them to fight against injustice and "judicial murder of Negroes" in the United States.[20]

In Cuba, workers from the Tobacco Workers Union planned a demonstration in support of the Scottsboro defendants, and presented a resolution which stated, "We protest against the proposed electrocution of eight young Negroes at Scottsboro by United States imperialistic murders and regard this massacre as an instance of Yankee capitalistic oppression of Negroes of the United States. We protest this proposed mass murder. We pledge ourselves to combat race discrimination and fight for equal rights for Negroes. We demand punishment for the lynchers."[21]

Prominent scientists, authors and public figures also began to make supportive statements and resolutions. The Theodore Dreiser Committee obtained support from individuals such as Thomas Mann, Albert Einstein and numerous others who were known for their liberal concern for human rights. Sending a cablegram to Alabama governor Miller from Berlin, Dreiser's committee appealed for executive clemency in this case for the eight youth. They also let it be known that, "hundreds of representatives of intellectual Berlin beg you in the last hour for the sake of humanity to stop sentence against the eight young Negroes of Scottsboro."[22]

It was Walter White of the NAACP, however, who in an article entitled "The Negro and the Communists" delineated the position of most liberal and reform black organizations of the day. In explaining how Communist "propaganda" (a term which in the depression had distinct pejorative connotations) attempted "proselyting among American Negroes," he noted:

> As I write, I sit in a large Middle-western industrial city. Yesterday I was told by a social worker of a case he had encountered a day or so before. A Negro Industrial worker employed by a large rubber company was about to be evicted from his tiny, humble home for non-payment of three months' rent amounting to sixty dollars. He owed a balance of forty-eight dollars on a loan, and the loan company had garnished his wages. With a wife and five children wholly dependent on his wages, his wife a chronic invalid, two girls in high school, and the entire family suffering from under-nutrition, the man's wages

are thirteen dollars a week. Less than two dollars a day to feed seven mouths, pay rent, buy clothing.

Two weeks ago I visited Alabama, Georgia, and other Southern States. The collapse of cotton prices will hit the Negro farmers — some four million of them — harder than any other group, inasmuch as they are now and have been for some time on the ragged edge. A recent survey by the National Urban League reveals that in Chicago Negroes form 4 per cent of the population but four times that percentage of the unemployed; in Pittsburgh Negroes make up 8 per cent of the total population but 38 per cent of those out of work; in Baltimore the percentages are 17 and 31.5; in Buffalo 3 and 25.8; in Houston, Texas, 25 and 50; in Little Rock, Arkansas, 20 and 54; in Memphis, 38 and 75; in Philadelphia, 7 and 25.

Usually the last to be hired and first to be fired, kept out of the skilled and semi-skilled trades even when amply qualified by ability and training to perform skilled work at correspondingly higher wages, the Negro unquestionably is suffering during this period of distress more than almost any other group. Lynchings have declined in number during recent years but are still frequent enough to hang ominously over the heads of Negroes, particularly in the Southern and border States, as a not unlikely fate should they stir the mob's hostility, ever near the surface. The benefits of unionization are denied them; the American Federation of Labor has even ceased passing perfunctory resolutions against the color line in union membership, while the majority of its constituent unions bars negroes from membership by constitutional provision or unwritten law.

...It is through such an embittered Negro world that the Communists shrewdly sought to spread their theories and to gain a large following. At first their efforts met with a success which amazed the more conservative leaders of Negro opinion. A man who is starving, homeless, exploited, and oppressed is always a fertile field for those who advocate a change. Many Negroes looked upon the Communist as a new Messiah, a new Moses sent to lead them from the bondage which had become almost unbearable. With jesuitical zeal and cleverness the American Communist agitator sought to fan this flame of discontent which the slave trader, the lyncher, the disfranchiser, the denier of decent jobs and wages and homes had lighted and kept alive through three centuries. He resorted to every possible means to impress upon the Negro that he had no stake in his own land, that a philosophy of complete despair was the only sane and intelligent attitude for him to take. All this was centered about the Scottsboro cases as the basis for a highly emotional appeal. Negroes and whites were urged to give vent to their resentment against the farcical trials accorded the nine Negro boys by sending telegrams to the Governor of Alabama or to other officials of the State, peremptorily demanding immediate release of the defendants. Often the industrious Communists volunteered to write the messages for less literate Negroes. It is reported that Governor Miller of Alabama has received more than seventeen hundred such messages.

When this campaign of threats was denounced by non-Communist organizations like the N.A.A.C.P., the vials of wrath of Communist publications were poured upon them and they were denounced as "traitors" and as conspirators to execute the boys.

White ends his analysis with an appeal to the moral conscious of white America. Ignoring the underlying social-political and historical exigencies of American racial economics, he exclaims:

> There is but one effective and intelligent way in which to counteract Communist efforts at proselyting among American Negroes, and that method is drastic revision of the almost chronic American indifference to the Negro's plight. Give him jobs, decent living conditions and homes. Assure him of justice in the courts and protection of life and property in Mississippi as well as in New York. Put an end to flagrant and unchecked disregard of the Negro's constitutional right to vote. Let labor unions—conservative and liberal as well as radical—abolish written or implied barriers against the Negro, doing so in sheer enlightened selfishness, if for no other reason, since it is self-evident that white labor will never be free as long as black labor is enslaved and exploited. Let employers of labor even in this time of acute depression see to it that Negro workingmen are treated no worse than white. In brief, the only antidote to the spread among American Negroes of revolutionary doctrine is even handed justice.[23]

Clarence Norris: All of this confusion and fighting over us continued right on throughout the early days of our trials. But while this was going on, we were in the dark about political differences of these two organizations. We didn't really know one organization from the other, and only really accepted the ILD in the beginning because they were there for us when we needed them. I said as much in a letter to a Mr. Fraenkle from Kilby Prison back in 1934.

> Mr. Osmond K. Fraenkle
> Dear Sir:
> Your most highly and appreciated letter received. Indeed happy to know that you are taking the case right ahead. It is true that I wrote Mr. Leibowitz telling him that I wanted him for my Attorney. But I only meant under conditions that he cooperate with the I.L.D. He is a fine and able Lawyer and I would like very much for him to be continued connected with my case in the behalf of the I.L.D. If not he is out for as I am concern.
> My mind will never lead me to drop this organization. They have did to greater work in this fight to see that I get justice for a crime I am absolutely innocent off. My mother was down to see me Saturday & Monday also Benjamin Davis. They straighten out things and give us advice what to do in the future.
> I do ardently hope that every wise step that be taken will be a step toward my freedom. I am not loosing my faith and courage but I do hope that this struggle will come to an close in the very near future. I want you and all others who are interested in my case in my behalf to turn a death ear to all gossip concerning Leibowitz and me.
> Wishing all much success in the near future.
> Very Truly yours
> Clarence Norris[24]

Clarence Norris: And I'll tell you something else: regardless of what anyone says about our indecision on who was going to represent us in court, if it wasn't for that communist organization trying to save our lives, we would have went to the chair on the 10th of July 1931. That for damn sure.

Chapter 4

House of Pain

Clarence Norris: Alabama's Kilby Prison, or the death house as we used to call it, was really a house of pain. I spent a total of some five to six years on death row at Kilby, so I can tell you things that would make you wonder about what it means to be human. First of all, once Judge Hawkins sentenced all of us, with the exception of Roy Wright, due to his youth, to be electrocuted on July 10, 1931, we were sent to Kilby Prison. At Kilby, we were caged in narrow cells with small windows which prevented you from seeing anything except a few cells directly in front of you and the guards when they came by. If I remember, there was only thirteen cells on death row. The thirteenth cell was the one they put you in just before you were killed. You could talk with prisoners on either side of you, but you were never allowed outside your cell unless all the other prisoners were locked in their cells. When you were allowed to take a shower, there would be two guards standing there as you left your cell, naked — one with a stick and the other with a gun. They would march you to the bathroom for a three- or four-minute shower. They would make damn sure you didn't leave that shower with anything in your hands, then march you back to your cell. By the time you returned, there would be clean linen laying beside your clothes.

My cell was situated so that over the years I could see many a man walk through a green door, behind which was the electric chair. Now, as sure as I'm talking to you now, I can tell you that I heard many a man crying for his mama and everybody else as they were dragged through that door. But more than that, when a person was being executed, you could actually hear it! You could hear the last words a man said, and when they put the switch on, you could hear the warden say, "You got anything to say before you go?" I've heard some say, "You're killing an innocent man." Some simply say "no, no, no," while others wouldn't have anything to say. The next thing you know, the old Negro state chaplain would be saying some religious words over their dead body.

This preacher was the only black man I ever hated in my lifetime. Though he gave the last rites to many a condemned man and witnessed their execution, whenever I saw him he always seemed like he was getting a kick out of seeing people die. Every time an execution was scheduled, he would enter death

row singing, "Swing low, sweet chariot, coming for to carry me home ..." While the man's being strapped in the chair, he'd then sing two or three verses of "two white horses, coming in line, coming in line, coming to carry me home. Swing low, sweet chariot ..." Yes sir, he'd be standing right there, in that little room where the chair was, singing this stuff about two white horses coming in line to carry you home! You couldn't see the chair, but man, you could hear everything. This preacher had to be sick, but back then we just called him an "Uncle Tom."

Now, that's a job I wouldn't have. Just think of it, how could a black man have a job like that when most of the people being executed were black? Let me tell you something. A few times when this hateful preacher thought we were surely going to die, he'd come around asking us if we wanted to confess our sins to him and all that nonsense. In fact, on one occasion when the Alabama Supreme Court turned down our appeal and set the 13th of May as our execution date, he'd come around singing "the clock has struck 13," and then start talking about the Bible. I would just sit there and let him preach all he want and let him say any damn thing he wanted. I figured he was thinking our souls were being prepared. Yes sir, that was a sorry-ass Negro preacher as I ever saw one.

For whatever reason, having "the chair" so close to my cell and being able to hear almost everything that was being said during an execution didn't bother me. In fact, one day an old guard by the name of Bill Gray and another cracker asked us if we wanted to see the chair. I was the only one who said "yeah." Some of the other boys didn't want to see it, thinking that it was going to worry them, but for whatever reason, it didn't bother me at all. They opened my cell, led me through the green door, and I saw up close what this chair really looked like and even sat in the damn thing! It weren't nothing but a big old straight-back chair. Man that old cracker looked at me like I was crazy, but there wasn't anything to worry about as long as the power was off and you weren't strapped to the chair. I knew the chair couldn't do nothing by itself. Ain't no juice up under your arms or your butt. Ain't but one way that juice could get to you. In any case, I was curious about how it operated. For example, every time there was an execution, I remember seeing from my cell that someone always brought a round brass cap, which I could now see was attached to a set of cables at the top of the chair. During the execution, electricity went through these cables, into this brass cap, through the mold of your head, and finally through the rest of your body. They had a strap that went around your chest to make sure you were upright, a strap to hold your head up, a strap for your arms, and a strap to hold your legs to the chair as volt after volt of electricity went through your head, into the rest of your body, until you were pronounced dead.

Opposite: **Kilby Prison, Alabama. Factory buildings are on the extreme right. The death house is on the extreme left (Department of Archives and History, state of Alabama).**

While I was on death row at Kilby I've seen some seventeen or eighteen people going to the electric chair, or what we would call doing "walk-bys." In fact, back there in February 9, 1934, I saw five men walk past my cell on their way to the electric chair. In one night, right behind each other, just like hogs going to the slaughter, they killed Ernest Waller, Solomon Roper, Harie White, John Thompson, and Bennie Foster. I'm not sure why all of them was put to death, but I do know you could actually smell burning flesh all up and down death row after they was executed.

But the damnedest thing happen back in 1938 a few months after Governor Bibb Graves commuted my death sentence to life imprisonment. By now I was transferred from the actual death-row cells at Kilby to regular population in another section of the prison. One rainy night in November a black youth by the name of Jimmy Brown was being executed, and as his last request he told the warden he "wanted to see Clarence Norris." A guard bangs on my cell, wakes me up, and yells: "Are you Clarence Norris? Get your clothes on." I said, "What in the world they want with me?" I put on my clothes, and they take me down to the front of my cell block. There's this big old guard sitting there. He tells me, "Warden wants to see you over in the death house." Man, I don't know why the hell they want to see me in the death house this time of night. Part of my mind is telling me, "They're going to kill you anyway, and that's going to be that!" Another part of me is saying, "I must have done something wrong." Man, I really didn't know what to think, and I sure enough didn't want to go, but I had no choice. I finally figured that they were going to kill me and be done with the entire matter.

When I finally get to death row, I hear this old nasty cracker, a real black man hater named Connie Vaughn, crying and hollering. Now I first ran into Connie back in 1933 at the Birmingham City Jail during one of our early trial dates. He was always yelling at us because we were continually singing and making noise while trying to keep our spirits up. Connie would always be cussing and calling us all kinds of names from his cell, which was above ours. He'd yell, "Shut up the noise and all that jive you goddamn niggers!" We would cuss him back by telling him he was a pot-gutted mother f__ker who was going to the chair anyway for putting that white woman in that lake." And he would just laugh at us.

Well anyway, there this sucker was, crying and yelling, "Oh Lord, I don't want to die, oh Lord, I don't want to die!" There was three Catholic priests standing there right outside his cell, his mother and father was up there, but old Connie didn't want to talk to anyone, he would just walk back and forth hollering, "Oh Lord, I don't want to die, oh Lord, I don't want to die!" Now, I know this ain't really funny, but that's the only time I ever got a kick out of seeing a goddamn white man going to the electric chair. That thrilled me to my heart. I swear before God it did. You got to remember, he didn't get the chair for killing a Negro, he killed a white woman, and during that time this was something totally different. It seems that he and another white guy drove this woman out by a lake, killed her, put heavy haywire in her car to weigh it down, then pushed it into a nearby lake somewhere near Birmingham, Alabama. The guy helping him got life, but Connie got the chair!

In any case, I was up there the night he went to the chair, as well as Jimmy Brown. As I walked towards the last cell where they kept you just before entering through the green door, I saw Jimmy Brown standing there holding onto the cell bars. I held out this same right hand of mine to him; he grasped it and said, "Clarence, you going to be free one day." I said, "I hope so, Jimmy." Now, I can't hope him no luck, because his luck has run out, now that's a hell of a thing. You can't hope no more because he's going to be killed in the next few minutes, but Jimmy kept on grasping my hand while talking to me for about five minutes. He kept repeating that he felt for sure that one day I was going to be free and that he had made his peace with God. Finally, the old warden said, "Okay Norris, go back to your cell." The guard took me back to my cell, but I guess Jimmy was dead before I got there. The cell block is damn near as long as a city block.

I got to know Jimmy pretty well because he was literate and I wasn't. He would read everything he could get his hands on and then tell me what was going on and who was saying what as it pertained to our case. In fact Jimmy would write my letters for me. Most of those letters that came from me up to 1938 were actually written by Jimmy. I would tell him what to say, and he wrote letters for me to all parts of the country. The tragic part of all of this is that he was only twenty years old, had just married a pretty little sixteen-year-old, who would visit him here in prison, but somehow right after their marriage Jimmy was arrested one night with a pistol in his pocket on some private railroad property. He was sentenced to ninety days for carrying a concealed weapon and trespassing.

On the night that he was picked up, some woman claimed that she was raped. The police went about picking anybody black they could get their hands on. Since he was arrested that night, they eventually put him and all these young black men in a lineup. Jimmy was in the line up to three times until the police finally got this goddamn woman to say this "boy" raped her, probably because he had a pistol in his pocket that night. That's what he got the chair for. Now tell me, how in the hell can you be serving time, a few months later have some woman put you in a lineup, and then charge you with rape only after being pressured by some crackers?

I tell you, people don't think about how desperate a goddamn cracker can be. He is a no-good son of a bitch they ever had who could shit between two shoes. I'm telling you, I get mad whenever I think of the crap my people have taken from crackers. And even today when people ask me if I have any hate after all I've seen, I say no. I don't carry hate towards no man cause of his color, although I'm hated. Since I got out from what I was under, I don't have any hate. I got my freedom and I am thankful for that. But I will never forget what the white man did to me and other black people. I can't forget. I don't carry any grudge, or desire to want to kill every white man or hate every white man I see, I just stay my distance as long as he stays his. I treat him as he treats me. But if he gets wrong, he's got something on his hands, you can believe that. That ain't hate, you're just taking care of yourself, that's all.

1

Trying to survive in Kilby Prison meant being able to find food that was eatable for humans. When I think about it now, it's very clear that the type of people who were standing on lines in the street waiting for an apple or bread were some of the same kind of people here in prison. Remember this was the 1930s. The country was in the midst of a depression. There was practically no food or work for most people, and if anyone was going to get the bottom of the barrel as far as food was concerned, it was certainly going to black folks, not to mention those of us in prison or on death row. Unless you had some money or some outside connection to purchase food for you, the only food they feed us which was barely eatable was beans and greens! In fact, dinner and lunch was always beans, greens, and no meat to be seen.

They would shove the food on a tray through an opening at the bottom of your cell door, just like they were feeding a dog or something. We complained about this to our support committee on the outside and eventually they fed us like everyone else, by opening the cell door. But man, this was no big deal. The food was still the same. For lunch and dinner, beans, greens, and no meat to be seen. Breakfast was different but still always the same. Rolls which they made there in prison, grits which they made out of corn, and a slice of something which looked like white pork. Man, you couldn't eat that stuff. I'd get sick just looking at it, but that's all they would give you for breakfast, lunch, and dinner, every single day. Luckily for us, we were getting some money from a support committee that allowed us to buy some canned food from a commissary within the prison. Years later, after my sentence was commuted to life in prison, if I gave the guards some money, they would go to the commissary and get some items such as sardines, crackers, potted meat, milk, cakes, pies, or whatever. I was continually writing people on the outside for money so that I could get some food and do some dealing in order to survive in this place.

> County Jail
> Feb. 16 1937
>
> Dear Mother.
> I receive your letter a few days ago. and it found me doing very well — and truly hope when these fews lines reach your hands will find you well and enjoying the best of life. listen mother I need a little money. this food they feds don't agree with my Stomach. You know I suffer with the stomach ache. if you

> send me a little money I can send out and get me something to eat. that will agree with my Stomach. of course the food if All Right. But it just don't suit my appitipe. So mother I will be looking for it Soon. Send me much as $2.00 are $3.00 any way—I am awfully glad to know the children are still going to school. And tell all of thems I say hello. And be good. I hope to meet you all again Soon. so I will close.
>
> from your Son.
> Clarence Norris
> County Jail
> B.Ham ala.
> Ans. Soon.[1]

CLARENCE NORRIS: The official procedure was like this: if you were on death row, you first had to see the warden and explain to him what you wanted to purchase, such as chicken, steak, or something on that order. If he had no problem with this, he would have an official who was picking up the prison mail in Montgomery, Alabama, stop off and purchase food for those of us on death row. You could then have this cooked in the prison's kitchen, but again you have to pay for this. But what the hell, you couldn't do nothing with the money anyway but buy yourself a good meal every now and then. So we had our "outside" food cooked in the kitchen.

When you consider that while on death row we weren't allowed to leave our ten- by twelve-foot cells, and the only exercise we were able to get was that which you managed to do inside this steel cage, if you didn't have any money to spend on some eatable outside food, you were in serious trouble. Though we were fortunate to got some money, it's still a wonder how we survived. Even with those cakes and steaks from outside, our health began to deteriorate, we began to lose weight, in fact at one time you would of thought we were starving. The problem was that all day long, every day, we simply sat in our cell with its little face bowl, toilet, bed, and a box to sit on thinking about our situation.

Death row was so crowded that at one time they actually had to place two men in a cell. However, if they brought a white boy in for the chair, rather than put him in a cell with a black, they would place him in a detention cell nearby rather than place him in a cell with a black. Once there was room, you know, after an execution, he'd have his own cell. That's right, segregation existed right there on death row. But I'll tell you something, I wouldn't want to spend a single solitary night in a cell with one of them. Everything you said, or anything someone else said to you, they would probably go right ahead and tell the guard, who would then tell the warden. Anything that might get their sentence changed from death to life or better they would do. In any case, with the exception of old Connie Vaughn, I never saw a white person executed. Every other white man that got the death sentence when I was there eventually had his sentence commuted to life imprisonment or less. And even then, this would happen only for murder. You never saw any of them up here for raping a white woman, only for murder. And as for them being charged for raping a black woman, well you can forget that. You never would see that or even hear about that, yet we all know they was raping and then killing our women all the time. In fact if you heard or knew of such an instance, it would be simply that only you knew of it, because they didn't care if the deal went down that way. They were above the law. Only black people ended up on death row for supposedly raping someone or for killing one of their own kind.

Serving time at Kilby Prison, meant that you were always subject to being cursed at or being beaten by the guards. First of all, they would always call you "nigger this and nigger that." I mean they just didn't know any other way how to call you or talk to you. No matter how old you were, they would say, "Boy, hey boy, come here." The only time they might call you by your name was when you had a visit or if they were enjoying some displeasure you were going through, like right before your execution. But you generally didn't have any conversation with them guards because there was nothing to talk about, unless maybe you and them had some little hustle going on.

There were, for example, prisoners who were not on death row, but in general population, who were making whiskey. That's right, some of these crackers were using the old empty shirt factory building as a whiskey still and selling this "moonshine" for 50¢ right to then have it sent out to downtown Montgomery! These cats were doing the same thing in Kilby Prison which they did on the street. But that was nothing compared to some other things. If it was necessary to murder someone, usually over some girl-boy thing, they would do it and think nothing else about it. Yeah, a whole lot of that went on right there in prison among both black and white prisoners.

But the hardest thing I had to deal with on a day-to-day basis at Kilby, both mentally and physically, was the sadistic guards. Man, they would beat you for the slightest thing. If you were placed in population it could be because you broke a prison rule, didn't reach your work task level for that day in the shirt factory or cotton mill, or simply because the guard felt you were acting like an "uppity nigger." It was there that you more than likely would get a beating. Of course, some of those guards would simply just want to beat on you, particularly the new guards, it helped them to get over their fear of being around so many blacks. It somehow made them feel good, you could see it in their faces.

They even had a special ritual for whipping you. First they would force you to lay a blanket on the floor, then lay stomach-down on it. One guard would hold your shoulders down while two others would sit on your legs. A third guard had this long leather strap which he would beat you with, or as they said, "lay on" whatever number the warden decided you needed. This was no whipping, this was a killing. The very first lash would cut right through your skin, I mean it would tear your flesh to pieces. From then on the succeeding lashes would be tearing up numb flesh. By the time they finished with you, you'd be almost dead. They had a habit of beating you on one of your buttocks so that you wouldn't be able to sit on that side for at least a month. Some men were beaten so badly they had to be admitted to a hospital for two or three days. Yeah, I know this for a fact because it happened to me.

I remember, one morning back there in 1933, I was laying down flat on my stomach in my cell minding my own business, when suddenly I heard a key unlocking my cell door. When I turned around, there was this big old cracker guard Bill Gray and another cat standing in my cell door. Gray tells me to get up and come to the cell door. When I get to the door he suddenly smashes me in the head with a pair of brass knuckles. While I'm laying on the floor nearly unconscious, he and this other guard begin to beat me all over my body. They kicked, stomped, punched me in my face, back, groin, arms, you name it. I was beaten so bad that I lost consciousness. When I came to, I couldn't remember who or where I was, my eyes were just about closed, bruises were all over my body, they actually tried to beat me to death, and almost did. But you know something, if I was to ever see that man today, even after all of these years, I'd kill him, so help me God. He could be bent over and have whiskers down to the floor, but I'll kill him as sure as I'm sitting here right now. That was one beating I got simply because I was black.

Years later while serving time at Birmingham's Jefferson County Jail I was punished again, but this time it was for fighting with another inmate who owed me some money. You see, inside prison, money is everything. You either owe someone or they owe you. Either way, one way or another, some dues were going to be collected, and yes, just like on the outside, people killed in order to collect. On this particular day, me and another inmate got into a fight over some money he owed me. He figured, like so many others, that you wouldn't really want to push the issue because a fight might cause the warden to simply add more time to your sentence. But the problem is that when you loan money out, you want to be paid back at a specific time and most important you want interest back as well. All of this related to your own prestige at Kilby. If someone thought they could chump you off by not repaying a debt, your reputation as someone who was easy could become a problem on many levels.

You see, they had white guys in prison who had as much as $5,000 or $6,000 stashed away someplace in prison. Now, when you consider that you were only allowed $5 as pocket money from the outside, much of this cash would be loaned out and of course used to pay off the guards for special favors, such as to look the other way during a prison break. That's right, whites did escape while I was there in Birmingham jail, even though there were guards with high-powered rifles and machine guns on the walls.

In any case, this guy refused to pay me my little bit of money, while badmouthing me all over the prison. So I planned to kill him with my dirtch [knife]. A friend of mine told me, "Say man, don't even bother to kill this guy, because all it's going to do is allow the state to do to you what they have been trying to do for the longest time." So I didn't use my dirtch, but waited for him one day and smacked him in the head with a piece of iron as he walked into the prison cloth factory where we both worked. The guards saw me when I smacked him and before I knew it they carried me up front to the warden office and beat me with a strap. But even after this, I still carried by dirtch because in prison everyone keeps murder in their heart. It's the only way you can be ready to defend yourself.

2

In 1934 while at Birmingham's Jefferson County Jail, I was placed in solitary confinement for about a year. They did this for two reasons. First, they wanted to make sure I didn't communicate too often with the rest of the prison's population. Secondly, they were trying to break my spirits and, literally, drive me crazy.

When they placed me in solitary confinement, they chose a section of the prison called "P" ward. I guess the "P" stood for psycho ward because damn well everyone in this section of the jail was psychologically disturbed, you know, just plain crazy. Most prisoners placed in this section were eventually "lost!" I mean, whether you were insane or just acting this way to get transferred from one section of Kilby to another, you were taking a big chance, because they would just lose your records or whatever. After a while they would transfer these inmates to Alabama's institution for the insane in Mount Vernon. So although I received the death sentence for a second time, rather than send me and the other Scottsboro boys back to Kilby Prison, they placed me in this crazy ward and scattered the others throughout the rest of the jail. I knew, for example, that Hayward Patterson, who also received the death sentence for the second time, was down on the seventh floor.

Now, these folks thought they were slick. They figured that if I was placed up there with these crazies, I would eventually be just as disturbed as them. But I knew the deal. However, let me tell you, this was some rough living. Although I had a cell by myself and didn't really have to come into direct daily contact with these folks, I could hear almost everything that was going on around me. All throughout the day and night there was constant noise, weird sounds, crying, and banging of heads on cell walls, everything, it was like pure hell. This went on for an entire year! Till this day, I still don't know how I was able to keep my own sanity while these people made every imaginable sound you could think of, while saying and doing things that just didn't make any sense. Now if that wasn't torture, I don't know what is. In any case I'm sure that the warden thought that after a few months in "P" ward, I might say something which might implicate me in the alleged raping of those white girls, or do anything to get out of there.

What I was able to do is to have one of the cell boys, who was really the warden's flunky, to find out where Andy Wright's cell was and to ask him to write folks on the outside about my situation. I wasn't too sure if this flunky was actually going to do this, but it seems as though he did because sometimes soon after, I was transferred along with Patterson over to the white prisoners' side of jail and placed in solitary confinement, or what they would call L lockup. I can only imagine why they would do this. Here we are, two black prisoners, who at this point didn't like each other at all and would be ready to fight in a second, locked up for allegedly raping two white women, now surrounded by white prisoners who were as racist as the guards. We spent about a year in this section of jail.

As bad as Jefferson County Jail was, if you could learn how the system operated you could live a little better than others. For example, earlier in 1933 there was always a lot of gambling going on. If you had some money, you could live there in a decent manner. You see, what they did was to put eight of us in one cage, but separated Roy Wright from us due to his age. He was placed in population with the rest of the prisoners. We had night cells where we would sleep three men to a cell, but during the day we would be in a dayroom which had a large steel table in the middle of the floor and off in the corner a shower. You could wash your own clothes and all that kind of stuff. It was during this time that we could get us some women right there in jail. We had it so that we could gamble all day long, and if one of us needed some money, he would get a loan from the other, then pay it back when he got some money.

I remember, there was this one guy, a prison "trustee" named Ernest, who basically looked like a white man. His pappy was a white man and his mother was a light-skin Negro. Anyway, one day Ernest was passing by our cell, looked in, saw all this money we was gambling with, and said, "I sure wish I could get in there and get some of that money you all got." You got to understand that we also knew that Ernest was a jailhouse hustler; I mean though he was a prisoner, he was the boss of the cell boys or jail flunkies who cleaned up the jail, including the women's side. In fact, because the women's jail was right across the way from us, we could see them walking in their cages and they could see us. There were always two cages full of these women, so we would wave at them and they would wave at us and all that stuff. Now and then the guards would let them out onto the sun parlor and we would holler and talk with them all day long.

Ernest asked us what would he have to do in order to share in some of the money. I told him, "Look you can share in this money, if you do the right thing." He said, "What's that?" I said, "Let me over there where the women's at." He thought for a moment, looked around, then said, "I just might take you up on that someday." Well, weeks passed and I forgot all about this, because I knew flunkies like Ernest were always trying to set you up on something, just to make their own little hustle on the warden look good. I figured he must have thought it was too dangerous and not really worth his while to get involved in my suggestion. But sure enough, late one night after we got back to our night cells, I heard somebody fooling with the combination lock on the door to our cell block. Finally the door opened and I saw Ernest walking down the cell block to my cell. He said, "How many of you want to go over there?" I said, "I for one want to go."

Willie Roberson and I decided to go over and visit our "girlfriends," who we knew only by hollering at them from the sun parlor which separated the male and female sections of the jail. His girl, whose name was Carey Bank, was serving life for murder. Mine, Lou Bertha Edwards, was a pretty little dark-skin girl who had this long hair down her back. Before I actually got a chance to actually talk with Lou, I would buy her some candy from the store man when he came around. Other times I would get in contact with one of the guards, give him some money so that he would get someone who was going into town to purchase me a "licking iron" for Lou, and then have her do my shirts or whatever. That's right, we had it so that our girlfriends would wash and iron our clothes, and if "Lou" was doing me right, I would send out for her favorite flavor of ice cream. We would call them our "old Lady." You see, if you had money you could buy and just about do anything you wanted to do in jail. That was one time in which we were "living" in jail.

Once the guards realized that Ernest was making some money off our little meeting with the women they transferred him to another part of jail and then began to cut in on this business. One night, this particular guard who knew we gambled heavy came by and said, "If you niggers will share some of that money, I'll fix you up good with these women for only $3.00 each." His angle was that rather than us going over there and take a chance of being caught, if we would give him the names of those women we wanted to spend some time with, he would bring them over to us and they could damn near stay the entire night.

We made a deal with this guard and pretty soon we were lowering the darkened part of the windows in our cell area so that nobody could see in and then we would do our thing. Once the women were brought over, he would leave, lock the door, and be on his way until the early-morning hours when they would be returned to the other side.

Like I said, this was living, but it didn't come easy. No sir, we had to fight for these privileges every step of the way. In fact, these advantages were the result of a previous run-in we had with the guards and the warden, one which almost turned into a full-scale riot or worse for us.

3

Newspaper accounts of the "jail riot," however, placed the fault of this incident at the feet of outsiders rather than the conditions at Birmingham Alabama's Jefferson County Jail. In an article replete with veiled threats, the *Birmingham News* reported:

The Jail Riot Staged by the Scottsboro Negroes

The riot staged in the Jefferson county jail by the nine Negro defendants in the Scottsboro case must be put down as just another unfortunate consequence of the senseless and vicious agitation of the case by the International Labor Defense and other radical groups or individuals.

There can be no doubt that the prisoners were aroused to their mutinous attitude by the Communist propaganda that has been bearing in upon them, and not by any grievance over the treatment they have received in jail. It is not surprising that the propaganda which has reached them should have had this effect. The fact that the Negroes, after their violent outburst and some hours of sulking, have abandoned that attitude and promise to behave themselves, indicates that their own better judgment has now prevailed over the incitements to which they have been subjected. Let us hope this better judgment will continue to rule their conduct. It is obviously better for them to behave themselves, and it is better for everyone and everything else concerned. It ought not to be difficult to persuade them of this. However they may feel about the case itself, they surely have no cause for complaint at the treatment they have received in jail.

If we realize that their spell of misbehavior was a more or less natural result of the propaganda which has surrounded the case, we may dismiss it as a matter of no serious concern. It is unpleasant for Alabama to have this sort of thing happen. But there has been much in connection with the case that has been unpleasant to Alabamians. Our people on the whole have tried to bear it all with patience, which under the circumstances is the sensible attitude for us to take, and certainly we can be patient with respect to this latest consequence of the reckless and unscrupulous agitation on the part of radicals who have sought to make of the case a cause celebre in the interest mainly of themselves, and not of the defendants.[2]

CLARENCE NORRIS: We had a habit of waving to the women across the hall from our dayroom especially during visiting hours. This of course was natural. Here we are, young men, full of life, cut off from any natural sex life, and the only females we get to see are those over in the women's jail which was directly opposite from our jail cells. We could see them clearly through this thick plate of bullet-proof glass which also separated us from visitors or anyone passing by. At that time, this was the only way we could communicate with anyone outside our dayroom. Anyway, this particular day, a big old crazy white guard decided that he was going to stop me from waving at the women by yelling, "Stop waving at the girl over there!" I looked at him like he was crazy and told him he was nothing but a "pot-belly son of a bitch" and a whole lot of other stuff. That night when they put us back in our night cell, the guards soaped up the glass partition so that we couldn't look outside our cage, but more importantly, we couldn't see our women. Furthermore, the very next visiting day they confined us to our night cells so that we couldn't speak with anyone. At this point we decided to get tough with them.

They would feed us on these old cast-iron trays which would be slipped under the cell door through a hole near the floor, just as if you were feeding a dog. After we were finished eating we were supposed to shove these trays back into the hallway, where the flunkies would collect them. This day we decided to hold onto our trays. Upset and nervous, this flunky goes running right back to the kitchen sergeant boo-hooing about we won't give him back the trays. Before you know it, the sergeant comes running down the hall yelling, "You niggers stop playing around, shove those trays out here!" We yelled back at him, "Come and get 'em you pot-bellied son of a bitch." That's what really started the riot we had back there in April 1933. Once this disruption started, we figured they were going to try and get us in the dayroom and then beat the hell out of us. However, by this time, the guards knew that most of us had knives, as did almost everyone in jail, and that we would be ready to use them in self-defense.

Haywood Patterson gets things going by setting fire to his mattress. He knew that the fire couldn't burn concrete, but the smoke would certainly cause a lot of problems for the guards. While he was doing this, we stripped the windows of their dead weights. Dead weights were those lead weights connected to chains inside of window frames which helped you to raise or lower the window. These weights made excellent clubs which we were prepared to use. Pipes were taken out of the shower and fashioned into a variety of weapons such as knives, clubs, and could even be made into a "zip" gun. We didn't have a zip gun, but we could have made one without any problem.

I really expected the guards to rush us because we couldn't lock the door to the dayroom, and all they had to do was to push it back and try to come on in. The only thing stopping them was their fear that we would cut them up in the process.

So, here we are, standing right on the inside of the door to the dayroom, yelling at them: "Come on in, come on in, come on in! You got your goddamn blackjack brother. You got your pistol, shoot! Causes if you don't, you had your mammy." Man, we raised hell that day. When Deputy Warden Rogers, who also hated our guts, eventually came up to the eighth floor with a bunch of sheriffs and guards from the street, we began yelling at him also.

Now before I go any further, you have to understand that this particular deputy warden, Dan Rogers, hated us with a passion, and he didn't hide it. If he could have figured out a way of killing us and not be blamed by politicians and outside folks he would have done it. He said as much a year later in 1934 when Benjamin Davis of the ILD visited us. Davis was a well-known supporter of the Communist Party and a member of the ILD. This, of course, did not sit well with these crackers. But more importantly, he was also black.

Ben Davis' recollection of this visit stated:

> The last time I visited the Scottsboro boys in Jefferson county jail, I carried them a carton of cigarettes, matches and stamps. Following the usual custom, I expected the packages to be examined and returned to me for distribution as I interviewed them. But this time Deputy Warden Rogers, refused to permit me

to deliver them. He took the packages and marked on them for "the Scottsboro Niggers." This was done plainly and conspicuously so that I might be intimidated into understanding the treatment accorded to all "niggers" whether they were lawyers or prisoners.

Then Warden Rogers, as he led me to the cells for interview, stated, "he didn't know what had gotten into them Scottsboro niggers. They're the worse bunch of niggers he ever saw. Always raising hell when they get the best treatment possible."

But the [seven] Scottsboro boys in Jefferson County jail tell a different story about the "best treatment possible." Andy Wright was confined in solitary for more than 3 weeks because he refused to go "outside" in the snow and sleet to catch a death [of] cold. This was at the request of Warden Dan Rogers. Then [Olen] Montgomery was placed in solitary because he kicked against the starvation portion put on his food plate. Warden Rogers considered this "the best treatment possible."

Warden Rogers asked one of the boys "who is that nigger lawyer who came in here, a son of a bitch? I wish I could catch him sitting in the court house here. I'd hang him." He also told the boys, that "as long as that nigger lawyer keeps coming down here swelling your heads you're going to stay in solitary. You'd better keep him away."

Once Warden Rogers brandished his pistol on one of the boys threatening to kill him. As the boy pleaded for his life, Rogers belched, "I ought to kill you now, they're going to kill you anyway, just like they're going to burn Patterson and Norris."

The boys all are mortally afraid that Warden Rogers will someday shoot them in cold blood. At every opportunity he curses them, brow beats them and attempts to provoke them into defending themselves in order that he might murder them for "resisting an officer of the law." He plants stool pigeons in their cells. These stool pigeons provoke fights which result in the boys being thrown into solitary while the stool pigeons are never punished. Then he boasts to the boys "that I'll always believe my stool pigeons in preference to you niggers."

A stool pigeon framed one of the boys a month ago, by claiming he had stolen 50 cents from him. This boy has been in solitary now for more than five weeks without change of clothes or a bath. This same torturer Rogers also claims that the boy has a razor in his possession, and threatens to keep him in solitary until the razor is delivered up. The truth is that this boy has never had a razor in his possession and obviously has no way of obtaining one even to secure his release from solitary.

Warden Rogers has repeatedly informed the boys that as long as people come to see them they will stay in solitary. Recently when Myra Page, well known writer, visited them, Warden Rogers called her a white whore and yelled "as long as white whores come down here to see you, we're not going to let you out."

In spite of all the concentrated terror and brutality unleashed upon them recently, the boys understand clearly that it is not accidental or spontaneous. As they said to me, "We know they're trying to divide us, but they can't. They're trying to force us to take the NAACP, but we don't want it. Warden Rogers is trying to find an excuse to kill us in jail, but we know we're going to stick together and watch him."[3]

CLARENCE NORRIS: Rogers was really looking for any opportunity to kill any one of us. He's told us this, as well as outsiders, and I for one believed him. But this was one time he just stood there as we yelled, "Go on, shoot, that's all you can do, shoot mother f__ker, shoot!" Rogers, however, told his guards, "Leave them niggers alone, ya'll just leave them crazy niggers alone." Sure enough, they left, but before doing that they brought about ten Negroes up there and tried to convince them to rush us. Them fellows took a look at what they were facing and decided they would rather take a beating from the guards than try to get past us. We told them: "You can let that white son of a bitch put you up to wanna come in this cell, but if you come in here, nigger, we're gonna kill you. If you darken that door, nigger, we're gonna to kill you." Man, once these cats took a look at what they was about to get themselves involved in, they began mumbling and milling around. We could hear the guards yelling at them for not trying to get in, calling them all kinds of worthless shit, kicking at them, slapping them upside their heads. At the time I thought this was really funny, but now, years later, when I think about how grown men can be reduced to another man's plaything or whipping stick, well, I really get kind of sad, almost sick. They finally sent these fellows back downstairs. But it just goes to show you, if we would have let Rogers and his henchmen in there on their own terms, we would have been beaten, probably nearly killed, in that dayroom. I tell you, them crackers were some dirty sons of a bitches. Yeah, you can believe that.

Anyway, the warden tells the guards not to give us anything to eat or drink until we give up all of our weapons. This meant that we had to rely on water from the toilets in our cells. Outside of that, there was no food for five or six days. They tried everything to get us out of that dayroom, but nothing seemed to work. During the night they would cut off the lights in the dayroom and throughout that entire side of the jail. Since all those prisoners on floors beneath us were moved somewhere else when our complaint began, we were now basically isolated.

I remember on one particular night when it was so dark you couldn't see your hand in front of you, we could hear the guards moving about, whispering to each other. In fact we knew that they were bringing up a fire hose to try and shoot water in on us. But man, those crackers were still scared of coming in there. We could hear them talking and debating what to do:

"Ain't them niggers asleep?"

"You know them damn niggers ain't sleep."

"We could take the fire hose and get it into the hallway and get in on them."

We finally recognized Warden Rogers' voice: "Forget the fire hose, the niggers will take that fire hose away from you, you can't do nothing with that hose."

They decided to do nothing.

On about the fifth or sixth day, the warden came up to the dayroom door and said, "If all of you put down the stuff you gonna fight with, and leave it all on the table and return to your night cells, we'll fix up this place and see to it that you will have house visits and be treated like any other prisoners." Suspecting a trick, we told them that this could work, but only if he, Warden Rogers, would agree to be the officer to search us. We didn't want to be set up by guards who were in a position to "frame us" over something petty during a search. Once this was agreed upon, we returned to our cells and from then on were treated somewhat like people, you can believe it. Now ain't that the damnedest thing you ever heard of? This is why I believe that you got to fight for what you believe in. There is no other way. Why else would we have a riot in prison we were doing time in?

When you're in prison, things do happen in which you have no control over whatsoever. For example, in July 1938, right after my death sentence was commuted by Governor Graves, I somehow became innocently involved in the damnedest riot you ever want to see at Kilby Prison. This was something I really didn't need, but when you're incarcerated, you sometimes get caught up in a process which you neither control or influence, but will be held responsible for.

Let me first tell you about my "job" at Kilby Prison. I worked in the shirt factory which was a part of the cotton mill at Kilby. For those of us who worked in the mill, day began at the first ringing of "the steel" at six o'clock in the morning. They had this steel bar which someone banged every morning which let you know it was time to get out of bed, wash up, get your clothes on. The next clang of this steel bar indicated the opening of your cell door in which you were expected to line up in twos facing the mess hall. The last clang was when you were marched off to the mess hall for breakfast. Once you got to the dining room you had to stand at the side of each table and wait for the signal to sit. This went on each and every day. If you didn't want to eat you could stay in your cell. However, in about twenty to twenty-five minutes after breakfast when the whistle was blown, you had to be out in that yard ready to go to work, or as they called it, do a task, in either the shirt factory, cotton mill, or whatever.

You were assigned a task after a series of physical examinations were done to see if you were fit. First they gave you an eye and heart test. Then you had to jump around a bit, I guess this was to see if you were fit. In any case, once this was completed, you were assigned a task and someone would be appointed to train you, just like any other job situation. My task was to make sure that all twelve cotton spinning machines I had responsibility for were running smoothly. Considering all the other types of nonsense they had you doing in Kilby, this wasn't a bad job. All I had to do was to make sure everything ran smoothly, and correct anything that went wrong. This work was simple enough, however you were still a prisoner without any privileges including moving away from your machines without permission. All day long I would place large rolls of cotton in the back of this "cord" machine which shredded it until it resembled a spider's web. It was on this machine I lost part of my middle finger while trying to repair a broken string. Somehow while I had my hand in there the machine started up. I was lucky only to lose part of my finger as this blade chopped right down on this finger.

In any case, you would then place this web-like cotton into another machine which spun this cotton into a piece of string a little larger than my thumb. There was another part of this machine which placed this string in a can, in a circular fashion until it was full. Once full this would be taken to another machine called the "drawing frame." At this stage, a string of cotton would be cut, placed in a device called "the slugger" which would spin the cotton onto a spool. Being careful not to cut your fingers, you would place this spool into still another machine which would cut the string down even smaller. This spool of string would be taken to the spinning room where it was converted into "ravel" which cotton clothes were made from. We would then carry this ravel down to the weave shop were prisoners converted it into a fine cloth material.

If your job was to monitor these machines, you had to make sure that every time the string would break you were there to change, or rethread the machine. Since they would automatically stop if something was wrong, thereby delaying the weaving process throughout the factory, you were given a certain amount of seconds to make any corrections needed. If you were slower than they thought was necessary, you would be taken "up-front" to the warden's office and whipped with a leather strap. If in the weave room your cloth was considered to be "bad" cloth or of inferior quality, you were whipped right there in front of all of the other prisoners. This was to set an example. And if it happened again, they would simply whip you again. You see, this prison was really a commercial factory, except that as with slavery the labor was free, and worse of all, we had no rights the guards were bound to respect. Consequently they whipped us whenever they felt like doing so.

The only payment we received for doing this work was 15¢ on a Friday evening when returning from work. I remember it as if it was happening right now. After being whipped, cursed at, knocked about, always knowing this cracker was waiting for you to make a mistake, they would line you up at the end of the day to walk between these two guards. The one on the left would have a sack of dimes, and the other would have a sack of nickels. When you passed between them, one gave you a nickel, the other a dime. This was your pay for a week of abuse. That's all you got unless someone sent you some money from the outside. And even then, the guards would try to steal some before you ever received it.

Even when I had this kind of job, I had to be careful of other prisoners who were either hateful or stool pigeons. Sometimes they would come up to you and ask stupid questions such as, "Did you guys really rape these women?"

I'd say, "What did I tell the jury? Why did you ask me that question?" And then others would come up and say, "I believe you all did do it," etc. All of this I believe was done to keep us jumpy, nervous, and distrustful of everyone, but you see, one must keep a level head especially in that part of the country if you are accused of raping a white woman. You become a target for every bizarre scheme by prisoners who are trying to wean favors from the prison administration which is also trying to break you into submission and possibly a false confession. I had to take all that kind of stuff when I was there. And yes, I believe it does begin to affect your personality.

Part of the problem, beside just being locked up like a wild animal, is that they are forcing you to work for nothing, and at the same time punishing you for a crime you didn't commit. This alone can make you hateful and evil. Sometimes this makes you want to rob, hurt someone, and even kill just to get some freedom, even if your chances of success are slim. They must have known this because I was never placed in a situation where I could realistically think of escaping.

This however never prohibited me from thinking about it or acting aggressive towards anyone who challenged me. Even among us Scottsboro boys we had some conflict and fights. Most of the time it was between Haywood Patterson and the rest of us.

> Benjamin Davis Reported:
>
> **Thursday, May 11th 1933,** Haywood Patterson on the one hand and Roy and Andy Wright on the other, became embroiled in serious mutual "kidding." Before the boys were arrested in 1931, they were interested in the same girls in Chattanooga. There was a sort of friendly rivalry between them. This rivalry has followed them through the whole three years of their imprisonment. On this occasion the kidding became extremely personal, and before either of the boys knew what had happened, Roy Wright the younger of the two Wright boys, seized a knife and stabbed Patterson. The wound while not serious, required the immediate services of a physician who closed it with two stitches. The wound is on the left side, on an approximate line with the lowest rib. Patterson is not seriously affected, the only serious consequences being fright and pain. There is a conflict between Patterson and the Wright boys as to where the knife came from. Patterson stated that the knife was slipped to one of the Wright boys by their friends at the jail; while the Wright boys say that the knife was taken from Patterson at the time of the incident.
>
> As a result of the incident the Wright boys and Charlie Weems have been moved to a separate cell from the other 6 boys. Weems was not compelled to go, but chose of his own volition to be with the Wright boys. I talked over the incident with Weems and the Wright boys, also.
>
> Patterson and the Wright boys both regretted sincerely that their tempers "got the best of them," and wish to be placed in the same cell together again. They stated that it is very likely that incidents of that sort will occur, inasmuch as they have no literature to read and no diversions to occupy their time and minds. They say that they are frequently nervous and irritable from the terrific strain from the "frame-up" ordeal.[4]

CLARENCE NORRIS: Patterson and I didn't really get along too good because every time you turn around he'd be into something or another with the rest of us. He just wasn't liked by most of us. Even when the both of us were put on death row for the second time, we would be continually arguing. I didn't like his ways and I didn't like him. He was the kind of person you couldn't tell nothing to. He was overbearing, always ready to fight, always into something, and always being punished whether it was his fault or not. The strange thing is that he would start a fight, I guess out of boredom, but then would end up getting the worst of it.

The fight between me and him is a perfect example. One day while in solitary confinement and locked up in separate cells next to each other, he yelled over to me that he wanted to borrow some money. I told him no because earlier I had asked him the same thing and he said no. Later that day, we were gambling with cards, you can do that with cells on either side of you by simply placing the cards on the walkway outside your cell. Anyway, he broke me, and I asked him to credit me some money. Later when I won that back and Patterson again owed me some money, he said he wanted to borrow $20 to send to his baby sister. I again refused to let him have it so he started putting me in "the dozens," calling me names and talking about my mother and sisters, etc.[5] So I took him up on this and eventually beat him at this because I can really rap when it comes down to doing this. Anyway he really got mad because I "sounded" on him really bad. You know how it is, when you get a rhythm going playing the dozens it can really hurt the other person, while being very funny.

Anyway the more I got into it and started to laugh, the madder he got. I started to tell him about his mama wearing combat boots, and her being so ugly she chased away daylight, you know all that sort of thing. So he said, the next day when they let us out to clean our cells he was going to "craw" [cut in the stomach] me! Now, it just happened that when I was placed in solitary, I found a knife, well really some metal wires that someone earlier had bound together into a pick-like object, sharpened and left hidden in my cell. I was now ready for anything Haywood wanted to do. The following day they let me out of my cell first, then him. No sooner did we step outside when he rushed me. So I just gave him what I had right in his stomach and chest. I must have stabbed him two or three different times. If it wasn't for the guards and one of the workers cleaning up there, ain't no telling what would've happened. I just might of killed him right then and there. That's basically how we related to each other. No real love lost there. But this was typical for Haywood. He had problems wherever he was.

In 1937, after the Alabama State Supreme Court confirmed our convictions, giving me the death sentence for the third time, Andy Wright ninety-nine years, and Charlie Weems seventy-five years, Haywood Patterson was given seventy-five years but sent to Atmore State Prison farm near Montgomery,

Alabama. While this left Weems, Andy, and myself basically behind the walls, it actually gave Haywood an opportunity to at least think about escape because Atmore with all its evil still allowed you to work outside those gray walls. You have to be locked up in a cage for a period of time to understand what I'm saying. When locked up, your entire world is limited by your cell, possibly your cell block, but definitely by those gray walls. You become used to these limitations. You begin to forget about what it means to look at things at a distance. Variations in colors becomes dulled by the experience. You become and begin to act just like a rat in a box, predictable and yet irrational. Patterson's stay at Atmore, with all its violence, sadistic guards, breaking of men's personality, and outright murder, ironically allowed him to look beyond the limits of those gray walls when he worked in the surrounding farms of Atmore Prison. His experiences down there made him realize that his life was in peril as the guards schemed with prisoners to have him killed. He was considered to be the true "bad nigger." His near-murder by another prisoner left him now a damaged lung after being stabbed repeatedly. This, along with a diseased bone condition in his left leg and increasing bad eyesight, forced him to think in survival terms that had but one objective, escape.

His first escape attempt was a failure and the way I understand it, when he was captured they nearly beat him to death in the warden's office with those leather straps. He was eventually sent back to Kilby Prison where after a while he was able to convince the administration that the only way he could keep out of trouble would be to work out on the farm system at Kilby Prison. I'm pretty sure they thought that he might try and escape again, but what they weren't ready for was Patterson's ability to play the role of the flunky, the Uncle Tom, the boy. I mean even before they sent him out on the farm he was scheming.

Patterson remembered:

> "Snake Eye" [Patterson's nickname], Burrs said, "you done overdone a good thing. You been having the cell-boy job a long time and now you got to be punished. We going to put you out on the farm and make you work you damned ass till it be thin."
>
> "Oh, boss, don't put me out on the farm. Please, don't put me out on the farm."
>
> "The farm is where you go!"
>
> "Oh, boss, I can't make it out there. I had so many years of that hard labor down there at Atmore! Please, don't put me out on the farm!"
>
> I was playing Br'er Rabbit with Captain L.J. Burrs. Old Pork Back, he didn't know he was putting me right in my briar patch. I was born on the farm. Once I got out there I'd scoot, sure as rabbits.
>
> He wasn't shitting me. I was shitting him.
>
> Burrs said,
>
> "Snake Eye, if you go out there and behave I'll put you back inside after a while."
>
> I figured I better not behave too good.[6]

Clarence Norris: Though we didn't see him during the day because he was assigned a job on Kilby's farm, we heard that he was kissing up to the guards, scratching his head, "yes'sa" and "bossing" them all day long when in reality he was outfoxing them with this buffoon role. He eventually got to the position of water boy. You know, whenever the guards wanted some water, food, or anything, they would yell, "Boy, bring me this, or that." Anyway Patterson played this role to the bust, and got over. The guards began to believe he was a broken nigger after the Atmore beating. This of course gave him an opportunity to slowly and patiently plan for a successful escape years later in July 1948.

The way I understand the escape, he and some old cat were able to take advantage of the guards out there in the fields, took their guns, and ran away. The biggest problem they had was figuring how to get away from them dogs that were kept out in the fields just to chase and run down Negroes trying to escape. In fact they had "dog boys" whose job was to take care of these dogs, help train them, and have them ready just to attack prisoners. That's right. They had niggers training dogs to chase after anyone trying to escape from the farm! Now, some folks did get away from those dogs, but man, those dogs will track you for days and not by ones but by packs. If you got to Montgomery, which was only about ten miles away, you had a chance, but man, you had to be good to get away. Patterson was.

Patterson recalled:

"We got to move and move fast. If we don't we'll get caught."

We took off. We were still on the state premises. We couldn't get off. We circled around on the farm down by the hog lot. Dillon, a Negro caretaker, he was a nice guy. He would do things for me. But I didn't go near him. The woods was thick with the posse hunting us and we were near the woods. We were also near the gardener's house. The kid got frightened. He said, "What we going to do?"

I said, "You take it easy. I'll tell you what we do."

The kid said, "We go to the gardener's house and steal his car."

"No."

"Yes."

He just kept insisting. I said, "All right, you go ahead."

No sooner he stuck his head around the garage, a guy shot about six times.

He didn't see me but he saw the boy. We ran then for the high corn near his house. We got back in the cornfield again. It was a different cornfield about a quarter of a mile from where we had run. As I got in there I lost confidence in the boy. He was reckless. He wanted to commit crime. That was his talk.

I decided to give him up right there in the corn patch because it was dark and he couldn't see me.

The dogs were right up on us then. I just detoured back — in the same direction I came from.

The dogs were pushing me too close.

There was a road leading down by the hog lot. I headed for it. As I tried to make it across the road I could see spy cars waiting there. I could see one guy

with a shotgun in the crook of his arm. And several waiting for me to cross the road. They knew from the way the dogs were coming that the dogs had my scent. Guards, they wouldn't go in the woods at night but stood in the road and waited for you to come out. I saw the dogs were overtaking me and the road was filled with cars. Men in them waiting.

I was determined they wouldn't get me.

I decided not to go up in the road.

I turned on the dogs and went to meet them.

Three of them came up. I just sweetened them. I called them, petted them, pretended like I was helping them seek what they're looking for. I used the same strategy that a dog boy would use with the dogs.

The dogs seemed to take notice and listen and they came right over. I kept saying, "Here, here, here." They figured I was one of the boys. They started smelling again. That gave me a chance to grab them. I didn't know which was the lead dog. If you get the leader the rest are no more good. An old dog always leads younger dogs. I got one by the collar and then grabbed the other.

They started to pull away.

They began to sense I was the wrong guy. But I held them. I tried to get the other one, but I had a handful and couldn't get him. He started running in another direction, but I called him. I talked kind of lowly to him and he came back and followed.

That gave me a chance to tie them all up.

I took off my shirt. One sleeve I tied underneath the collar of one dog. Put a good knot in it. The other sleeve I tied the other hound in the same way. Took the back of the shirt and tied the third with that. Then I tied them good to a tree.

They didn't bark. They were the sweetest dogs I ever met. I could hear the dog boy calling them. After the dogs ceased barking the dog boy started hollering. You could hear him for a mile.

I laughed every time he hollered because I had the dogs. The dog boy, he blew a bugle that the dogs knew and they jumped like they wanted to go, but I sweetened them and they stayed right on there.

The people on the road, they couldn't see me, but I could see them. The main thing was to keep the dogs quiet and I kept them that way.

When I saw the hunters weren't going to leave the road, I left them.

I eased away and went down along the stream of water to where it was a little better than waist-deep. I could see cars in all directions making a circle around the farm.

They were busy. That was a busy night for them.

They didn't want anybody but me. They didn't care if all the guys got away. They wanted me.

I waded through the water until I got about a mile away from the dogs.

All of a sudden here came the dogs again. That impressed me a great deal. I wondered how they got away from the vise I put them in. I knew that was serious.

I was down in the water. The dogs jumped in. They scented me off the water. I just said, "I'll get rid of you this time."

It was the same three dogs I tied. I don't know whether the dog boys had found them and released them or whether they got free themselves. I knew they were the same because they had some portions of my shirt on their collars.

I figured the dog boys must be pretty near behind the dogs.

> When the first dog got to me I grabbed him, carried him under the water, and held him there till he ceased kicking.
>
> When I knew he was dead, I turned him loose and he stayed under the water.
>
> I called another. He swarm over to me. I carried him under the water. I could feel him kick.
>
> I had all I could do to hold the rascal under. He was terrible. He was hard to die. He scuffled so he got his head up out of the water.
>
> I knew it meant life or death for me.
>
> The third dog was wise. It was the same little fellow that stayed away from me before. Seemed like he had an understanding what was going on. I tried to sweeten him, but he wouldn't come out on the water. Instead he turned and went back the other way.
>
> But that settled it. Thereafter I had no more trouble with dogs.[7]

4

Though Patterson's escape from Kilby Prison was extremely difficult for the prison officials to explain, it was predictable. Patterson was in no way a "model" inmate. He rebelled, orchestrated, exploited anyone and everything in his struggle to survive Alabama's strategy for his execution, "legal" or not. Thus it was with pain and maybe some relief, as in good riddance, that the *Birmingham News* on July 20, 1948, some three days after his actual escape on the seventeenth, announced:

> **"Scottsboro" Felon Escapes**
>
> Haywood Patterson, one of the defendants in the famed Scottsboro criminal attack case in the early 1930s, escaped from Kilby Prison late today along with eight other Negro convicts.
>
> Patterson, now 35 years old, was serving a 75 year term. He was convicted in 1937 and had escaped once before tonight. That was in 1943 when he got away from Atmore Prison Farm and was recaptured two days later.
>
> Five of the nine Negroes who fled today were taken into custody a few hours later but Patterson and three others were still at large.
>
> Patterson's escape brought a promise of an investigation by State Prison Director, Frank Boswell.
>
> "That Negro had no business working on the farm," Boswell declared. "He should have been kept inside the prison. I don't know how he got out on the farm but I'm going to find out."
>
> Boswell said the nine convicts were returning to Kilby in a truck after working in a field. As they rounded a sharp curve, he related, they fled into a corn field. Patterson was the first to run.
>
> The guard fired once with his shotgun and emptied his pistol at the fleeing convicts but failed to stop them, Boswell said.[8]

CLARENCE NORRIS: The pressures of imprisonment were so intense that any little incident could set off a series of response by the guards. Any escape attempt or, worse, a successful escape, complaints about the food or workload, anything at all, simply made it harder for all of us. For example, I knew that many of the prisoners were complaining about the bad food and the constant diet of beans and greens, but what could we do?

In Kilby Prison, a prisoner committee of sorts was actually formed. Within a short period of time they organized a strike to petition the prison administration about our bad working conditions and the inferior quality of food we were given. What I didn't know was that these strikers were also going to attempt to close down the entire cotton mill at Kilby.

On this particular day around noon, everybody agreed they weren't going to eat due to the bad food. Before I knew it, guys were running around smashing machine parts and breaking the keys which were used to start either the cotton or thread machinery. In no time flat the entire place was in revolt. The guards began to force everyone out of the factory into the prison yard, hoping that they could stop some of the machines from being damaged, but by this time the factory was in total chaos.

After they got us into the yard they then tried to force us back to our cells but by this time it was too late. There must have been close to one thousand men in the prison yard. Nobody was returning to their cells, and if you even appeared to be thinking about returning you knew that you'd have to explain your actions to the other prisoners. When caught up in something like this, you really have to just lay back, act like you're in with the crowd, observe, and know when to move in the right direction, otherwise you might find yourself in a tight spot.

I really wasn't ready for this action, and in fact, Andy Wright, Charlie Weems, Ozie Powell, and me were together out there in the yard, but as far away as possible from the leaders of this action. As I remember, it was the white prisoners who got this thing going and the Negroes just followed along with them. In any case, it's a good thing Haywood Patterson was in Atmore Prison at the time, otherwise he probably would have been right up there in the middle of this action and the officials would surely have blamed this whole affair on us, the Scottsboro boys as they now called us.

After about an hour of this, the prison guards along with what seemed like the National Guard marched in through the back gate right into the yard. They began to yell, "Everybody to your cells, ... everybody to your cells!" Some of these prisoners began chanting back at the guard, "Nobody going back to their cell, ... nobody going back to their cell." When you're in a spot like this, you go along with the crowd, otherwise you just might end up getting killed by who knows what. So here we are, chanting along with everyone else, "Nobody goes back to their cell." The National Guard begins to march slowly towards us with shotguns and rifles at the ready. All of a sudden, we heard shots and quickly realized that the Guard was firing right at us. Man, it was just like stampeding cows. These guardsmen were firing buckshot right at us. I saw some fellows bleeding from head wounds, falling all around me, others running past me, knocking me down, and I'm saying to myself: "What am I doing here? These guardsmen are going to kill us all." After the first shots, I got up and start running along with everyone else.

Then there was a second series of shots, and I can see the walls I'm running towards begin to peel from the impact of the bullets hitting them. We're all running and these soldiers are firing again and again. We can hear someone yelling, "Go to your cells, ... go to your cells!" By now we have reached the doors to the dining room but due to the frenzied rush to get back inside, people were trampling, fighting, and actually blocking the entrance as they tried to get inside and away from the shooting. I'm running as fast as I could go and suddenly I'm knocked down just as the guard fires again. I notice little bits of sand jump up all around me and realize that these were bullets hitting the sand. As I'm trying to grab onto anyone passing me by I hear someone yell, "They're only firing tear gas!" I almost laugh at this ridiculous statement as I found myself crying out for help to anyone running past me. By now it was truly an every-man-for-himself situation, and that's a bad position to be in while in prison. So at this point, since all the skin on my knees were scraped off, the only thing I was able to do was to somehow drag myself up and stagger to the dining hall. Once inside the dining hall, they told everyone to get back to their night cells.

Man, you never seen a bloodier or miserable-looking bunch of people in your entire life. There were men with buckshot wounds all over their body. When they took those of us who needed some kind of medical treatment to the prison hospital, I just had to laugh at the pitiful state that some of these fellows were in. Now I know this isn't funny, but I saw grown men laid up there with buckshot all in their backside simply because they wanted some decent food. I tell you it's sad, but back then I just had to laugh at the crazy things you had to do in order to get some respect, and even then it doesn't always work out in your favor. This strike sure didn't. They locked us up that night, and the very next day to prove a point, marched us back to the dining hall, fed us the same old beans, greens, corn bread, and no meat to be seen. From there they marched us back to the yard and dared us to riot again.

For the guards this was important because they were trying to make sure that the riot didn't establish any strong bonding between the black and white prisoners. You see, when you're in the yard, blacks had to stay on one side of the yard and the whites on the other. This was done purposely because, quite naturally when you're in prison, the psychology is such that you begin to look at other groups as your potential enemy, your competitor, especially if you can't communicate with them. And of course the guards would always be there to keep this conflict going. In fact, often the guards would ignore a card game between blacks and whites, knowing that sooner or later a fight would break out and that this would eventually be viewed as a racial fight. This would then support the prison administration's claim that it had to keep its prison population separated. The fact of the matter is that all prison populations have groups, some good, others bad.

In prison you have to quickly learn which groups to stay away from and which might help you to survive. Neither one of these groups may be all that good, but that's the only choice you have. You can't be a loner unless you're constantly in "the hole" or in solitary confinement, and that can drive you crazy. You must learn how to pick your jailhouse friends. Those who you want to deal with. Someone who you can sit down and talk with, without compromising your safety or your life. But I got to tell you something about these groups: it is here where you get in trouble. It's one thing to have someone to talk with, read magazines, or even listen to the radio and another to find yourself being setup by the supposed friend who's really all about betrayal. Listen man, I've seen how this thing works and I've seen how people get killed dealing with these groups.

When you first enter prison, the guards tell you: "We got all kinds of people in here, you pick your own associates. However the best thing to do is to mind your own business and don't be associating with anybody." Now that sounds good, but it's a lie. The guards know damn well that the only way they can keep any order in prison is to work the various groups that exist. In fact, they even promote this so as to make their job easier, not to mention their own racist feeling about this person and that group. When you're in population, you pick your own kind of trouble and your own kind of friends. I know, I was there.

For example, there were some cats who every time you turn around were either in the hole or receiving some kind of punishment. They were usually busted for trying to beat the system without paying off the guards, such as the group that tried to make money while in prison. Yeah, that's right, these cats were making real silver half-dollar pieces right there in the old shirt factory. They had a place up in the ceiling where the mold for the coins and everything was hidden. I know, man, because I've seen these half-dollar pieces before they were busted, and these coins were real. Another group had a whiskey still with some good whiskey. Now I tried to stay away from these groups but of course in prison this is not always easy. So you learn to see and don't see. You hear and don't hear. You know but don't know, otherwise you going to find extra time and trouble hanging all over you. It's just like out here in the streets. You see and hear, and don't see and hear. Once you start seeing, hearing, and knowing everything, you find out that you're a problem to someone. The irony of all of this is that if you don't know exactly who your enemies are, you're in big trouble. Anyone can then slip up on you with a dirtch or knife, and sometime, somewhere later they will find you dead after you've bled or starved to death. You see, one really has to be very smooth in prison, almost like a con artist in order to survive behind those walls. It's no joke.

Of course, if you choose not to associate with any particular group, you're still going to be tested by someone because it's all about power and your ability to defend yourself against becoming a flunky or worse. So you act just like you did in the street. You move around in a bunch and you rely on your wits to let everyone know that you belong to such-and-such group. Today's young people use the word "crew," well we did the same thing by running crews in the joint, saying "this is my buddy" and all of that. It was all about protection.

Now the biggest thing going on in prison is either money or sex. You got cats in the penitentiary who turn out to be girls, and other cats who turn into what we called "wolves" who would attempt to convert other men into "girl-boys." Then there is another group who enter prison with either a drug or alcohol habit, have no money, and are therefore susceptible to all kinds of pressures from both the prisoners and the guards to comply with the demands of wolves or other prison predators. It was basically a war of the strong against the weak, and quite naturally if you don't have any willpower, someone is going to hit on you.

I've seen new prisoners come in there, no money, no nothing, beg for a cigarette, borrow some money, and then find themselves "obligated" to pay back the favor via sex. Of course, as the law of the jungle dictates, the guards knew what was going on, however they didn't report it. In fact they would try and set this up so that they could play off power groups against each other for money. The only time they would interfere is when it was for their benefit. If they wanted to catch you, they would, if they didn't, they wouldn't. Yet there have been riots and killings in prison over these "girl-boys," or what the wolves would call their "Old Ladies," when one of them would be "ripped off" by another wolf. This would usually happen if the girl-boy was offered more candy, cigarettes, money, or whatever. Yeah, they would fight just like out here in the street when there is a lovers' quarrel, except that in prison it usually ended up very quickly with someone being seriously hurt or killed. So as I said, most of us generally tried to stay clear of most of these groups, but then, us Scottsboro Boys were seen by the guards and prisoners as a group all by ourselves and were often picked on simply because we were supposed to be some "bad niggers."

Several conflicts with prisoners occurred due to this "Scottsboro" reputation of being "bad niggers." The first time I almost got into a fight with a white boy was basically because someone got him to try and set me up in the cotton factory. The rules were if they caught you fighting or doing something to destroy the machinery, you would automatically be sent to the hole. So, you had to "walk a chalk line," as we used to say, meaning you couldn't respond to every little instigation. If someone antagonized you or tried to set you up, it was best to simply walk away or hope that you could explain it to the guards. However, to do so would also be to jeopardize your reputation and possibly set the stage for more trouble.

One day while working in the cotton factory I noticed that one of the machines started to make a whole lot of noise. When I went over to it to see what was causing all of the racket, I noticed that rocks were placed inside one of the machines. Nearby there was another set of machines that this white kid was working on. I asked him if he noticed anyone fooling around with my machines. He said he seen this other white guy put rocks in the machinery. As he's telling me this, a guard yells at me, "Why you putting rocks in the machinery?" I said, "I haven't put no rocks in the machinery," but that this white boy and I were talking together when we both heard this noise at the same time. While it wasn't exactly the truth it was something the guard could accept. It was the old southern thing, a white person must be there to validate a Negroe's statement. Without that, it would be assumed I was lying. In any case, this white boy then tells the guard he also saw who was messing around with the machine. Once this other white kid was picked up for jamming my machines and sent to the hole for I think ninety days, I began to prepare for a major fight when he got out by stashing away a large steel pipe. When he did get out, I was waiting for him, figuring he might want to get even, but nothing happened. Now I was really surprised that this white kid did not come looking for me or the one who squealed on him because spending ninety days in the hole was no joke. In fact I don't know which is worse, a beating or the hole. If you get a beating, they would simply tear your ass up. If the infraction was that you dared to fight back against a cruel guard, you'd get beaten two or three times by the guards and then again before the warden in his office. When you were brought to the warden's office, they had you put a blanket on the floor, then lay on it with your stomach down. Two guards would hold your shoulders and legs down while a third would be whipping you with this leather strap on your behind. To make sure you didn't die in his office, they would have the prison doctor in there. After usually twenty or thirty of these lashes he would take your pulse and recommend how many more lashes your body could withstand. That was a hell of a punishment. I had one of these sessions in the warden's office and man, that strap cut through my skin like a razor blade. Blood was flying all over the place, I mean even on the walls. Once you got that, they would then throw you in solitary confinement where you'd have to lie down on your sides. I have those scars to this very day as a result of this sick shit.

Now the "hole" was something else and should not be confused with solitary confinement. I ended up there several times myself and nearly died in the process. The first time was over some money this boy owed me which he said he wasn't going to pay back. So me and this cat got into this fight. We both got dirtches, jabbing at each other, but nobody's really getting cut up. When the guards saw what was happening, they took our dirtches, gave each of us a leather strap, and told us to start whipping each other! They made us do this until we were both bloody and tired. For the guards this was like a game. They would cheer us on like we were contestants in some sort of sporting event. Yeah, that's right, we were their entertainment. When they got tired of watching us beat each other nearly to death, we were placed in separate concrete cells they called the hole.

The time you spend in the hole is determined by the offense. If you get into a fight with another inmate like I did, you'll get ten or twenty days. If you used a knife to seriously cut someone, depending on how bad they were messed up and if the guards dislike you, your sentence could be anywheres from thirty to ninety days in the hole. Thirty to ninety days is rough business. I lucked up and got only twenty days.

First they make you drink a large cup of castor oil. A little spoonful of this stuff would have you shitting all day long, so they gave us a full cup before locking us up. You get a bucket to sit on to move your bowels, a blanket to sleep on, and once a day someone would come down and give you a piece of bread and a cup of water. Now you can't really see anything in there, not your hands, legs, or anything, but you can sure smell your own shit. So you sit there hour after hour, day after day, just thinking about how you are going to survive this madness. There's nothing else to think about. Soon you begin to lose track of time as day becomes night and all sense of the outside becomes strangely vague and almost irrelevant. There is nobody to talk with besides yourself. If you're not strong you can easily begin to give up as your mind goes blank. At this point you feel like some damn animal anyway. Even when they fed you your bread and water, it was shoved to you like they were feeding something in the zoo. You take it, eat it, sit, shit, and wait.

When I finished my time in the hole I lost so much weight and was so weak I must have looked just like a man who was starving to death in someone's concentration camp, and this was only twenty days in the hole. You can imagine what a man who spent sixty or ninety days must have looked like. By being so weak I could hardly stand up to walk out of there. Yet there are some people who were constantly being sent to the hole for all kinds of reasons. Some of them would eventually lose their health in there and simply die as a result of being constantly treated so harshly. That's the way it was back then, maybe even today. In any case, if you had any sense, you were going to try and stay out of the hole, because man, that was pure hell. Now you can believe that.

Chapter 5

Against Judicial Murder

Though Clarence Norris spoke on the importance of staying out of the hole while in prison, the very structure of prison life seemed to mandate that every step taken to ensure that this would not happen actually brought one in direct conflict with the anomie of being incarcerated. Much of what we view as abnormal conditions within prisons, that is, maximum security, is but a reflection of lifestyles in society at large. Minimum security considerations are established to ensure societal stability, or at least an adherence to prescribed social relationships, which are often administered in ways analogous to those found behind prison walls or in maximum security.

For example, during the 1930s, an era of depression and economic deprivation for millions of Americans, the test of judicial justice was very often weighed against the leaden and cumbersome needs of scapegoating and racism. Within this context, part of the problem for judicial defense teams representing southern African Americans was getting a presumably unsympathetic white jury to realize the innocence of a client who historically, simply by his existence, had already been deemed a social outcast and therefore guilty of anything. Though this was primary for the defense, of equal importance was getting the uncommitted observer of social justice to understand that the pain of being incarcerated unjustly is one thing, whereas dealing with the psychological pressures is quite another and had direct implications for Americans irrespective of race. It was the latter occurrence that millions of southern whites had convinced themselves was the social lot for blacks while ignoring the political consequences that such beliefs had on their own lifestyle. What they overlooked was that this negative reality was experienced jointly by both the jailed and the jailer. The effects of racism could not be quarantined because it does not exist within a social vacuum.

A prison guard once commented on this phenomenon:

> These prisoners are lucky, they'll leave here one day, one way or another. I'm stuck here. This is my job. This is how I feed my family. I get a good salary, but I have to come here everyday and voluntarily lock myself up behind these walls. I too feel convicted though I haven't done anything. Sometimes I find

Underground cells in a Georgia convict labor camp in the early 1930s. Eight hands can be seen sticking through the iron grating (Library of Congress).

> myself doing things that are just crazy. I used to laugh at the prisoners having races with captured cockroaches or water bugs, then one day I found myself capturing them also but I wouldn't race them. I would get a piece of paper, place the roach on it, then put a paper cup over it and light the four corners of the paper with a match. Watching the roach trying to get away as the fire burned closer to the cup and slowly roasting this helpless bug really excited me. When I eventually realized after a few months what was happening to me, I really became scared. I began to ask myself, if this is happening to me, what in the hell is going on with these prisoners? This kind of violence is all over this place and it's scary.[1]

Understanding the pressures of national economic destabilization can be challenging and dangerous if one empathizes with those who so often become the scapegoats for a failing social ethos. Similarly, when law cloaks itself in the reflective mood of a frustrated and enraged populace, the incarcerated are sacrificed on the altar of state power and social order. If race, an American dilemma, is added to this milieu, a public's ability to understand or even empathize with those pressures faced by the entrapped disfranchised becomes muted by declarations to maintain white American hegemony. Consequently, for the nine black Scottsboro defendants, living year after year under the administrative authority of southern white prison officials, the question of guilt or innocence was secondary to the question of white racial prerogative. Race, in this case white political consciousness and social experiences, would determine the question of guilt or innocence.

As the nation, both black and white, struggled with the devastating effects of national economic depression, racial strife increased, as did the number of state-sponsored executions, some sixty-two at Kilby Prison alone during the 1930s.[2] Similarly, when a growing army of the poor in the early 1930s placed demands on President Herbert Hoover's administration to address a growing national economic crisis, only to be countered by state authority in the form of the National Guard—or, as in the case of the Henry Ford auto complex, his private police force—intimidation, outright force, and murder became the weapons of the strong. This was complicated by a reality that as the depression of the thirties gained a full head of steam, racism, which always existed in its most repugnant form throughout the South, found a socially acceptable scapegoat in the Negro. Politically active Negroes viewed historically as a conceivable enemy of social tranquillity, and in the thirties as a potential Communist dupe and therefore enemy to the state, may require incarceration, many whites argued, if not public execution as an example to other blacks. In fact, though the traditional lynching of blacks in the 1930s from tree limbs stayed in fashion throughout much of the South in lieu of execution by the state, the electric chair itself became a symbol not only of "official" execution but also of an execution that transferred the public's psychic need for killing to the state. In doing so, the state, in this case Alabama, could placate growing levels of economic and political frustration by handling that which the mob would have accomplished in its own unique fashion. In this sense the nine Scottsboro defendants were victims not only of the whims of an enraged, misguided, and racist posse of Alabamian country folk or of the devious manipulation of two hoboing white women scared to face the vagrancy laws of a southern state. They were victims also of a society that needed assurance that its traditional resources would not have to be shared in a time of scarcity with blacks, who were fighting their own struggle against racism, economic exploitation, and physical brutality.

Therein exists an interesting dichotomy in that although southern blacks at this time were the South's most valuable labor resource, they were a resource that had little or no control over its own labor. This lack of control extended into other areas of southern black life. In fact in many respects, for white southerners, blacks existed as an anathema to white society, as a contradiction to the notion of all that was good about the South, America, and Western civilization. Translating this into notions about black bestiality, low lifestyles, and the need to "keep them in their place" was critical for white southerners in that their own regeneration was ensured as long as they didn't have to sink down to the level of the despised black race. Being able to continually define blacks as such became essential and mandatory for their own sense of salvation.

Nevertheless, there were some southern whites who, for a variety of reasons, refused to have their own personal integrity compromised by what they considered to be the intellect of the "rabble." For them, blacks might not be their social equal, but they were unwilling to compromise their own intellect in order to maintain social control, political advantage, or racial hegemony. In Alabama during the thirties, these few were clearly viewed as the absurd minority by those who knew better.

1

SCOTTSBORO TRIAL MOVED 50 MILES
Negroes Will Face Second Prosecution at Decatur on Change of Venue

SCOTTSBORO, Ala., March 7 —
The new trial which the United States Supreme Court ordered for the eight Negroes sentenced to die after conviction of attacking two white girls nearly two years ago will not be held in Jackson county, still embittered, in which they were first convicted.

In a courtroom crowded with mountaineers, Judge A.E. Hawkins granted a defense motion this afternoon for a change of venue and set the place of trial in Decatur, the seat of Morgan county, some fifty miles west of Scottsboro.

Judge Hawkins, who presided over the first trial, declined, however, to rule on a defense motion to quash the indictments on the ground that Negroes were excluded from the grand jury which indicted the defendants and the petit jury which found them guilty and decreed their electrocution.

He left that issue, which leading members of the bar of Jackson county said never had been raised since the reconstruction period, to be decided by the judge before whom the new trial will be held. Judge Horton of Athens, Ala., is expected to preside at the new trial....

The State, represented by its dapper young Attorney General, Thomas E. Knight Jr., a son of the Supreme Court Justice who wrote the opinion of the highest court in Alabama affirming the conviction and sentence of the accused Negroes, but was reversed by the Supreme Federal Tribunal, did not oppose the motion for a change of venue.

"I am not opposing this motion," he said, "because I want the people of all these United States to know that these defendants will get a fair trial. They had one when they were tried here and convicted and they will get a fair trial, regardless of what county of Alabama is chosen for their trial now."

"The people of Jackson County are to be commended for their restraint in this case. They have not sought to influence any one half so much as these outside organizations which have come in here and tried to influence the rest of the country to believe that an injustice has been done here"....

Feeling is still very strong and there are many in Scottsboro who declare regretfully that the old way of the rope was better than the newer way of the law. Yesterday when the motion to quash the indictment was offered and there

> were rumors that the prisoners might be brought from the penitentiary to the court house a large crowd gathered in the square outside.
>
> Many of them had shotguns and their presence caused some anxiety to timorous visitors from New York. Old-timers reassured them, however, explaining that it was an old Scottsboro custom on the first Monday of every month to barter for farm implements and produce. It just happened that there were a lot of mountaineers who wanted to swap guns for things they needed more.[3]

Some two years into the trial of their lives, on March 27, 1933, the Scottsboro defendants found themselves in front of Judge James E. Horton. Arguing innocence for his clients, attorney Samuel Leibowitz realized that a ray of hope did exist with this apparently rational judge, who was to preside over a case in which most white Alabamians and possibly even some blacks had already been convinced in their hearts and minds of the defendants' guilt. Judge Horton was clearly one of the few who resisted the racist banter that prevailed during the early thirties, although his resistance would place a heavy penalty on his career.

With Decatur as the site for this second trial, the defendants were placed in a new environment. As one writer described it:

> A quiet little town of twenty thousand people, of whom about three thousand were Negroes, Decatur was supported by several hosiery mills and an iron foundry. The mills were still operating, although at lower wages and shorter shifts, but the foundry had been closed, putting another three thousand workers on the rolls of the unemployed.
>
> Shade trees lined the narrow streets of the white residential areas, composed of rows of rather modern frame houses, but the white slims and "Niggertown" were replicas of their counterparts in Scottsboro and Huntsville and throughout the South: a veritable breeding-ground for unspeakable squalor, hastily thrown together on land where even weeds grew sparingly. "Niggertown" in Decatur was referred to with a snicker as "buzzard's roost."
>
> Now the population had almost doubled. The main street, the courthouse, the jail, and the Colonial Hotel were studded with over two hundred National Guardsmen, installed to keep order among the townsfolk and the curious visitors, and to prevent rioting and lynching.
>
> The courthouse building was solidly constructed of huge gray stones and pillars; one look at the front, and a walk through the interior was convincing proof of its permanence. The main "white" jail was in this building.
>
> The nine defendants had been moved to Decatur from Birmingham, but the jail where they were housed was another story. A crumbling old edifice made of brick and pine logs, it had been condemned as a city jail three years earlier, and now was only used for Negro prisoners. The bricks were turning to fine red sand, and the heart of the lumber had rotted long ago.[4]

In a more personalized manner, Blaine Owen, a white ILD organizer, described the area surrounding Decatur as a "gaunt country where cotton stood only a foot and a half or two feet in the drab fields, the boll scrimpy and hard." Impressed by the rigors of a basically rural, economically depressed, and racially segregated populace, he was also able to sense what

The Scottsboro defendants under the watch of the Alabama National Guard, March 20, 1931. The defendants from left to right: Clarence Norris, Olen Montgomery, Andy Wright, Willie Robertson, Eugene Williams, Roy Wright, Charlie Weems, Ozie Powell, and Haywood Patterson.

the community saw as necessary for their survival, be they black or white. Ironically, crossing the racial lines that physically separated southern communities, hamlets, and towns in the 1930s was not only suspect by most liberals, black or white, but dangerous due to its implied threat to the established mores that separated whites, poor or otherwise, from an ever-present danger of black uplift.

Although this "threat" had been institutionalized by years of mythology before the depression of the 1930s, it was a threat ground into the psyche of southerners as a result of the historic relationship between those who were once an enslaved race and now found it difficult to shed that mantle and others who could not forget the social benefits that were accorded them as being members of a slave-owning race. For southern whites in particular, social dictates of this kind, premised on color, became the only "saving grace" that prohibited them from facing the reality of their own peasantry. However, for blacks, rising above those dictates, which defined them as being the official "pariah" race, was essential, if not providential. Herein existed the basis for social crisis, in that the former saw their position as a permanent reality, whereas the latter viewed their position as a temporary state of inequality.

In Morgan County, Alabama, during the 1930s, challenging the established mores of a hamlet, town, county, or state was to risk censorship of the most violent type, that is, lynching. In this atmosphere, Organizer Owen set out to ascertain public opinion on the grass-roots level and, in doing so, uncovered a sensitivity among people that is often lost in the din and confusion of battle. Graphically describing the interactive experience of rural folk with their social environment, Owen recalled:

> Stopping to pick up a pebble, I glanced back between my legs. No one in sight. I stepped quickly across the ditch and into the unpainted, square building with the rough wooden cross nailed up over the door. This was the place.
>
> The preacher went right on, reading verse after verse from his great Bible, his chest swelling out of the too-small morning coat. One day a week he preached the word of the Lord, six days heaved cotton bales in the mill. There were the few moments during which Grace, buxom and stiff in a starched white dress, saw me and came down the aisle, happiness glowing from her broad face, wide eyes and startling, strong teeth.
>
> Many turned to stare as she shook my hand, clothes rustling.
>
> "I knew you'd come, comrade Blaine, I just knew it," she told me in a choked whisper, still squeezing my hand hard in both her great, dark ones, tears welling up in her eyes.
>
> The preacher coughed and Grace flustered, nodded, smiled more broadly than ever, nodded some more and sat down beside me. I believe some there were a little scared. A white man shakes hands with a black, sits beside one, talks to black people about — well, there are certain things black folks talk about only among themselves, rights, freedom, equality. No white folks want that — why, they'll lynch you.
>
> The verses again went on and faces turned again forward. We listened. It was the story of Jericho, and the deep, full voice of the worker-preacher filled the little church with the trumpet sounds of a people pounding against high walls.
>
> "One of our beloved Sisters," he said slowly, after the reading was over and we had stood together to join in song, "has made arrangements to have with us a distinguished white speaker for today..." I don't remember the rest. It was most polite. Then Grace got up and simply said, "This is Comrade Blaine, brothers and sisters, an' he's coming to us from the ILD, that has been saving those Scottsboro boys." There was a great sigh in the little church and a shifting forward in the seats.
>
> What I said is not important now. I spoke of Scottsboro, of what must be done about it. I spoke to the old gray-haired man who leaned on his knotted stick and cupping his hand over one ear to catch each word.
>
> I spoke to the slim brown girl in the fifth row who sat still and serious beside the tall, rangy Negro youth and held his hand tightly, never moving while I spoke. And, "Amen, Brother," the old man said, when I paused. "Hallelujah," three others exclaimed at once, when I spoke of the growing and ever more necessary unity.
>
> I said things which were not new to these people, the men in the rusty black suits, the folds showing where they had been laid by for the week, or just in plain, laundered overalls.
>
> It was the eyes, the faces, the stillness of every big-knuckled hand that said more things to me than I could find words for, that day.

"Hear what has been said," the preacher boomed when I sat down again, "and harken, you people. This here's the voice of an angle sent down by Jesus to save us poor colored folks from our trials and tribulations."

And Scottsboro flamed alive there in a tiny church on the outskirts of Decatur. Men and women walked out of that day with new hope and new confidence with a sudden realization that there were white men too, who were marching with them against the high walls of Jericho.

Huntsville is no better, I believe, or worse than the average textile town of the south. Except in a very few small mills, Negro workers are allowed only cleaning and loading jobs. Jim Crow lines are sharply drawn. The lynch spirit is carefully nurtured.

It was early evening and Taylor's wife, Clara, had gone inside to mix dough for biscuits and put coffee on the oil stove. We sat out front and talked.

"That Labor Defense outfit," he asked of me, a reporter for labor papers that had "been around,"—"they say that's a nigger outfit, but they defend all sorts of working men, like in strikes for instance, don't they?"

I said they did. Taylor is a white textile worker, a weaver, and secretary of his union local. We had been talking of the last great strike.

"Now the Scottsboro case for instance," he said. "It's too bad so many folks around here got the idea that was all they done."

We talked about the Scottsboro case. I explained how the "rape" cry was just a cover-up for the whole Jim Crow and special oppression structure and that it was directly out of this that the wage differential and lower living conditions of the southern toilers was nurtured.

He nodded. "I went up there to Paint Rock that day," he said. "They come around and told us, 'rape,' and a whole gang went up. I reckon we was aiming to do them in right then."

I didn't say anything. He sat on the steps, his elbows on his knees, picked up a twig and broke it carefully in his strong weaver's fingers.

"You know," and the words were slow. He cleared his throat and again the twig snapped in the twilight silence. Clara walked across the bare board floor inside and lit the oil lamp.

"They tried to pull something like that right here not long back, right in the middle of the strike, to be exact.

"There is a little store at the edge of the mill village, owned by a woman who was known to have attempted to recruit scabs. During the height of the strike the Negro helper on the Coca Cola truck was accused by a girl working in this grocery store of having asked her for a date while delivering a case of bottles.

"No one did put stock in what she said, anyhow, but the law come and took the nigger down. Guys come out from town that night and started talking around about stringing him up, 'fixin' to get the strikers to do it. But we could see how we was being wire-worked," my narrator continued, looking up at me. "They just wanted to get us off the track and in trouble and give us a black eye."

About a week later the Negro was released on a $25 bond, an absolutely ridiculous and unheard-of procedure with such a charge in a Southern court. The trick—the usual attempt to raise the Negro scare to break the unity of white and black workers—just didn't work in this case.

"You know Arnolds?" Taylor asked me as we sat down to eat.

"Hell, yes," I popped out, then remembered and excused myself for the cussing, but just recalling Arnolds' huge, good-natured bulk excited me.

"Now, there's a guy for you," Taylor added, taking a forkful of the greens.

I had met Arnolds on the picket line during the textile strike. He was president of a local in a nearby town and proud of the hundred-percent organization that had been achieved there. He had a right to be proud, too, of the love in the eyes of men and women, boys and girls that followed him as we walked around.

But most of all he was proud of what workers had done. When things got tough and the law jugged some of the union men for beating hell out of a scab and there were preparations to smash the picket lines and open the mill, Negro workers from a steel mill in the same town came around.

"Mister Arnolds," one of them said, "we sure want to see yu-all win out now, and we figured maybe we could help yu- all out a-picketing, if it'd be all right with you."

"All right!" Arnolds roared when he told me about it and his head tilted back as he laughed. Then he grew serious again.

"You want to know why they done that, son?" He tapped my chest slowly with his calloused forefinger. "Cause when we started out to organize our union, we went at it to have it one hundred percent.

"One hundred percent," he repeated. "And that means the colored folks, too."

As I was leaving I had asked him if there were any Communists in the union. The papers had been full of Red- scare accusations and even some of the union leaders had echoed these things. As a matter of fact, I knew there was only a single Communist Party member in the town at the time.

Arnolds looked at me shrewdly. Then he suddenly smiled and put his arm across my shoulder. "Well, now, I guess we're all Communist in a way, aren't we?"[5]

2

In this setting, Judge Horton demanded that an atmosphere of judicial impartiality exist within his courtroom, something that under presiding judge E. A. Hawkins in the first trial was nonexistent. As a consequence of Hawkins' continually rapping his gavel and his impatient push of the "speedy trial" concept, he unwittingly provided the basis for a successful appeal of the death sentence by the defense attorneys in the U.S. Supreme Court. Under Horton's judicial gaze, the first defendant, Haywood Patterson, for the second time was found guilty and sentenced to death; however, attorneys Samuel Leibowitz, Joseph R. Brodsky, and George Chamlee were able to establish a record of appealable motions, which assured that his case would have to be reviewed again by the Alabama and eventually the Federal Supreme Courts. A major factor in this appeal was Ruby Bates' retraction of her original rape charge. This reversal, by a key witness for the state, sent a message throughout the mythical yet dangerous world of race relations: that white southern women might reject the burden of alleged eternal "purity" placed upon them by southern white males and that the encapsulating social apparition of white womanhood in the midst of an agonizing depression was no longer sacrosanct, even in the rural areas of the South.

Bates' revelation not only tested both the black and the white communities' presumptions about the case but also placed the state's primary witnesses at odds when Victoria Price continued to maintain her original testimony of being raped by these nine black youths.

STATE OF NEW YORK
COUNTY OF NEW YORK

RUBY BATES, being duly sworn, says: I was continuously present on March 25, 1931 with Victoria Price during the time when it is charged that Eugene Williams committed rape upon said Victoria Price for which charge he has been indicted. Said Eugene Williams is entirely innocent of said charge. I further state that said Eugene Williams did not commit rape upon said Victoria Price nor upon me on said date or at any other time.

I further state that Eugene Williams is completely innocent of any misconduct whatsoever toward me or toward said Victoria Price in any form, shape or manner whatsoever.

RUBY BATES

Sworn to before me, this
17th day of May, 1933
Morris A. Greenbaum[6]

The basis for this sworn statement occurred in early January 1933 when a controversial letter from Ruby Bates to her boyfriend, Earl Streetman, was obtained by ILD attorneys. At a court hearing with Judge John P. McCoy in Birmingham, Alabama, a writ of habeas corpus was presented, asking for the release of Roy Wright, who was underage when jailed and indicted as an adult but up to this point was still unsentenced. On January 30, McCoy dismissed the writ in behalf of Wright and sent him back to jail, still unsentenced. The "Earl Streetman" letter was eventually presented in March as part of the defense's evidence, but it was not until June that Wright, along with Eugene Williams, was sent to juvenile court.

The controversial letter stated:

Jan 5 1932
Huntsville, Ala.
215 Connelly Ave.

Dearest Earl

I want to make a statement too you Mary Sanders is a goddam lie about those Negroes jazzing me those policemen made me tell a lie that is my statement because I want to clear myself that is all too if you want to believe me OK. If not that is okay. If not that is okay. You will be sorry some day if you had to stay in jail with eight Negroes you would tell a lie two those Negroes did not touch me or those white boys I hope you will believe me the law don't, i love you better than Mary does or anybody else in the world that is why I am telling you of this thing. i was drunk at the time and did not know what i was doing. i know it was wrong too let those Negroes die on account of me i hope you will believe my statement because it is the gods truth i hope you will believe me. i was jazzed but those white boys jazzed me. i wish those Negroes are not Burnt on account of me it is those white boys fault that is my statement, and that is all I know i hope you tell the law hope you will answer

Ruby Bates

Huntsville Ala
215 Connelly Ave.
P.S. This is one time that I might tell a lie But it is the truth so god help me.[7]

A second major argument for an appeal started with the beginning arguments by both the defense and the prosecution on the motion to quash the indictment by defense attorney Samuel Leibowitz. Up to this point, no African Americans were to be found on petit juries throughout the state of Alabama. To demonstrate this point, Leibowitz called thirteen witnesses to provide evidence that blacks had been excluded from the grand jury that had returned a twenty-count indictment against the Scottsboro defendants back in April 1931.

Some of these witnesses—such as Dr. Frank S. Sykes, Dr. N. E. Cashin, and Dr. N. M. Sykes—were physicians who stated they had never served on a jury. Similar accounts came from Hulett J. Banks, bill poster; W. G. Wilson, lay preacher; William James Wood, dentist; and J. D. Picketet, school principal—all of whom claimed that they could name countless other blacks who were just as qualified as they were but who had never served as jurors. At this point Leibowitz informed the court that he could provide at least four hundred other similar blacks who on prima facie were qualified to sit as jurors. In one redirect examination of two black witnesses who were never summoned to be jurors, it was revealed that both had served in World War I, with one being a graduate of the Phillips Exeter Academy and Howard University, the other a leader of the local Negro Civic League. Leibowitz went on to explain that blacks' Fourteenth Amendment rights had been so abridged that voting rights were secured only by demonstrating one's memorization skills in reciting the federal constitution for qualifiers.

Mr. Tidwell, who was appointed by Governor Miller to the jury board as commissioner, testified in behalf of the state and, in doing so, was forced to present the county's jury roll-book and to identify, if any, the names of blacks in it. Prosecutor Knight objected to this procedure on the grounds that this was immaterial evidence and that county commissioners had discretional powers, "which no one can go behind," in attempting to show that an absence of blacks from these rolls was evidence of an arbitrary misuse of power.[8] Judge Horton, however, ruled that the evidence was proper. Seizing the moment, Leibowitz asked, "Isn't it true that you and your fellow commissioners are required to place on that roll [book] the names of all citizens who possess the qualifications prescribed by law—all citizens—isn't that true?" Agreeing that this was his understanding of the law, Tidwell was then sharply asked, "Now isn't it a fact that all the names written in that book are names of white citizens?" "I don't know," responded the jury commissioner.

While the defense's argument centered on the jury-selection system in Jackson County, the county seat for Scottsboro, it was also hoping that the judge would see the relevance of the contentions to Morgan County, where Decatur was located. After arguments by both sides, with the defense threatening to summon every known person on the jury roll-books, some twenty-five hundred persons, to prove that they were all white, even if it financially broke the state in the process, Judge Horton finally brought the proceedings to a halt by declaring that further testimony along this line would be merely cumulative and that the court had "decided not to hear further testimony on this question. The motion is overruled."

Although some questioned the wisdom of Horton's decision, Leibowitz did not. Clearly preferring to have blacks on the jury, Leibowitz was not naive to the severe intimidation that whites would place on any black chosen for the grand jury. However, he also concluded that by allowing the defense to make an argument against jury-selection bias, Judge Horton was providing a basis for appeal by the defense in the likelihood that the defendants were found guilty by the jury. This was a judicial window of opportunity that any competent defense could not ignore.

For most white Alabamians, the idea of blacks sitting in the jury box was so strange that it was viewed as an incitement to riot, if not murder. An editorial in the *Jackson Sentinel* prophesied soon after the issue was raised:

> The plot thickens.
>
> We have no editorial this week on the "Negro trial matter." We just couldn't do one without getting mad as hell. And why? We refer you to the statement by the "New York defenders," appearing in *The Chattanooga Times* and *The Sentinel* today. Its arrogance is most astounding. It smacks of trouble. It is the most dangerous movement launched in the South in many years — it brands Jackson County citizenry as little short of being cold-blooded murderers.
>
> After we forget "the rope" to pick up "the code" for the safety and benefit of the Negroes, we are told that we must have Negro jurors on any jury trying the blacks if they are to get "their rights." A Negro juror in Jackson County would be a curiosity — and some curiosities are embalmed, you know.
>
> **Cannot Recall Negro on Jury**
>
> The oldest citizens of Scottsboro said today they could not recall a time when a Negro had sat upon a jury. There was nothing odd about that, they explained, for there are only about twenty-five Negro voters in the county's population of 36,000.
>
> The commissioners of Election appointed by the governor have plenary power to decide on who is eligible to vote. White men are presumed to be competent, but Negroes have to prove it by doing something easy like reciting the constitution of the United States from beginning to end, if they are so bold as to apply. The twenty-five or so who do vote are eligible because of the "grandfather law" which guarantees the suffrage to any descendant of a soldier of the Confederate or Union Armies.
>
> From a legal point of view, attorneys maintain that since a white man has no right to object to a Negro on his trial jury, a Negro cannot legally complain

about the presence of whites. The ratio of whites to Negroes in Jackson County is about three to one, but in counties further south the Negroes outnumber the whites nearly ten to one.

Not only were there no Negroes on the first trial juries but the white men who sat in judgment were nearly all from what is known as the Sand Mountain section where the natives boast of signs reading: "Nigger — don't let the sun go down on your head."

No doubt exists in Scottsboro that the result of the second trial will be the same as the first, regardless of the change in locale. However, a new complication has arisen. Sheriff T.W. McBryde received a report today from a deputy at Huntsville, who said that Ruby Bates had disappeared from her home there. She was reported to have sent a letter home saying that she was tired of the unwelcomed publicity and did not want any more to do with it. The State's attorneys, however, were confident that they could find her.[9]

3

Now two years older, taller, and clearly more aware of their predicament, "the Scottsboro Boys" faced a bewildered white populace who clearly found it difficult to understand why the state and counties were spending all this money on a bunch of "guilty Niggers." Even the jail itself was a reminder that they were on a social treadmill that countless others before them had trekked.

The Decatur city jail was not only old but had walls laced with the grime and filth of prisoners who spent their time in steel cages with nothing to keep the mind busy except the intrigues of a caged mind. Although the Decatur jail was no longer used as "the death house," in its courtyard stood the old gallows, standing there as a reminder to the present inhabitants that the rope was always a part of Alabamian justice.

In the courtroom itself, a trial full of twists and turns was beginning to unfold. With no blacks on the jury or as spectators, a few black reporters were allowed to sit in a special section off to the side. One reporter, from the *Afro-American*, described the courtroom:

> Two high, narrow windows, half-covered by yellow shades … hid the sunlight. Three windows back of the judge's bench are completely shaded. The benches to accommodate 425 spectators are filled.
>
> The air is foul, for the windows are closed tight, though they have screens over them. Spectators, lawyers and newspapermen smoke during adjournments and the place has a grayish haziness over it.
>
> Whites sit in the majority of the seats, mostly young boys out of work. Here and there are lean bony men of the South with hard looks in their eyes staring steadily.[10]

As before, Victoria Price took the stand; she maintained her previous testimony that she had been raped, though on many points she contradicted her earlier testimony. In direct examination, the Jackson County solicitor for the state, H. B. Bailey, carefully led an impetuous Victoria through the following testimony:

Mr. Bailey:
Your name is Mrs. Victoria Price?
A: Yes sir.
Q: Where do you live?
A: Huntsville, Alabama.
Q: Where were you living on the 25th day of March 1931?
A: Huntsville, Alabama.
Q: What was the very first violence that was done to you?
A: They grabbed me and asked me was I going to put out, and I say "No sir, I don't know what that means" and he says "You will or die" and I said "I would rather die."
Q: That is talking, I am asking for violence?
A: I pushed them back, and when I pushed back, one of them grabbed me and hit me on the head, and pulled me down.
Q: Grabbed at you,—where did they put their hands?
A: The first that grabbed me?
Q: Yes?
A: My legs and shoulders and held me over the gondola.
Q: Was that before you were hit or after?
A: I wouldn't say which it was.
Q: Did any one of these negroes grab you by the breast when he was raping you?
A: I don't remember whether he did or not.
Q: Some of them held you by the shoulders while having intercourse with you, did any grab you around the waist?
A: No, not while they was raping me.
Q: Any one of the six?
A: No sir.
Q: Did some one of them grab you by the private parts, or manhandle you in that way?
A: No sir.
Q: Was it painful, did you suffer pain?
A: I don't know what that is?
Q: Don't you know what pain is?
A: I don't know what it is to a man.
Q: Did you suffer pain?
A: I did, sure.
Q: Were they rough with you?
A: Sure they was kinder rough.
Q: They were tearing your insides wasn't they?
A: No sir.
Q: Did some of them kick you?
A: I don't know whether they did or not.
Q: A portion of your skin was scraped while they were raping you, a portion of your body was scraped?
A: The skin was torn in several places on my body.
Q: Where was it, on what part of your body was your skin torn, give us some of the places?
A: Well, on my throat and on my face. (indicating)
Q: On your side?
A: No, I didn't say on my side.

Q: Where else?
A: On my back.
Q: Where else?
A: I had one spot on my leg.
Q Where the skin was torn?
A: To the best of my remembrance it was skinned a little bit.
Q: Where else?
A: I wouldn't say about where else.
Q: How about the skin on your stomach?
A: I wouldn't say.
Q: Was your stomach bruised?
A: Yes sir, I had some blue spots.
Q: On your stomach?
A: I wouldn't say.
Q: Was your stomach sore?
A: Yes sir, kin'ly.
Q: Hurt when you touch it?
A: Yes sir.
Q: Were you black on your hips while lying on the rocks while these six negroes raped you?
A: I don't know whether I was or not.
Q: Don't you know afterwards,—your hips were sore wasn't they?
A: Kin'ly.
Q: Your back, that was sore from lying on those rocks, wasn't it?
A: Yes sir.
Q: You stood up in this gondola, didn't you, when the train stopped at Paint Rock?
A: After the train stopped, I did.
Q: You sat down while it was coming along, until it stopped, and then you got up on the edge when it stopped?
A: Yes sir.
Q: You are sure of that?
A: I was lying in Gilley's lap until it stopped, with my head in his lap.
Q: When was it that you put your head in Gilley's lap?
A: After the negroes had quit raping me.
Q: How long before the train stopped?
A: Five or ten minutes.
Q: The intercourse was over then?
A: Yes sir.
Q: What were you doing?
A: I wasn't doing anything.
Q: Just standing around?
A: No I wouldn't say positively that I did.
Q: Where was Ruby?
A: She was with one of the negroes with his arm around her neck.
Q: Standing up?
A: Sitting down.
Q: You were lying down and she was sitting down?
A: Yes sir.
Q: Were you lying down when the train passed the station?
A: No sir, I was standing up then looking.

Q: The car that you were in, did that pass the station or not?
A: I don't remember.
Q: After the train stopped you and this Gilley got up?
A: Gilley did.
Q: You too?
A: I did in a couple of minutes.
Q: You were still lying in the gondola on the chert for two minutes?
A: I said for a couple of minutes.
Q: Wait a minute lady, I want you to be clear on that, I want to know if you are telling us that you were lying on your back for a couple of minutes after the train stopped, and then got up, is that what you say?
A: I was sitting up when the train stopped.
Q: You said you were lying down, isn't that what you said?
A: I was lying down when it stopped, when the train stopped Gilley got out of the car, and I sat up like I am now.
Q: Did you continue to lay in the gondola after the train stopped?
A: No sir, no sooner than the train stopped than Gilley got out, and I sit up.
Q: Did Gilley climb out of the gondola after you got up?
A: No, he didn't stay in there.
Q: Did you or Gilley call out to any man along there for help, or say "Hay," and call the attention to any one?
A: I don't know anything about that. They were all hollering and going on around there.[11]

Much of Victoria Price's testimony was contradicted by Dr. E. R. Bridges, who examined both Victoria and Ruby Bates soon after their departure from the train at Paint Rock, Alabama. Bridges, a licensed general medical practitioner, was questioned by Defense Attorney Leibowitz as to Victoria's physical condition when he examined her after the alleged rape. Though some portions of his testimony were objected to by the state and court for submission in the subsequent trial of Clarence Norris in November 1933, those excerpted portions are presented here. Clearly indicated are the juxtaposed judicial positions of Judge J. Horton, who allowed the defense some latitude in presenting its case, and Judge W. W. Callahan, who rejected much of this evidence later, in Norris' trial.

Q: After she removed her clothes, you gave her a physical examination?
A: Yes sir.
Q: Did you find any cut on the top of her hand from which any blood came?
A: I don't remember seeing any.
Q: Did you find any bruises on the face?
A: No.
Q: Did you find any puffed up lips, or swollen lips?
A: No, I don't remember that.
Q: You mean that if you had seen that you would have noticed it?
A: Yes, we were looking for those things.
Q: Because you wanted to find out if the woman had been choked or mistreated?

COURT: I don't think that you ought to ask that question.
MR. LEIBOWITZ: There was no objection from the state.

COURT: I am the judge, and it's my business to see that improper questions are not asked.

Q: Were you instructed by the authorities of Jackson County to make the examination?

MR. KNIGHT: That is objected to.

COURT: Sustain the objection.

Q: Just what part of the face did you examine?

A: I made an examination of the face. I didn't see anything. I didn't see any blood.

Q: Were you examining her for the purpose of finding marks, if possible?

A: Yes sir, and make note of everything I saw.

Q: You didn't find any scratch on her face?

A: I don't remember it.

Q: Did you examine the chest of this women?

A: Not that day; I did the next day.

Q: You examined her the next day?

A: Yes sir.

Q: Did you examine her abdomen?

A: Yes sir.

Q: Any cuts on the chest?

A: No.

Q: Any cuts on the abdomen?

A: No.

Q: Did you examine her back?

A: Yes.

Q: Were there any cuts on the back from which blood would come?

A: No.

Q: Any cuts on her legs?

A: No.

Q: Any abrasions or skin rubbed off on the legs?

A: No.

Q: Any tears of the skin near the privates at all?

A: None near the privates at all.

Q: Was the vagina torn in any way?

A: No.

Q: You did find a couple of scratches on the wrist?

A: On the wrist of one arm, and on the fore-arm of the other.

Q: These were scratches?

A: Yes.

Q: Did you know that this woman had been riding freight trains?

A: I knew they were taken off a freight train. I heard that, I didn't know it.

Q: Outside the scratches on the wrist and forearm. Did you find any lacerations of any kind?

A: No.

Q: When you examined this woman, did you examine her pulse?

A: Her pulse was not fast; it was in the bounds of normal.

Q: Was the respiration about normal too?

A: Yes sir.

Q: That is the breathing, isn't it?

A: Yes sir.

Q: A person under excitement, especially a woman, would show a rapid pulse, wouldn't she?

A: As a rule, yes.
Q: Would she show rapid breathing?
A: Yes.
Q: Suppose a woman came into court and made believe she was fainting, threw herself over in this fashion, if she was just faking or shamming a faint, a doctor could find that out by feeling her pulse, couldn't he?
A: As a rule, but not always. They can fake it sometimes mighty well.
Q: Tell us doctor, supposing a woman had been hit in the head with the butt end of a gun, — let me put it this way, suppose that a woman came into court and testified, that is assuming a state of facts for the purpose of a hypothetical question, — assuming that a woman came into court and testified that she had been hit on the head with the butt end of a gun, the wound from which bled —
MR. KNIGHT: I object to the question.
COURT: I will wait until he gets through.
Q: (continued) and supposing further that she states that she was seized very violently, and states further that she was struck several blows in and about different parts of the body, including the face, and supposing she was picked up and held over the sides of a gondola car by her legs, and then pulled back around, and thrown down on some rough material known as chert, and supposes then and there one of the assailants pushed her head, that is the head, in a violent fashion, put his hand on her face roughly, and supposing further that this man that threw her down had intercourse with her, and supposing that while the intercourse was going on, he tore at her breast, taking hold of her in and about the breasts, and suppose that six men in succession had intercourse with this woman, against her will, while she was struggling and squirming, and resisting, on this rock, or chert, and suppose, doctor, that she lay on this rock or chert on her back and on her side for over an hour, screaming and struggling with these heavy men on top of her, and suppose after that, she was taken off, and suppose that she claimed that she was in a faint, for a few moments, and was taken to a nearby point to a doctor's office, — what would you expect to find on her body, — can you state with reasonable certainty what would be found on her body, would you not find more evidence of violence and assault than a mere couple of scratches on the wrist and forearm, or the throat?
MR. KNIGHT: We object to that.
COURT: The objection is well taken. The question is not based on the evidence.
MR. LEIBOWITZ: We except.[12]

After Leibowitz completed his examination of Dr. Bridges, it was clear that major inconsistencies and implausibilities existed in Victoria Price's description of her "rape" as well as her description of her physical condition afterward and her condition as described by Dr. Bridges. However, in a further dramatic and electrifying fashion, Leibowitz then called on the "missing" Ruby Bates to take the stand.

Everybody gasped when the girl, missing since February 27, walked nervously into the old Morgan County courtroom. Clad in a new, tight-fitting gray cloth coat and hat to match, the slender girl took the stand and produced sensation after sensation in the crowded room.

> She revealed that she recently visited New York. The Rev. Harry Emerson Fosdick, distinguished pastor of the fashionable Rockefellar Church, gave her the money to buy a new hat, she said.[13]

Keeping her eyes away from the glare of pure shock, then hatred, coming from the courtroom spectators, Ruby Bates retracted her first testimony from Scottsboro and proclaimed, "Those boys never touched me." Describing how she had traveled to New York City in search of employment and how she finally located Rev. Harry Fosdick, who gave her advice on the importance of clearing her conscience, Ruby Bates forced the Scottsboro "rape case" into a new dimension. She accomplished this by braving intense feelings of racial bigotry and began to testify for the defense against Victoria Price, who still charged rape.

Not wanting to miss a word of her testimony, even Judge Horton left the bench so that he could hear every word of her testimony. Savoring the moment, Leibowitz questioned Bates:

> Q: What is your name?
> A: Ruby Bates.
> Q: How old are you?
> A: Nineteen now. I will be twenty on my birthday, March 4, 1934.
> Q: Do you know Victoria Price?
> A: Yes.
> Q: When and where did you meet her?
> A: In a textile mill in Huntsville, Alabama, in the year 1929.
> Q: Do you know Lester Carter?
> A: Yes.
> Q: When and where and under what circumstances did you first meet him?
> A: Well, I met him on a city chain gang in January of 1931 in Huntsville, Alabama.
> Q: Do you know Jack Tiller?
> A: Yes.
> Q: When and where and under what circumstances did you first meet him?
> A: I don't remember the date when I met him. I met him with Victoria Price in a cotton mill in Huntsville, Alabama.
> Q: Where did you reside in 1931?
> A: At home in Huntsville, Alabama.
> Q: With whom?
> A: With my mother and brother and sister.
> Q: Prior to March 24, 1931, were you in company of Victoria Price, Lester Carter and Jack Tiller or either of them, especially in said month of March?
> A: Yes, I was in their company on March 23 and 24th, 1931.
> Q: State specifically what occurred between you and them or either of them.
> A: On March 23rd in the afternoon about 5:30, it was nearer 6 o'clock, Victoria Price, Lester Carter and Jack Tiller and myself walked up the Pulaski Pike and then we turned off at the Pulaski Pike after we had gone something like a mile or two miles. I don't know exactly how far it was that we walked up the pike. We went off into a side road. We walked along this road until we came to a big ditch and then we saw these vines on each side of the ditch where we couldn't be seen. We got over in the vines. There were sexual intercourse

between both couples, Lester Carter and myself and Jack Tiller with Victoria Price. Later in the night it began raining, so we moved from there and walked to the N.C. & St. L. Railroad and at first we couldn't find any empty box car and then we went to the Southern railroad, where it crosses the N. C. & St. L. Railroad and we found a box car there on the side track. We got into this box car and later in the night there was sexual intercourse again. We also built a fire in the box car so to keep warm, with paper that was in the box car.

Q: What conversations, if any, did you have, prior to March 24, 1931, and in the said month of March with Victoria Price, Jack Tiller and Lester Carter, with reference to a proposed trip out of the city of Huntsville, Alabama?

A: On the morning of March 24th, early in the morning about five o'clock, Victoria Price, Lester Carter, Jack Tiller and myself were together and it was discussed between us about leaving that day, which was on Thursday, March 24th, and we planned to meet at 11 o'clock that day on the Southern Railroad at the Athens Crossings.

Q: Did Victoria Price have intercourse with Jack Tiller a day or two before March 25, 1931, in your presence and in the presence of Lester Carter?

A: On the night of March 23rd, yes.

Q: What occurred on March 24, 1931, in your presence between Lester Carter, Jack Tiller and Victoria Price?

A: I don't know what they mean. Unless this is the answer. Jack Tiller did not go with us on account of his wife. Of course, we was all talking. There was nothing done except talking and Jack Tiller said for us to go ahead and that he would join us in a few days and that he did not go on account of his wife.

Q: Did you, Lester Carter and Victoria Price board a freight train in the city of Huntsville, Alabama, and proceed on said freight train to Chattanooga, Tenn.?

A: Yes.

Q: State the details and circumstances concerning the said ride mentioned in the preceding paragraph.

A: When we first got on this freight train going to Chattanooga, we got in a box car. The box car had a lot of white men and also there was some colored men in the car — but did not speak to us for a long time. There was one boy in the car who knew myself and he came to where we was. We was in the other end of the car and he was at the other end of the car with the rest of the hobos. When he got off the train he said "Good Luck" to us. The train pulled into Chattanooga that night about 8:30.

Q: Upon arrival at Chattanooga, did you meet one Orville Gilley? State circumstances of such meeting, who was present, and what was said by Victoria Price, Lester Carter and you and Orville Gilley.

A: Yes. We was looking for a box car to stay in that, because we knew no one in Chattanooga, Tennessee, where we could stay. While we was looking for this box car, Orville Gilley was coming meeting us, coming in a direction to us and we coming meeting him. Lester Carter and Victoria Price and myself were present and Orville Gilley was by himself. Lester Carter asked him for a match. Then he wanted to know what we were doing and where we was going, — so we told him we was looking for a place to stay for the night and he joined our group to try and find a box car that was fit to stay in. Most of them was dirty on the inside and some were almost rotten down. When we couldn't find a box car, Orville Gilley said that he knows a place, he knew was the hobo jungle, a

Victoria Price and Orville Gilley (UPI/Corbis-Bettmann).

place where we could rest. So, we all got arms full of shingles from the box cars and took them over and built a fire.

Q: State in detail what occurred during your stay in Chattanooga between you, Orville Gilley, Lester Carter, Victoria Price and others, until the morning of March 25, 1931.

A: On the night of March 24 after we had built a fire, Orville Gilley and Lester Carter went to get something to eat. Of course, we couldn't see where they went, because ... I don't know. When they came back they had something to eat and also some coffee and a small lard bucket to make the coffee in. After we had eaten what they got, we were sitting by the fire and Lester Carter and myself spread out on Lester Carter's overcoat on the ground and laid down and we dozed off to sleep. That's all that happened that night that I remember.

Q: What transpired on March 25, 1931, between the hours of 6 A.M. and 3 P.M.?

A: On the morning of March 25th, Lester Carter and Orville Gilley went again for something to eat and while they was gone, Victoria Price and myself got some water from a branch stream that was running near the place where we stayed that night. After we finished washing, we was sitting there and talking and two men spoke to us and said, "Good morning" and asked us if there was anything they could do for us. We told them there was nothing they could do. Then they went on. Later, there were two Negro men went by and they spoke to us and said "Good morning." They asked if they could bring wood to put on the fire for us. We told them we was letting the fire go out. Then they wanted to know if we were alone there. We told them we was not alone. That's all that was said between us and they left.

Then Victoria Price looked over into another place where there was a bunch of hobos and she said, "If I knew that Lester and the other boy [who introduced himself to us as Carolina Slim and later told us his name was Orville Gilley] would not come back soon we would go over there and make some money from these boys." Then we went up on the railroad and we were sitting on the railroad and we saw Lester coming down the railroad, and when Lester joined us, Victoria Price told Lester that we had been insulted by a Negro and it made Lester Carter mad. Lester Carter said he would kill him if he could find him. So, Lester Carter hunted all over the swamp and he couldn't find anybody that had said anything to us but "Good Morning." Then he went over to a bunch of Negro hobos and asked them had they saw us or said anything to us. They said "No." So he cussed one of the Negroes out and called him dirty names. That was what he told us when he came back to where we was. After this I got a chance to tell Lester Carter better, that there was no Negroes insulted us or any one else. Then Orville Gilley joined us. Only a few minutes after Orville Gilley joined us, we went down to the freight yards. We sat at the freight yards until the freight train pulled in going west.

When the train pulled in we caught the train. We got on this train. We got between a box car and an oil tank. We sat down on the end of this oil tank and there were two other men and I neither saw them since nor have I ever saw them before they got on the train at the same time we did and sat down with us. Then we had been going for some time when there was a bunch of hobos coming on the train and they were just walking on the train. When they passed us, they said "Hello" or something like that. They spoke to us and walked on. Then when the train pulled into Stevenson, Alabama, we got off the train. We tried to find an empty box car and failed because there was no empty box car that we could find on the train. When the train started to pull out, we got into a gondola and besides this gondola there was several other gondolas. We was all sitting on this gondola, Victoria Price, Orville Gilley and Lester Carter and myself. Shortly after the train pulled out from Stevenson, Alabama, there was some white boys come to the next car from where we was, a gondola, and they said something and Lester Carter was talking to them. I don't know what was said between them, but I noticed that there was some Negroes come into this car from the top of the box car from the direction of the caboose. Then when these Negro boys got to where these white boys was, there was a fight. I don't know what the fight was about, but most of these white boys got off the train. Lester Carter also got off the train. Orville Gilley started to get off. I don't know why Orville Gilley or Lester Carter wanted to get off, but Lester Carter got off. Gilley started to get off, but was pulled back in the car by one of the Negro boys. After then the Negro boys disappeared. I did not see them any more until there was some boys taken off the train at Paint Rock.

Q: Did you arrive on a freight train at Paint Rock, Alabama, at or about 3 P.M.? State in detail what transpired at Paint Rock.

A: Yes, there was some Negroes taken off the train and placed under arrest and Victoria Price and myself was also placed under arrest and Orville Gilley was also put under guard by the sheriff. Victoria Price made out like she fainted. She was taken into a store where I was also taken a few minutes later. When I was taken into the store there was a doctor with Victoria. The doctor said there was nothing wrong; only that she had just gotten scared and that she had high blood pressure. When she began to talk, she was asked about what happened. So she told them that we were attacked by some Negro boys. There was one man who told her to tell the story and there was another man who told her to shut up until she got to Scottsboro under protection of sheriffs. We was arrested by the sheriff at Paint Rock, Alabama, but those others were higher sheriffs. When we first arrived at Paint Rock, there was a big crowd there.

Q: State in detail what transpired on March 25, 1931, on a trip from Paint Rock to Scottsboro, Alabama.

A: There was nothing happened, only that we was taken from Paint Rock to Scottsboro in an automobile with a few men in the car. I think it was about five or six men. I don't know exactly how many. The Negro boys was also carried to Scottsboro. I saw them when they left for Scottsboro, and then I saw them again in Scottsboro.

Q: State in detail what transpired during a physical examination of yourself and Victoria Price by doctors Bridges and Lynch.

A: Victoria Price was examined first by these two doctors in Scottsboro, Dr. Lynch and Dr. Bridges, and then I was examined by these two doctors. The doctor only asked me if I had ever had any children and I told him: "no." (He asked me when was the last time I had sexual intercourse and I said "the evening before"). That's all that was said between the doctors and myself. There again was an examination.

I don't know what they did to Victoria Price. I suppose they gave her the same examination. They just gave us an examination and painted us with mercurochrome. That was all that happened. They didn't examine my whole body that day. They just examined the lower part of my body—my vagina.

Q: State what transpired in the Scottsboro jail and conversations had by and between you and Victoria Price and certain white boys confined in Scottsboro jail after March 25, 1931, up until the trial of Haywood Patterson and others.

A: After we returned from the doctor's office to the jail, there had been seven white boys arrested at Stevenson, Alabama, and had been transferred to Scottsboro. Lester Carter was also there at Scottsboro jail. (Victoria Price told the high sheriff, who was also the jailer, that one of these boys, who had been arrested and brought to this jail, was her half-brother.) Then she told again that we was attacked and raped by the Negro boys. She told that to the sheriff. She said that there was twelve of the boys. There was not very much said about it that afternoon, because it was late and that night Victoria would not rest. I didn't know what was wrong. She was scared and we was both frightened. The next day we was examined again by the doctors and there was a few scratches on our bodies and there was a few bruised places. They were caused by the freight train riding (because anybody will get sore from riding in a freight train and staying in a hobo jungle.... This boy, who Victoria claimed is her half-brother, also told that Victoria was his half-sister and kept making noise and kept trying to break out of jail, until they put him in the same cell with Victoria Price and myself.)

Then my mother appeared at the jail. First she asked the jailer why that man was in there with us two girls and Victoria Price was standing there and she answered: "He is my half brother." The jailer said he wouldn't be quiet until he was moved into the cell with Victoria. My mother tells the jailer that unless he removes that man from the cell she would see what she can do to him for having the man locked up in jail with two girls, when it was against the law. After the boy was removed, Victoria said to me that I must remember to tell the same story as she was telling me. She was at that time telling me what all she had told the sheriff. She had told the sheriff that we had been raped and she made up the story of how we had been raped and she was telling me the story. I told her that I do not know whether I will or not, because it is not true. She was telling me that I must tell these things, as she was pointing them out to me. She said we had been raped each of us by six Negro boys and that one of the Negro boys was holding her feet, another held a gun and a knife at her throat and another had intercourse. She also stated that she had some money on her and that it had been taken off, also a pocket knife, that she had on her when she left home, had been taken off her from her pocket. We had men's clothing on. We had clothes underneath. We had slips and a couple of dresses. As I remember, Victoria Price had a sweater—and we had overalls over the dresses. We also had lots of visitors who came to the jail to see us. They would always ask Victoria Price what had happened and she would tell them that we had been raped by these Negro boys. We were then removed on Sunday from the small cell to the large cell.

There was also a cage in the middle of both cells where the men prisoners was, but there was more men prisoners in the larger cell. The seven white boys that were arrested was in this large cell. Victoria Price would have conversations with different one of the boys that was arrested and placed in jail for witnesses against the Negro boys. I do not know what the conversations was about, only in one conversation she had with one of the boys, the boy with whom she claimed was her half-brother and with whom she had been making love affairs since she had been in jail, told her that he was going to tell the truth about it at the trial and that he was not going to lie for anybody, her or any one else. I don't remember what he gave his name, but I remember that Texas was his nickname. I know his name now, Odell Gladwell. I also heard her tell Lester Carter that he must tell that we had been raped by these Negro boys.

During this whole time that we had been in jail, there had been many Negro men brought in by the sheriffs for identification for the other three Negroes who had not been arrested, which Victoria Price said there had been twelve. There was only nine arrested at Paint Rock. Lester Carter told her that he knew nothing about it, whether or not we had been raped by those Negro boys.

Victoria Price reminded me during all this time that I must tell what she did. She said that unless I did tell what she did, I would get her in trouble. She would have to serve a jail sentence. (She was then expecting to be prosecuted by my mother for carrying me across the state line when I was under twenty-one years of age and because my mother knew nothing about my going away from home.)

We was also taken out into the hospital apartment of the jail, hospital ward, to identify Negro boys. Victoria Price identified a knife which she said was hers; that it had been taken off her body by one of the Negro boys. Victoria Price did not have any knife when we left Huntsville, neither did she have any money. There was a lawyer by the name of Stephen Roddy, or Stevenson Roddy. He had the nine Negro boys brought into the hospital where he also had us brought to identify the Negro boys.

Then he asked me if the other three was the ones that had raped me. I was at this time frightened very badly, because there had been threats made against my life and I said "Yes." (The lawyer then asked the boys if they was guilty and the boys said "No." The lawyer told the boys that from the evidence that he had they was guilty and the best thing they could do was to plead guilty and beg for a life sentence). Victoria Price had also told that there was two guns that the Negro boys had, I remember as being thirty-two calibre, that's what Victoria Price said. I remember her as saying there was a thirty-eight or forty-five calibre.

Victoria Price and Lester Carter had a conversation. Lester Carter asked Victoria Price why she wanted to tell what she did on these boys for. Victoria Price said that she didn't give a darn for all these niggers, let them hang them all and Lester Carter told her that she should be ashamed of herself. I don't remember whether there was anything else.

Q: Did Haywood Patterson, Ozie Powell, Willie Roberson, Andy Wright, Olen Montgomery, Eugene Williams, Roy Wright, Charlie Weems and Clarence Norris, or any of them, have intercourse with either of you or Victoria Price on March 25, 1931?

A: No, not any of them, with either of us, Victoria Price or myself.

Q: Did Haywood Patterson, Ozie Powell, Willie Roberson, Andy Wright, Olen Montgomery, Eugene Williams, Roy Wright, Charlie Weems and Clarence Norris, or any of them, assault either you or Victoria Price on March 25, 1931?

A: No.

Q: Up to the time you reached Paint Rock did you see Haywood Patterson, Ozie Powell, Willie Roberson, Andy Wright, Olen Montgomery, Eugene Williams, Roy Wright, Charlie Weems and Clarence Norris, or either of them?

Q: Of course I saw some Negroes in a fight with the white boys in the next car on the train, but I could not say whether any of these nine was in this fight or not.

4

The April 1933 trial of Haywood Patterson was a judicial template for Clarence Norris's trial and for the trials of the rest of the Scottsboro defendants. Although their guilty verdict was in no way surprising to the citizens of Decatur, Alabama, Judge Horton's opinion on the merits of the case was.

On June 22, 1933, Horton addressed Haywood Patterson's motion for a new trial and his appeal against the death penalty. In answering this appeal, Horton reviewed the merits of the case and its importance: "As human life is at stake, not only of this defendant but of eight others, the Court does and should approach a consideration of this motion with a feeling of deep responsibility, and shall endeavor to give it that thought and study it deserves."[14]

With this as his premise, Horton began to discuss the social basis of law and its significance to at least some notion of fairness and impartiality in its application. He noted, "Deliberate injustice is more fatal to the one who imposes than to the one on whom it is imposed." Horton suggested that the court, as he viewed it, should not become involved in what some may have viewed as "southern justice" via the mob. Clearly the court "recognizes the passions, prejudices and sympathies that such cases as these naturally arouse," he commented, but justice should not be deferred from accomplishing its purpose due to these emotions.

Approaching a key element of this case — Victoria Price's testimony and its apparent contradictory recollections as to the alleged rape — Horton noted that according to the examination and observations of Drs. Bridges and Lynch, neither of the complainants had wounds that would be suggestive of the crime they claimed occurred. Central to this point was Dr. Bridges' statement that: "I did not sew up any wound on this girl's head; I did not see any blood on her scalp. I don't remember my attention being called to any blood or blow on the scalp." And this was the blow that the woman claimed helped force her into submission. Second, "semen found in the vagina of Victoria Price was of small amount" but also "nonmotile, or dead." Furthermore, if such an attack had occurred, the women's composure was not "hysterical or nervous about it at all," and "their respiration and pulse were normal." However, "the evidence does tend to suggest that they spent the night in a hobo dive; that they were having intercourse with men shortly before that time. Those few blue spots and [this] scratch would be the natural consequences of such living; vastly greater physical signs would have been expected from the forcible intercourse of six men under such circumstances."[15]

In this regard, Horton noted that with the exception of Lester Carter, who contradicted Price's statements on the stand, none of the other seven white boys who could have possibly testified in Ruby Bates' or Victoria Price's behalf were ever brought to trial by the state. Then, in dramatic aplomb, Judge Horton explained:

> Rape is a crime usually committed in secrecy. A secluded place or a place where one ordinarily would not be observed is the natural selection for the scene of such a crime. The time and place and stage of this alleged act are such to make one wonder and question did such an act occur under such circumstances. The day is a sunshiny day the latter part in March; the time of day is shortly after the noon hour. The place is upon a gondola or car without a top. The gondola

according to the evidence of Mr. Turner, the conductor, was filled within six inches to twelve or fourteen inches of the top with chert, and according to Victoria Price up to one and one half feet or two feet of the top. The whole performance necessarily being in plain view of any one observing the train as it passed. Open gondolas on each side.

On top of this chert twelve Negroes rape two white women; they undress them while they are standing up on this chert; the prosecuting witness is then thrown down and with one Negro continuously kneeling over her with a knife at her throat, and one or more holding her legs, six Negroes successively have intercourse with her on top of that chert; as one arises off of her person, another lies down upon her; those not engaged are standing or sitting around; this continues without intermission although that freight train travels some forty miles through the heart of Jackson County; through Fackler, Hollywood, Scottsboro, Larkinsville, Lin Rock, and Woodville, slowing up at several of these places until it is halted at Paint Rock; Gilley, a white boy, pulled back on the train by the Negroes, and sitting off, according to Victoria Price, in one end of the gondola, a witness to the whole scene; yet he stays on the train, and he does not attempt to get off of the car at any of the places where it slows up to call for help; he does not go back to the caboose to report to the conductor or to the engineer in the engine, although no compulsion is being exercised upon him, and instead of there being any threat of danger to him from the Negroes, they themselves have pulled him back on the train to prevent his being injured from jumping off the train after it had increased its speed; and in the end by fortuitous circumstances just before the train pulls into Paint Rock, the rapists cease and just in the nick of time the overalls are drawn up and fastened and the women appear clothed as the posse sight them. The natural inclination of the mind is to doubt and to seek further search.

Her manner of testifying and demeanor on the stand militate against her [Victoria Price]. Her testimony was contradictory, often evasive, and time and again she refused to answer pertinent questions. The gravity of the offense and the importance of her testimony demanded candor and sincerity. In addition to this the proof tends strongly to show that she knowingly testified falsely in many material aspects of the case. All this requires the more careful scrutiny of her evidence.

The court has heretofore devoted itself particularly to the State's evidence; this evidence fails to corroborate Victoria Price in those physical facts; the condition of the woman raped necessarily speaking more powerfully than any witness can speak who did not view the performance itself."[16]

In judicial defiance to parochial racism, mob rule, and a state attorney general's inability to separate regional social mores from the morass of deleterious biases and solicitations to riot, Judge Horton announced his own judicial demise by challenging Alabama's racist judiciary system. He concluded:

History, sacred and profane, and the common experience of mankind teach us that women of the character shown in this case are prone for selfish reasons to make false accusations both of rape and of insult upon the slightest provocation, or even without provocation for ulterior purposes. These women are shown, by the great weight of the evidence, on this very day before leaving Chattanooga, to have falsely accused two Negroes of insulting them, and of almost precipitating a fight between one of the white boys they were in company with and these two Negroes. This tendency to make false accusations upon any occasion whereby their selfish ends may be gained.

The Court will not pursue the evidence any further.

As heretofore stated the law declares that a defendant should not be convicted without corroboration where the testimony of the prosecutrix bears on its face indications of unreliability or improbability and particularly when it is contradicted by other evidence.

The testimony of the prosecutrix in this case is not only uncorroborated, but it also bears on its face indications of improbability and is contradicted by other evidence, and in addition thereto the evidence greatly preponderates in favor of the defendant. It therefore becomes the duty of the Court under the law to grant the motion made in this case.

It is therefore ordered and adjudged by the Court that the motion be granted; that the verdict of the jury in this case and the judgment of the Court sentencing this defendant to death by, and the same is hereby set aside and that a new trial be and the same is hereby ordered.[17]

5

Sainthood should not be placed on the heads of Ruby Bates or Judge Horton, yet their recognition of their own self-worth as humans with a sensibility above that of the mob must be noted. Ruby Bates' recantation in a social climate as repressive as that of Huntsville, Alabama, in 1936 must be understood as part of an evolving southern political perspective in which economic incongruities gripping Alabama and the rest of the country played a major role. Notwithstanding this, historically Alabama, like much of the rest of the South particularly after the demise of Reconstruction in 1877, cultivated an ethos that defined the social pariah not only in terms of the African-American populace but also in terms, when expedient, of its "poor white trash." Yet, even at this juncture, whites who were clearly assigned an economic level equal to that of blacks were forever mindful that their sharing of unwelcome poverty and economic exploitation in no way eradicated the importance of race in all things social.

For example, southern white Americans who suffered throughout the depression were more often than not viewed as the economically misfortunate. However, they were always expected to strive for and eventually achieve upward mobility and, most important, always existed as a historical bulwark against God's eternal fallen, "the Negro." Consequently, it was relatively easy for white Americans to surmise that given enough time, their deliverance over economic inequities would occur within the social and political arena of American society. For blacks, plagued by suppositions of racial inferiority and deeply rooted anti-black ordinances, any anticipated social resurrection, it seemed, would occur either by heavenly intervention or by a direct challenge of the political and judicial system in general.

Sensing rather than fully understanding the nuances of this social history

Ruby Bates (center) seated with the mothers of the Scottsboro defendants on the platform at Madison Square Garden during a May Day celebration, May 1, 1934 (UPI/Corbis-Bettman).

and its subtle function in sustaining aspects of American folklore, Ruby Bates' defiance in the face of these cultural mores and Victoria Price's willingness to exploit these same ethics for personal gain raise questions as to the formation of the southern collective consciousness.

Similarly, Clarence Norris' social experiences, as limited as they were, were also influenced by aspects of an American social consciousness that cared to know as little as possible about Norris' perspective as a black beyond that of his dependability in service to others. Inevitably, in such a social climate, race and the business of survival consumed his attention on a daily basis, in the process limiting many of his dreams to gain control over his own destiny. While life for the Norrises of America was an exercise in the art of service to others, the physical act of traveling from one city to another looking for work suggested another threatening possibility for unreconstructed whites: eradication of the notion of the lethargic, apathetic, weak, inept southern black male.

The depression years of the 1930s wrought havoc among white family relations as it did with blacks. Patriarchal family relationships that extolled traditional roles for southern urban and country women were severely tested in this time of extreme need. Southern white women, sensing that the myth of southern white womanhood was more a creation of white male posturing than substance, soon discovered that in times of economic peril, they too were exposed to abuse, manipulation, and dual standards of moral judgment. Moreover, women in general concluded that survival need not correlate with the puritanical mythology of a licentious male-dominated social system. Such an awareness placed the southern white woman face to face with the black woman, either as a gender compatriot or as a social-economic competitor. While both were imbued with an awareness that their existence, survival, and function had been intricately bound with males' interpretation of society, they now faced the option of following that prescribed social script or ever so dramatically, search for another. This was as true for Ruby Bates and Victoria Price as it was for Ida Norris, Janie Patterson, and the rest of the mothers of the Scottsboro defendants.

Being nineteen years old, and defined by the press as "poor white trash," Ruby Bates found herself trying to live down the accusation of now being a "nigger lover." In her first interview outside Alabama she stated, "I'm trying to live it down — I mean what I told against the colored boys in their first trial." Continuing on she explained, "I feel like it's something I've got to live down, … I feel like I made up some by telling the truth in the second trial, but I'm still willing to make up for the two years I helped cause the boys to suffer in jail — I know that much."

Attempting to pull her life together by learning stenography, she declared that this would be fine, if she "didn't have to work for nothing for three years afterward." Explaining further, she asserted: "Down where I live you learn shorthand at a college, the bank runs it. You can go to school for two years and they guarantee you a job afterward, but they work you and take all your money except $3 a week. If they ain't got room in Huntsville [Alabama] they send you to a branch. If you git somebody to board you for 50 cents I reckon you could git some clothes. They offered my sister a college course, but she had to go to work in the cotton mills."

The notion that Ruby Bates or even Victoria Price was simply a white woman selling her body to survive and consequently was bound to eventually come into some conflict with the law, or that they were both social trash, ignores if not obfuscates their social background. Consequently, though Victoria until her death maintained that she was raped by the defendants, a half-literate and shy Ruby Bates explained her retraction by discussing working conditions on the night shift in the cotton mills of Alabama and her resulting dawning social consciousness as a young girl.

Having up to a fifth-grade education, she worked in the mills for $2.75 a week. Sometimes, "I didn't know how much we was gettin' because the mill store took it all up." Her mother earned sometimes $5 in the same cotton mill. Supplementing her earnings on Saturday nights with sexual jaunts with boys, Ruby not only earned a few dollars more but also, from her perspective, made a statement against what society had deemed was her social lot.

In May 1933, Ruby Bates' political horizons began to expand as her relationship with the National Scottsboro Action Committee, an offshoot of the International Labor Defense, involved her in a series of speaking engagements and an eventual march in Washington, D.C., the purpose being to demand some recourse to the events in Alabama concerning the Scottsboro case and to ask President Franklin Roosevelt to enforce the Thirteenth, Fourteenth, and Fifteenth Amendments to the Constitution.

Electrifying events such as this caused her to recall: "Before the first trial I used to think of having to go into the mills so young [she was fifteen when she began to work on the night shift] and about all the people having to work so hard and getting practically nothing for it. I'd wonder what could be done, but I didn't know there was anything ... I had to work under the boss and his place was so much higher than I was — I was considered 'poor white trash,' you know. Now I understand that if the people would all work together instead of against each other it would help everybody. Well, I guess it wouldn't help the bosses, but it would help all the workers."

When questioned about her first testimony. Ruby admitted she was influenced by her friend's insistence that they protect themselves from being jailed, but that she didn't realize that "the colored boys might be hung for it."[18]

Chapter 6

Ozie's Sacrifice

Not me alone ...
I know now ...
But all the world oppressed
Poor world,
White and Black
Must put their hands with mine
to shake the pillars of those temples
Wherein the false gods dwell
And worn-out alter stand
Too well defended.

— *Langston Hughes,*
Negro Worker, July 1934

1

Decatur, Georgia, like much of the rest of the south in the 1930s, was an extremely dangerous place for African Americans—not that it wasn't the same as far back as anyone could remember. But now, with white passions rising above the surface and blacks insisting on challenging if not breaking some of the mores of southern etiquette, both anger and blood were to flow in the streets and fields of the South.

Much of the ensuing violence of the 1930s undoubtedly stemmed from blacks' reluctance to continue suffering economic deprivation under a social mandate known as "Jim Crow" or to accept peacefully the growing levels of violence via lynching by pseudo-legal organizations or spontaneous white mobs. Organizing on both a national and an international level to relieve racial injustices affecting every aspect of their lives, groups whose ideological orientations would ordinarily not be linked together were, out of necessity, coming together.

For example, the Scottsboro case demonstrated that blacks in the United States, with sufficient support from sympathetic whites, could receive and were receiving substantial international support in their resistance to racism and murder. As noted earlier, this support provoked numerous rallies and vigorous demonstrations throughout the world. For many, this elevated the question of direct political action as an appropriate response by an aggrieved and often despondent African-American citizenry. This was a question that, interestingly enough, would be raised again some twenty-five years later by another generation of blacks.

Others, however, argued that to do so meant assuming the risk of being considered disloyal to a surrounding paternalistic social order or, worse, considered criminal by violating the sacraments of state or national law. To be a black demonstrator in the social environment of the 1930s meant to risk everything: one's standing among peers, one's status within the larger community, and one's life in a cause emotionally shared but not necessarily physically chanced by others.

In the midst of this ensuing human drama, the press began to highlight an essentially brutal drama about blacks' survival in a national depression and about the honed edges of violent racial conflict. One reporter, emphasizing the struggle for enfranchisement, noted:

> Having come into Decatur a few days ago to get the sentiment of the people in regard to the Scottsboro Case, I find that there has been a reign of terror let loose against the Negro masses at the hands of the white ruling class. A Negro, Thomas Brown, was framed up and accused of attacking a white woman Monday, arrested two hours later on Vine St., taken to jail and identified by the white woman as the attacker. A mob gathered at the jail to take the Negro out and he was spirited away to some unknown place, according to the capitalist press; although it is known to everybody here that this boy has been going with this woman for several months, and it could not be rape.
>
> A Negro boy of 16 years of age was shot dead on Vine St. by a mob of Mack men about 50 feet from the place where Brown was arrested.
>
> The Klans paraded in the Negro sections. Negroes were barred from going through white sections on their way to work. A Negro drug store was broken into.[1]

Similar articles were published in other areas of the South such as Chattanooga, Tennessee, when a local branch of the Ku Klux Klan sought to intimidate a witness for the defense in the Scottsboro Case. A local newspaper reported:

> The vengeance of the Ku Klux Klan against those who fought to cheat the lynchers of their prey in Decatur, Ala., reached into Chattanooga, Monday, April 17, and while E. L. Lewis, Negro witness for the defense in the Scottsboro case was attending court at Decatur, waiting to be called in the trial of Charlie Weems, his house here, at 220 Central Ave., was burned to the ground and all its contents destroyed.
>
> Fiery crosses burned in northern Alabama while this outrage was perpetrated.
>
> Lewis was the witness for the Scottsboro boys who testified that Victoria Price spent the night before the arrest of the boys at Paint Rock in the jungle at Chattanooga. The girl has said she spent that night at the home of "Caille Broochie"—a non-existent person.

> Lewis was able to show that he had seen and spoken to her, Ruby Bates and two white boys early in the morning in the Chattanooga jungle.
>
> Ku Klux Klan threats, both officially from the organization and from individual members, have been received by defense witnesses and their lawyers.
>
> Already in Jackson county [Scottsboro], a reign of terror against the Negro witnesses who testified for the defense on the exclusion of Negroes from juries, and two have been terrorized into signing repudiations of their testimony.
>
> By October 17th of the same year, E.L. Lewis is mysteriously poisoned and dies in Chattanooga.[2]

Resistance by blacks to unmitigated poverty and to violence aimed at them as a race came to a head in the deep southern Alabamian cotton-growing counties of Dallas, Lowndes, and Greene. With enough squalor and poverty to share among both the black and the white communities, and with an annual per-capita education expenditure for whites at less than $25 but for blacks so minimal that it was inconsequential (white schools were valued at $24,515, compared with $1,500 for blacks schools), black sharecroppers organized themselves on the basis of economic issues and a need to survive.[3]

One such organization in Alabama's Tallapoosa County in 1931 was the "Society for the Advancement of Colored People," which some claimed was in reality a sharecroppers' union. Coming from the same peasant milieu as Clarence Norris and riling against the same inequities that had sent Norris looking for a better lifestyle, these men of the soil would inevitably have to cross paths with Alabama's Jim Crow system of racial segregation and brutality.

After one bloody incident at Camp Hill, Tallapoosa County, influential newspapers such as the *Pittsburgh Courier* and the *Chattanooga Daily News* took different perspectives and, in doing so, reflected the political abyss and tragic nature of the Scottsboro Case itself. For example, in April 1933 the *Pittsburgh Courier* reported:

> The men on trial here, indicted March 30 for assault with intent to murder, are: Judson Simpson, Sam Moss, Clinton Moss, Ned Cobb and Alf White.
>
> Trouble between Negro sharecroppers and officers of the law began early in 1921 when it was observed that radical propaganda was being distributed among the share croppers. Slight, surreptitious efforts were made to organize them in their own behalf.
>
> Not much headway was made. The disposition of white officers in this section is to prevent by force any demonstration they disapprove of whether the demonstration is legal or not, if Negroes are party to it. Thus, although the Constitution of the nation guarantees the right of free speech, sheriffs and their deputies, as soon as they get wind of possible organization among the Negro farmers, began snooping around and scattering warnings. Wherever two or three Negroes gathered together to discuss their own improvement, the deputies tracked them down and ordered them to break up.
>
> The first trouble occurred in July 1932, when blustery J. Kyle Young, who

> "has no use for niggers," pounced upon a meeting being held in a church and ordered the men to disperse. When they were slow about doing it, the Sheriff and his deputies began maltreating them and a general fight followed. Young himself was severely injured as a result.
>
> In the next two days, many Negroes were arrested. More than a dozen of these men have never been heard of since. The International Labor Defense charged that they had been secretly carried away and disposed of.
>
> The affair involving the five men whom Schwab is defending now, had its inception in a debt owed by one Cliff Jeans to a white man named Parker. Jeans had contracted in 1924 to purchase a 77 acre farm from Parker for $1,600. He paid $650. Then the depression came and like many southern farmers, Jeans found it impossible to keep his payments up.
>
> He saw Parker and the two of them discussed the matter. Parker asked Jeans to pay $80. Jeans did not have the money. Parker suggested that he sign a note for the money and left Jeans to "think it over."
>
> Before either man had seen the other again, Deputy Sheriff Clofford Elder showed up at Jeans' home with an attachment for two mules and two cows which Jeans owned. Jeans protested against the deputy taking them, holding that the cows were his food and the mules his only means of working his land. The two men argued and the deputy in a huff announced that he was going away and get enough men to "kill all the d__ned niggers."
>
> When a band of deputies returned they found a number of farmers at Jeans' house who had stopped by there after a rabbit hunt. They had their shotguns with them. The deputies fired into the house. Some of the men fired and others ran. Three men in the house died as a result of the fight and four deputies were shot.
>
> The five men ... were rounded up and charged with being participants in the so-called riot.[4]

The *Chattanooga Daily News*, however, reporting on the same incident, constructed a somewhat different context by placing the shooting between deputies and farmers as akin to the Scottsboro case:

> Let us examine the Scottsboro case again and see if The News claim is true that the ILD has sought to have the eight Negro boys executed for allegedly attacking two white girls, in order to manufacture propaganda for their own selfish purposes....
>
> Let us be candid about this affair. The ILD is a Communist organization, whose theories of social and governmental control run counter to southern thought. Furthermore, the attorneys it selected to handle the case were New Yorkers. If the ILD were seriously concerned about the outcome of this case, can there be any question but what they would have selected southern attorneys of ability, who could handle the case without the objection of bitterness, without appealing to race hatreds, and without the irritating influence of New Yorkers with Russian names?
>
> But that is not all the story. In July 1931, while the case was on appeal to the Alabama Supreme Court, Communist organizers went to Camp Hill, Ala., and formed a share croppers union of Negroes. Their literature urged Negroes to "demand what you want and if you don't get it, take it." After sowing their seeds of discord, the organizers left.
>
> Then, according to a communication in the New York *Herald Tribune* from

> Welbour Kelley, "shortly thereafter and no inference is intended, the sheriff of the county was advised in a mysterious telephone message that the Negroes were plotting an uprising. Officials investigated, and shots were fired on both sides. A Negro was killed and two officers were wounded."
>
> Mr. Kelly further relates that in December, 1932, one hundred armed Negroes gathered at Reelton, Ala., to prevent legal attachment of two mules owned by a white man. In the pitched battle which followed, three Negroes were fatally shot and four officers were wounded. Mr. Kelly adds this enlightening bit:
>
> "In neither case was a Communist within gunshot. As one of the sharecroppers put it, with inevitable Negro wit: 'When we had de meetin's and de peer-ades, dem white boys (the organizers) was at de head of de line. But when I look in de coffins, I couldn' see nothin but black faces.'"
>
> This is the result of the "direct action" which the organizers have been urging the Negroes to take.
>
> Are not the above facts sufficient to convince any one that the I.L.D. is determined that the Scottsboro Negroes shall be executed in order to supply their campaign of race hatred with flames for the fire? The presiding judge at the recent second trial of the case at Decatur, Ala., rightly refused to go on with the case, declaring that the I.L.D. attorneys, with their inflammatory tactics and their unfounded criticism uttered in speeches in New York, had become a "millstone" about the necks of their clients, and had made it impossible to secure a fair trial.
>
> The *Chattanooga News* again insists that the I.L.D. retire from the case. If it continues to refuse to do so, it will stand convicted before the world as being interested solely in propagating racial strife, and having no desire to secure the freedom of these Negroes.[5]

In an interesting twist of southern journalism, the *Jackson City Sentinel*, attempting to discredit northern journalistic excesses, charged the ILD with publishing "scurrilous and lie-filled propaganda" that, in a manipulative manner, "always winds up with a plea to the ignorant whites and negroes to pour money into the treasury of the I.L.D. which is now trying to exploit the Southern negroes for a bag of gold."[6]

Part of the "scurrilous" lies that the editor disliked was the following claim by the ILD:

> People of the boys' race and nationality are illegally excluded from the jury and are warned that negro jurors are a curiosity in Alabama and "some curiosities are embalmed."
>
> The most savage wave of race hatred has been launched throughout the south. Edna Davis, a defenseless woman, was murdered while on her knees at prayer, by police officers in Birmingham; Levon Carlock was handcuffed and then shot to death by police in Memphis; George Jeter was lynched without any case being brought against him in Aiken, South Carolina; Sixteen year old Will Sanders was legally lynched in seventy-seven minutes by a jury at York, South Carolina; In Hazard, Kentucky, a Negro man and woman were murdered in cold blood without provocation; three negro fishermen on Travernier Island were lynched on January 19.[7]

2

Throughout the political struggles, Clarence Norris and the rest of the Scottsboro defendants sat and awaited their fate as if in the eye of a raging hurricane. Their interest was elevated by events unfolding around them, but information was still meager and too often unreliable. Only a keen sense of who their immediate enemy was kept them alert to the business of day-to-day survival.

By the fall of 1935 the Scottsboro Case had moved beyond the charge of rape. After Clarence Norris' second conviction and death sentence and Haywood Patterson's third conviction, issues pertaining to whether or not blacks should sit on the jury panel occupied the attention of the U.S. Supreme Court. The justices now acknowledged, "The question of forging Negro names on Alabama jury rolls could not be ignored." Putting aside all precedent, the justices agreed to examine the original evidence and, in doing so, ascertain if "constitutional violations are pointed out—forcefully [and] clearly." Weeks later the decision was handed down. Unanimous, and with the decision read by Chief Justice Hughes, the death sentences of Norris and Haywood were put aside and new trials were ordered, "because all previous trials were illegal!" Noting that black jurors had been "systematically" prohibited from being placed on Alabamian juries, this statement by the courts was truly historic but dangerous for blacks trying to implement the Court's decision.[8]

On November 13, 1935, Creed Conyer became the first African American in sixty years to sit on the grand jury in the state of Alabama. However, with twenty-four men on the grand jury, his appearance is insignificant, since it took only two-thirds of a vote to return indictments. When, for example, Victoria Price appeared before them and repeated her story, the jury returned two indictments against each of the nine youths: one for raping Victoria and the other for Ruby Bates, despite the latter's disclaimer that the youths touched her or Victoria. A fourth trial scheduled for January 20, 1936, took place in a courtroom typifying Jim Crow segregation policies.

> One hundred "good men and true" are called for jury service. The edict of the U.S. Supreme Court is translated into life. Twelve Negro citizens are included on the jury panel of 100—but special Jim Crow arrangements have been provided right in the court room. The Negro talesmen are not permitted to sit in the jury box with the white men. They must sit in specially provided chairs—over to one side. Even the lone Negro reporter is segregated from the white newspapermen.[9]

Raymond Daniel of the *New York Times* noted that these twelve Negroes "diffidently and uncertainly" took their seats before Judge Callahan and, with upraised hands along with white jurors, swore that they would weigh the available evidence until a "true verdict is rendered," if they were chosen to sit on the Patterson case. More interesting, however, was the new talesmen's outward appearance of deference.

> The Negroes did not presume to seat themselves in the jury box, even when they were called in the groups of twelve to face the questioning of the attorneys for the State and the defense.
>
> Some chairs were placed for them alongside the jury box and in them they sat even when there were vacant chairs in the jury box, which for three generations the dominant white citizens of Morgan County have kept more free of Negroes than the rolls on the Democratic party below the Mason-Dixon Line.
>
> Once a stage-struck Negro, whose name was called at the head of a group of twelve, stumbled into the jury box and was about to seat himself when Judge Callahan, who a little earlier had denied a defense motion for a change of venue and had cut short an attempt by defense attorneys to oust the Lieutenant Governor, Thomas E. Knight Jr., from his role of prosecutor, called out sharply:
>
> "Here, boy, sit over there!"
>
> The Negro docilely left the jury box and seated himself in the chair the judge had indicated....
>
> One colored man, who described himself as a laborer, said that he could not serve because his "boss" had shot himself in the foot while hunting last week and had to have his leg amputated. Without him, the Negro said, there would be none to look after the business. The excuse did not suffice, but later the Negro talesman recalled a conscientious scruple against capital punishment and was sent home....
>
> Two other colored men were excused from service on the jury when it was revealed that they were over the legal age limit of 65. They left the court room looking anything but regretful. The Negro janitor of the court room, a colored teacher and two others found varied but valid reasons why they could not serve.[10]

To those present, the courtroom decorum was part judicial burlesque, part southern justice. The judge, William Washington Callahan, a strict constructionist as opposed to Judge Horton concerning the rules of evidence, would charge, through law book after law book, to find "reasons for excluding a great deal of testimony." These actions tended to play havoc with the defense while allowing the prosecution time to adjust its clients inaccuracies and falsehoods. For example, "Judge Callahan held repeatedly that the defense had no right to show that Victoria Price might have the physical appearance of having been attacked entirely as the result of her own willing indiscretions with white men on the night before she accused the Negroes of attacking her, after a posse had stopped the freight train on which she and her momentary lover were hoboing."[11]

Furthermore, Judge Callahan's decision to not allow the defense permission to interrogate Victoria Price on her activities in Chattanooga and with whom not only reached an accord with the regular courtroom spectators of Morgan County but also established a "line in the sand" attitude to the questioning of a white woman's word against that of accused blacks. Melvin

Hutson, a "fat, flabby and shifty eyed" Morgan county prosecutor and Sunday school teacher, summed it up well when he ranted and raved before the jury about the need to protect white womanhood, as personified by Victoria Price, from the ravages of individuals such as Norris and Patterson.[12] The jury retired and in less than eight hours returned with a verdict. However:

> It cannot come into court to give the verdict because Callahan is busy choosing the jury for the trial of Clarence Norris. The new jury files out. The old jury files in — Verdict — **guilty**. Sentence — 75 years in prison.
>
> The next morning — Friday — the Norris trial is postponed along with all the others. The Patterson sentence will be appealed to the Alabama State Supreme Court. Postponement is won by the defenses on a technical question revolving around the absence and illness of the most important material witness — Dr. Bridges of Scottsboro, Alabama.
>
> Judge Callahan calls Haywood Patterson. Tall and erect, Haywood stands before him. Asked whether he has anything to say before he is sentenced, Haywood Patterson speaks up:
>
> "I'm not guilty. Justice has not been done me in my case."[13]

Five years of bitter imprisonment, days in solitary, sleepless nights on the concrete floors of the Kilby death house, and beatings have steeled these black youths to a life of pain whereby acts of survival need no justification beyond the demands of the moment. Handcuffed in threes, the nine black youths were loaded into three cars, day in and day out, as they traveled across the icy-winter roadways of central Alabama from a Decatur courtroom back to a Birmingham jail.

3

On January 24, 1936, at approximately 3:00 P.M., Deputy Sheriff Edgar Blalock was wounded by inmate Ozie Powell while Powell and the other Scottsboro defendants were being escorted back to Birmingham's city jail. After the attack, Powell was seriously wounded by another sheriff. The defendants — who were placed three in a car, with the Alabama state police as their protection from whites who would rather just lynch them, or as it was often referred to, "hemp them" — were being transported each day to court. Though different accounts of the attack intrigued both the police and the public, one fact was dramatically emphasized: black inmates struck back at their perceived tormentors when given the opportunity and, in doing so, raised questions as to the justification of their imprisonment. For Clarence Norris, who was a close friend of Ozie's, the events were indeed traumatic.

CLARENCE NORRIS: I was in that car the day when Ozie Powell cut the deputy sheriff's throat. We were all handcuffed when traveling back to Birmingham, except that since I was sitting in the middle, each of my hands was cuffed to either Roy Wright or Ozie. That left Ozie's [right] hand and Roy's

[left] hand free. Now, we all carried something to protect ourselves with. In fact, throughout the trial, all of us kept a little blade in the seam which covered the buttons on our trouser fly just in case it came down to simply a case of having to defend ourselves. Of course the guards would never search us there, it was just too close to our privates for them to start feeling around. They'll pat you down everywhere but there, you understand. The funny thing about this is that in the initial stages of this trial they searched us twice a day. Once when we were leaving for Decatur, and when returning to Birmingham. Pretty soon it got so that they assumed there was no way we could get hold of anything without them knowing about it, so they stopped searching us. They would simply handcuff us, put us in cars, and take us where they were going to keep us. By January 24th, they weren't searching us at all, and Ozie was carrying a knife right in his pocket.

On this particular day while returning from Decatur, High Sheriff J. Street Sandlin was driving and discussing our case with his deputy, Blalock, who was sitting in the front on the passenger side. About ten miles down the highway Blalock starts running his mouth about the case and how our lawyers were not handling the case correctly and that "if you all was to put on and let them Eastern lawyers get you some Southern lawyers, you'd come out much cheaper in the trials. You'd get a better break in the trials. But then ... all you niggers should've been killed long ago, every damn one of you!"

None of us was saying anything, but I could feel that Ozie was getting tense and getting ready to say or do something. He suddenly blurts out, "I wouldn't put down the help I have for no damn southern lawyer I've seen."

I don't know why he told this old cracker something like that, at a time like this, but he did. No sooner had the words left his mouth when Blalock turned around and slapped him hard in the face.

I could actually feel the rage building up in Ozie as he twisted and turned while facing Blalock's half-turned back in front of him. A few minutes passed before I became aware that Ozie was slowly reaching in his pocket with his free hand for his knife.

Before I knew it, Ozie's pulling me forward as he reached around Blalock's neck and cut his throat. It seems as though he was trying to pull the deputy's head off. I started to yell at Ozie, "Don't do this, don't do this!" He finally stopped, but by now blood was gushing from Blalock's throat all over the place. The high sheriff slammed on the breaks while steering the car with one hand, draws his pistol, wheels around in the car trying to shoot us. Roy and I reached forward and hooked his head with our handcuffed hands and pulled it back against the car seat and said, "Son of a bitch, you don't get anything here, you understand." We knew he wanted to kill us right there and then, but we weren't about to make it easy for him. While all of this was going on, the sheriff was able to step on the siren and bring the car to a swerving screeching halt. Blalock staggered out of the front seat and kind of fell towards the front of the car and

Deputy sherriff Ed Blalock of Morgan County, Alabama, knifed by Ozie Powell (UPI/Corbis-Bettmann).

flipped over on the hood. We figured he was going to die right there. Funny thing though, he had a big old .38 on his belt, but he wasn't even thinking about it after that knife was pulled around his throat. Suddenly the sheriff breaks out of our grasp, jumps out of the car, forces down the window and fires right into the back of the car, hitting Ozie. He really didn't give a damn who he shot, because there wasn't but three of us back there.

The sheriff is just about to fire again when another state patrol car rolls up and someone yells, "What the hell's going on?" The sheriff yells, "One of these black sons of bitches cut the deputy, and I'm going to kill all of them!"

Again he takes aim and is getting ready to shoot when another car carrying the now lieutenant governor for Alabama, Thomas Knight, Jr., and the assistant attorney general, T. S. Lawson, pull up alongside us. I believe it was Lawson who yelled, "What's been happening here?" The high sheriff turned around to see who that was and because of that didn't fire his gun. It was just that close. Another two seconds and we would have been dead or close to it.

Lawson and Knight jumped out of their car and were immediately confronted with a chaotic scene, with Ozie bleeding and lying there looking like he was dead, the deputy on the highway gushing more blood, and Sheriff Sandlin yelling about how the deputy was cut and how he was going to take care of these "niggers." Lawson orders the sheriff to "uncuff that nigger from the rest of them, put him in the car and run him to the hospital." Knight, the senior official, countermands Lawson and says, "Let that black son of a bitch stay in there, let him stay handcuffed to the rest of them, rush the deputy to the hospital." And that's what they did.

Now Ozie was shot, man. The bullet went in here on the left side of his head and come out and went through the corner of the car. Yes sir, shot clean through his head with a .38. The doctor said that if the bullet had went a fraction of an inch deeper either way, he would have been a dead man. Anyway, I stayed handcuffed to Ozie and Roy all the way on that highway to a place known for its hatred of blacks and one which proudly claimed, "Nigger, don't let the sun catch you in town." In other words, you weren't going to find any black folks living in Cullman, Alabama.

When we got to Cullman, Knight's car pulled alongside of ours, and he hollered at the sheriff: "Take all these niggers out the cars and take them up to the damn jail and leave the doors open. Let the mob get them." Well, the man who had charge of these cars was the chief of the Alabama State Highway Patrol. He informed the lieutenant governor that the governor told him directly to "bring these boys to Birmingham and start out with them as fast as you can," because he was sending the National Guard to meet us on the highway. Furious, Knight conceded, and we proceeded on towards Birmingham. Obviously, Knight was hoping that once the townspeople of Cullman saw the blood on the side of the patrol cars they would get upset and that as soon as they knew the Scottsboro "niggers" were in their jail, they would do what comes natural to crackers, simply lynch us. However, the white folk we did see didn't seem interested in us for some reason, and if they did see some blood, they probably thought the police had beaten some Negroes. They didn't know we damn near killed one of the sheriff's men.

While we were sitting there in Cullman, the highway patrolmen goes to get the high sheriff of Cullman to replace the deputy who was cut. Once this was done, we take off again for Birmingham, but this time we're the last car. Ozie's head is bouncing off my shoulder so much, I just assumed he was dead. But slowly he begins to come to his senses, though he can't move because he's paralyzed. A few miles down the road I can hear him saying, "I ain't never been shot before." But he couldn't move his head. It laid right there on my shoulder.

About halfway between Cullman and Birmingham there are some mountains which you have to drive through. The high sheriff, who is now raging about what he would like to do to us, is saying: "Them people back in Cullman must not have found out what it was all about back there.... When I get out here behind these mountains, I'm going to kill them all." And sure enough, when he got out behind them mountains he began to slow up until we was separated from the other cars. He grabbed his gun out his holster and went to wheel around in the car to shoot, when the sheriff from Cullman knocked his hand down and told him, "Look here, this is a hard proposition you're going up against. You better get youself together." Yeah, that's right. He was intending to finish us off in that damn car, and let the devil beware!

When we got to Birmingham, they opened the car door on Roy's side. Roy tries to get out but he's still handcuffed to me. I'm handcuffed to Ozie, who is shot; he can't move because he's paralyzed, and all these crackers are yelling at us to get out the car. I'm trying to pull Ozie but he's like dead weight. Neither of us can move. Using his foot, one of the sheriffs on Ozie's side begins to push him out on Roy's side of the car. He pushed and pushed against Ozie until he got him out of the car on the ground. Almost as if you were pushing a sack of potatoes. When Ozie finally rolled out of the car and smashed onto the ground, the handcuffs tighten even further and cut deeply into both of our wrist. I got that scar on me till this very day. They then handcuffed Roy and me, put us in jail. The last we saw of Ozie at that time was seeing him stretched out, face down on the jailhouse ground. We didn't know if he was going to die or not.

Later we found out that the governor rushed Ozie Powell to the hospital and called upon the staff to make every effort possible to save his life. It turned out that after the operation, the surgeon stated that he had a fifty-fifty chance of surviving only because the bullet missed his brain and other vital arteries by a fraction of an inch. Two days later our attorney, Samuel Leibowitz, visited us to find out exactly what occurred in the car [see Appendix F]. Months later when Ozie Powell was eventually released from the hospital we could see that he was not the same. His personality was totally different. It seemed as if he was in a daze or something. He paid a high cost for our dignity as black men.

Newspaper accounts of this incident differed, from one extreme to another. An Associated Press story in the *Montgomery Advertiser* just two days after the attack attempted to give a balanced view by printing Clarence Norris' and Roy Wright's version along with Sheriff Sandlin's recollection of the attack.

The paper reported that Norris and Wright stated, "Ozie had sassed, Mr. Blalock and the officer slapped him." Norris reportedly stated: "Ozie and Mr.

Blalock had been talking about the attorneys in the case.... A few minutes after, Ozie reached his free hand into his pocket and got his knife. He opened it and then reached over and cut Mr. Blalock's throat. That was when the trouble started.... Roy Wright did not have a knife and did not try to cut Sheriff Sandlin. We thought that after Ozie had cut the officer so bad, that they was going to kill us all. They didn't shoot any of us though, except one.... I was not hurt and Roy was not hurt. We had not planned to escape because we feel now that we won't have to try to escape. We believe we will get free anyway."[14]

The same article also reported that Sheriff Sandlin was positive that "white persons were responsible for the plot to kill us." He went on to say: "It was all planned Thursday night, and no negro did the planning. We never had a cross word with any of those negroes and not a word had been spoken for 10 miles when they suddenly pulled knives and jumped on us." Supporting Sheriff Sandlin's contentions, Lieutenant Governor Knight added that from his vantage point from a car right behind Sandlin's, "Every Alabama officer present took every possible step to effect safe delivery of the prisoners to Birmingham, even after the attack on the two officers."

In another report, Thomas Norman, a socialist leader associated with the Scottsboro Defense Committee and the ILD in New York City, commenting on the professionalism and sincerity of Alabama police officers, stated that "the passion, prejudice and incompetence displayed" in the latest incident was itself reflective and "typical of the whole proceedings" known as the Scottsboro Case. He added, "The object from the beginning has been not falsity of the charges against these nine youths, but to exterminate them."[15]

Even two and one-half years later, papers such as the *Birmingham News* carried an Associated Press story titled "Red Plot to Slay Scottsboro Case Figures Charged." The story outlined the argument of the solicitor for the state of Alabama, Melvin Hutson, against pardoning four Scottsboro defendants. Claiming an ongoing Communist conspiracy against the state of Alabama, Hutson charged that the 1936 incident was a Communist "deep laid plot to murder the sheriff and his deputies in connection with the unsuccessful escape effort of Ozie Powell." He further opined, "I am convinced that this knife was slipped to this Negro [Ozie Powell] by a white man for the purpose of causing a race riot, hoping thereby to promote the cause of Communists." Hutson stated that these "convictions" made him "shudder to think what would have happened to many of our good and faithful citizens, both black and white, had the nefarious scheme of these white Communist been successful in this plot." Hutson concluded that "the blackest conspiracy that was ever formed in Alabama" was averted, and due to Ozie Powell's refusal "to tell the truth about this knife, he should be required to serve every day of his sentence."[16]

4

On February 3, 1936, Mrs. Josephine Powell visited her son Ozie in Birmingham's Hillman Hospital. Her account of this visit indicated a heightened level of tension and intimidation consistent with what one would expect among most southern whites and blacks, especially when specific interests were at stake. Part of the problem was that racism and the power to enforce compliance invariably structure communication and social action in a contentious manner. In such a situation, understanding how racial groups interpreted their role in reality also indicates how they fashion strategies to placate immediate exigencies in any subsequent interactions. For example, the context in which Clarence Norris gave his account to the press and surrounding deputies was similar to Mrs. Powell's situation when she visited her son in a hospital full of police, deputy sheriffs, and black workers who, if sympathetic to her plight, dare not indicate it. Their statements were evidence of a victimized people who have learned how to modify recollections while in the presence of victimizers who felt the need to exhibit control. Consequently, perceptions of reality existed in conflict and deference to each other.

In a sense, degrees of contempt are often demonstrated by victims in relationship to the "paternalistic powers" of their nemesis. Some have referred to this as "playing the fool," "playing the man," or "Toming." Dialogue between individuals is shaped by their historical relationships and is therefore suspect in the contemporary context. Undoubtedly, this occurs not only in black and white racial circumstances but in any social situation where communication is premised on hierarchical notions of authority and institutional forms of public deference, that is, segregation. In this case, subterfuge existed as an avenue for escape and expression, an avenue known very well by Mrs. Powell, her son Ozie, Norris, and the rest of the Scottsboro defendants, as well as by those who acted as facilitators of power.

The following account by Mrs. Powell, of her visit to her son's bedside, lends itself to this analysis when one reads a letter she dictated to Joseph S. Gelders, an ILD labor organizer, an ex-professor of physics at the University of Alabama, and an individual reputed to have a broad knowledge of Alabama's political, religious, and civic leadership:

> I went to Birmingham with James Thomas in his car. With us were Ozie's sister, Charlie Ray; his brother, James; his sister's "baby," Ruby Ray; and his girl friend Emma Lou Rucker.
>
> They wouldn't let anybody go to the hospital but me and the Sheriff didn't want me to go but he let me go after I made him know I was Ozie's mother. I showed him a furniture receipt (to identify myself).
>
> Two deputy sheriffs took me to the hospital in their car. One of the deputies said there were two things he wanted me to do. One was not to "break down" and the other was that he wanted me to question Ozie concerning where he got those knives from. [Note: there seems to be three knives now].

When we got to the door of the room, a nurse (Negro) said, "Is that your son in there?" I shook my head. Just then a deputy stepped up and told me not to talk with any of the nurses.

The sheriff (probably deputy) went in and asked Ozie how he was feeling. Ozie said, "very well," in a feeble voice.

Then he let me go in.

He was lying there like asleep, most likely doped up sleep.

The deputy said, "here's your mother."

Ozie jumped up and then fell back and started crying.

I said, "Hey, boy." He said, "Hey, Momma."

I said, "How you feeling?" He said, "Very well."

I said, "Anything hurt you?" He said, "Not now."

I said, "How long were you unconscious," he said,

"I haven't never been unconscious, only when I was asleep."

"Then I sort of started away and looked around and the room was most full of deputies."

Then I asked him, "Why did this thing just now come up when they been transporting you from jail to jail and from town to town?"

He said, "Well, Mama, I don't feel that there's no need for me to express any further cause. I done give up."

I asked him what he give up for and he said, "Cause, I feel like everybody in Alabama is down on me and is mad with me."

"What they mad with you for?"

"Because I done what I did."

I asked him what had he did.

He said, "Well, I won't talk any more about it."

I said, "you have told everybody else why don't you tell your mother?"

He said, "Mama, ain't but one thing I want to tell you right now. Don't let Sam Leibowitz have anything else to do with my case."

He said, "Will you write to that effect." I told him I will.

One of the sheriffs broke in and said, "It's not left up to your mother, you're supposed to have any lawyer you want."

One of the sheriffs bent over the bed and said, "Now Ozie, tell your mother the truth. Who gave you this knife?"

First Ozie said, "I don't know now."

The sheriff said, "Here's your mother, now, ... won't you tell her the truth about the knives?"

Ozie said, "I think it was a boy named Ernest that gave me the knife."

While I was talking to Ozie, there were about 20 deputies in the room and all out in the hall. They all had guns and black-jacks and I didn't know what they was going to do to me. I was scared they was going to shoot me down.

Then we left and went back to the courthouse where James was.

The sheriff and James started talking and I walked off.

The sheriff called me back and said, "Nothing to hurt you Auntie, this is just a news man" (another man, a reporter had joined the sheriff). The sheriff and the news man were standing there. The news man asked me some questions about who I was and where from and then he asked,

"Your boy wants another lawyer, doesn't he?"

"Yes, he asked for one," I said.

He asked was I going to get him a lawyer. I said,

"I'm going to try to, when I see further."[17]

Gelders' cover letter to Morris Shapiro, the Scottsboro Defense Committee secretary, reflecting his perceptions of the pressures being placed on both Ozie and his mother is also instructive:

Atlanta, Georgia, February 3, 1936

Mr. Morris Shapiro
320 Broadway
New York City

Dear Morris,

I just had a long talk with Mrs. Josephine Powell. I am enclosing, herewith, her statement as nearly as I could get it down and partially organized.

She seems to realize now, that the officers were using her as a tool (partially against her will, partially without her knowledge) in their effort to break the solid defense. She kept saying, as we discussed the matter, "I looked around and the room was full of sheriffs." Or "I just give up. I haven't got the strength to fight, I was scared, I didn't know what they was going to do to me," which indicates that she pressed her questions on Ozie unwillingly and under duress.

She is now anxious to continue with the Scottsboro Defense Committee and Leibowitz & Watts. But she is an exceptionally weak, emotional and vacillating person.

She is anxious to go back to see Ozie again this week, possibly Wednesday or Thursday. I urged her not to do this but to wait and come to Birmingham on February 12 which she agreed to do. In the meanwhile I think it *very important* for Ben Davis to come to Atlanta and see Mrs. Powell. She has complete confidence in him and I think he can restore her hope and will to fight. If so, she can have a good influence in rally Ozie when she does see him. I think the next visit should be in the presence of Watts, who can, in some measure protect her and Ozie from the pressure of the armed guards.

Everything points to the fact that enormous and brutal pressure has been exerted on that poor boy and that under this constant bombardment she has lost courage.

I'm going to get to the Negro nurses in the hospital in Birmingham while there. They will have a story to tell or I'm no judge.

Please show this to Anna [Damon] and make proper financial arrangements for Mrs. Powell to get to B'ham on the 12th if you so decide.

Sincerely, Joseph Gelders[18]

A week earlier, Carleton Beals, a columnist covering the Scottsboro Case for *The Nation*, received a somewhat more poignant response from the same hospital environment. Momentarily cloaked within the convenient white skin of one allied against "the nigger," Beals quickly became cognizant of what could be described only as the unmasking of southern white males' psychic fear of losing control over what they perceived as the black males' sense of being emasculated. Ozie's attack was a vivid reminder to Alabamian authorities that their physical control not only was indeed tentative over "their negroes" but also was one that required constant monitoring.

Beals described the hospital scene:

> In the Negro ward on the fourth floor of the Hillman Hospital on Sunday afternoon I was with Ozie Powell, the Scottsboro boy who was shot in the head by Deputy Sheriff J. Street Sandlin in the mysterious scuffle on the road between Decatur and Birmingham. Ozie lies in the first room after one steps from the white ward into the ill-kept black quarters. At his doorway are stationed highway patrolmen, sheriffs, and gum-shoe men, who survey all comers with suspicious eyes. Ozie was lying on his left side asleep, a white bandage on his head, his right foot chained to the bed.
>
> I was speaking to the nurse when a lanky sheriff poked me in the chest with a hard finger and snapped, "Who are you?"
>
> I explained, and almost at once he became loquacious. "I'd give a fifty-dollar bill," he repeated several times, "if you could talk to that nigger. But it's against the governor's orders. I'd like you to see for yourself that New York lawyer Leibowitz is a damn liar. Why, we had a man planted outside Ozie's window when he and Watts wuz talkin' to the nigger, and we know everything that was said."
>
> "What do you think of these niggers?" asked a fat gum shoe man. "They're guilty, ain't they? You'd shoot a nigger that knifed your buddy, wouldn't you?"
>
> I managed to convince him that I thought as any good Alabamian does, and the sheriff grew mellow with the idea that at last he had found a friendly New York newspaperman. "Stand right here in the doorway," he said, and have a look at him."
>
> Before I could protest, he strode over to the bed, woke up the boy who had undergone a serious brain operation less than forty-eight hours before and whose life was still in the balance, and began firing questions at him. There was fear in the spasmodic twitching of the Negro's body and his rolling dazed eyes; he answered respectfully in a weak voice. Even so, he refused to incriminate Roy Wright, one of the other two manacled Negro boys in the car where the trouble started. When the sheriff insisted on an answer, saying, "That Leroy Wright's a bad fellow, isn't he? He put you up to this, didn't he?" Ozie groaned out, "Naw, he didn't have to put me up to it."
>
> Similarly Ozie refused to answer the question, repeated again and again, "Leibowitz was mad at you, wasn't he?" This in a triumphant tone.
>
> "Naw, he wasn't mad," the Negro boy managed to groan.
>
> "But he was different toward you, wasn't he?"
>
> "Naw, I guess—" And Ozie's voice drifted into unintelligibility.
>
> "He didn't talk to you very long, did he?" persisted the sheriff.
>
> "Guess—he didn't have much time."
>
> "He was in a hurry, wasn't he?"
>
> Merely a negative sort of groan answered this question. The Negro boy was perfectly lucid, but he seemed to grow weaker from the prolonged questioning, of which only a sample is given here.
>
> The sheriff, with several others who had crowded into the Negro's room, came back to me with a gloating expression. "Now you can tell the truth about this, can't you? You seen for yourself that Leibowitz was lying when he said this nigger wasn't in a fit condition to be questioned. You seen that he knows everything he's saying."[19]

The thought that this too is American justice warps the conscious mind and its discernment of those processes that help formulate the due process of law in a segregated society. Are there limits to what can be expected from individuals whose notion of justice is envisioned only on the lowest corruptible level? Answering this question and others is often resolved by observing the process and those factors that help to implement policy on the micro level of social interaction. In this regard, Beals' observation is germane: "At the recent trial, watching the half-illiterate talesmen shuffle forward in response to Judge Callahan's sharp calling of their names, surveying their shabby clothes, their dull eyes, their vacant countenances, their malformed bodies, and seeing them fill the spittoons with tobacco juice, one felt a sense of shame. These are of our purest American stock. What has brought about their degeneracy?"

The answer is not easily found or learned, because it is entwined in the mythology of social development and those traditions obtained at the expense of the most vulnerable. To even ask the question is for many to risk social censure. Accordingly, "as one rides through the countryside and sees the shacks in which they live, the boards warped and rotting, the windows broken and stuffed with rags, as one looks at the stony hillsides and the pine trees standing in swampy pools, one realizes that many of these people in America in the twentieth century live worse than most peasants in the Balkans and certainly have fewer cultural attainments. They fear the Negroes. It is an economic fear. It is a physical fear. It is a cultural fear. It is a blind fear."[20]

The state of Alabama did drop the rape charge against Ozie Powell some sixteen months later, in 1937, but gave him twenty years for assaulting the deputy. The court also dropped the charges against Roy Wright, Olen Montgomery, Eugene Williams, and Willie Roberson.

When Ozie Powell was paroled on September 27, 1946, he went to live with his mother in Atlanta, Georgia. And that's where he died.

Chapter 7

Correspondence, Epistles, and Dispatches

CLARENCE NORRIS: Receiving letters from home or wherever made you feel that you were not alone and that what you were experiencing was appreciated by people on the outside, especially when a letter came from home. The problem was that I couldn't write and my reading wasn't the greatest. I knew that with a few lucky breaks, such as not having to work in them fields as a kid, and paying a little more attention to the little bit of schooling I did have, things might have been different. But like the old folks say, "That's water under the bridge."

At different times, either Roy Wright or some other prisoner would write letters for me. I would of course tell them my thoughts and ideas, they would read it back to me to make sure that was exactly what I wanted to say. My mother had the same problem. She would get someone to write to me, but the ideas and thoughts were hers. These letters were extremely important when I was on death row because they helped me to maintain confidence in others; however, it was very selfish of me to make demand after demand on her as I did others. Yes, she was concerned about me but she was also raising two younger kids and no one there to help her. However, it is a sad thing to admit, but when you're in prison your personal needs become the most important thing to you in the world. And when you were as famous as we were, receiving letters, newspapers, packages, and all kinds of promises from people around the world who we would probably never meet but who related to our struggle to survive and be free, one does become demanding. In this kind of situation your status in prison can be very threatening to others who already hate you for a variety of reasons. So here we were, nine black youth caught up in a situation we had no real understanding of until we received that first death sentence, and now a few years later, people in other countries were rioting and doing all sorts of things in our behalf!

Man, we received mail from places I never heard of before. I personally received letters from all parts of the United States, as well as England, Germany, you name it. From people who were black and those who were white. These were the things which made us always feel that we would be free and even strong.

But I'll tell you something, I would also get upset at the folks outside. You see, as I said before, when you're inside prison, time seems to move at a different pace than outside. Our day or week behind the walls was different than a regular day or week. The very space around us, limited as it was by walls and steel cell blocks, dictated where we could or couldn't walk. It was as if our bodies were encased within steel coffins. There was a constant need to beware of dangers all around us, and this affected how we saw each other and even the concept of time itself.

Occasionally mail did intrude upon this feeling of being in another world, a cold impersonal world. This too was welcomed, for it was a reminder of another reality with different people, places, and emotions. However, communicating with this world was very difficult, though it was our only lifeline.

The following sample of letters, official reports by the state of Alabama, and memoranda covering the years from 1931 to 1944 represents only a portion of the correspondence concerning Clarence Norris during this period.[1] Though Norris was limited in vocabulary, one can sense his frustration and anger as well as his sensitivity to others throughout these letters. It is also important to realize that, being illiterate, Norris was forced to dictate his letters to Andy Wright or any other prisoner who could write his thoughts or feelings on paper. And though replete with spelling and grammatical errors, these letters reflect the intensity of day-to-day struggles and frustrations to survive a reality not of their own making.

1.

From Olen Montgomery May 25-31
Kilby Prison
Montgomery, Ala.

My dear Frind Mr. George
Why sitting down warred nilly crazy i want you all to rite to me and tell how is things going on a bout this case of us 9 boys bee cause i am in here for something i know i did not do my pore mother has no one to help hur to make a living but me she had a little girl luft only 5 years old to take of and she has nop job at all and i gozt you all know how times is on the out side i hard is did all i cud for my pore mother to help hur live and my little sister i was on my way to Memphis on a oil tank by my self a lone and i was not warred with any one un till i got to Paint rock alabama and they just made a frame up on us boiys just cause they cud any way them grond jurys come out of the room and said us five boys punishment shall bee like time in the Kilby Prison and the judge sesnt them back in the room and they came back out the next time and said their punishment shall bee by death in the chair
Eugene Williams

Haywood Paterson
Charlie Weems
Clarence Norris
Ozie Powell
Andy Wright
Willie Roberson
We want you all to send us some money so we can bye us something what we can east this food dont degree with me at all i suppoosed to be at home any way i did not do whay they gat me for i ant give no one any cause to mist treat me this way i know ant and i hope you all is doin all you can for us boys please sur and we supposed to have a nother trial be cause it was not a fair trial i ant crazy no way either lost my mine

2.

May 2, 1934

President Franklin D. Roosevelt
Washington, D.C.

Dear Sir:

On May 13, 1934, on the day when the American people will celebrate Mothers' Day, we are asking the President of the United States to receive five American mothers, Mrs. Jane Patterson, Mrs. Josephine Powell, Mrs. Mamie Willimas, Mrs. Ida Norris, Mrs. Viola Montgomery. They are the mothers of five of the nine innocent Scottsboro boys, who three years ago were condemned to die, and whose lives were saved by thousands of Americans, Negro and white, who have protested their innocence and supported their defense. (Their innocence has been proven in the courts, and admitted by Judge James E. Horton, in his opinion of June 20, 1933.)
These mothers have suffered great unhappiness. In their suffering they symbolize thousands of mothers today, whose young sons and daughters, unemployed, despondent, demoralized, during the long period of the crisis, have left their homes in search of work, in the hope of recovering lost manhood and lost womanhood.
These mothers have long known this deprivation. For three long years they have known the torture of the threat of death to their innocent children. These are mothers to whom the government owes the safeguards for the realization of their right to "pursuit of happiness."
This appointment with the President on Mothers' Day is made at the request of the five Scottsboro mothers named above. We ask that acknowledgement be made to them in care of this organization.

Yours truly
INTERNATIONAL LABOR DEFENSE
National Secretary

3.

PA129 35 GOVT

THE WHITE HOUSE WASHINGTON DC 347P MAY 11 1934

WILLIAM PATTERSON
NATL SECRETARY INTERNATIONAL LABOR DEFENSE 80 EAST 11 ST

THE CASE TO WHICH YOU REFER IN YOUR LETTER OF MAY SECOND AND YOUR TELEGRAM OF MAY SEVENTH IS ONE OVER WHICH THE STATE OF ALABAMA HAS JURISDICTION I MUST THEREFORE RESPECTFULLY DECLINE YOUR REQUEST
MARVINE H MCINTYRE SECRETARY TO THE PRESIDENT.
405P

4.

Clarence Norris
Kilby Prison
Montgomery Ala.
8-18-34

To the members of the
American Federation of
Musicians Local 802.

Dear Friends it give the greatest of pleasure to try an show my appreciation toward you all for making it possible for me to have an guitar.
I was imform throu mine lawyer Mr Brodsky that your all are fighting for local autonomy.
I trust that you all will have the greatest success in your stuggle.
For the last three years a great fight have been going on for my freedom. But I have not lost my faith in the ones that are putting in every effort of their time to bring about my freedom.
I am sure that this worthy cause which you all are struggling to accomplish will end and be a great benefit to all.
The Guitar will help me a great deal during these trying days.

So again I thank you all. And my appreciation.

Wishing the A.F.M No. 802

Much success in the
future to come.
Sincerely yours
Clarence Norris

5.

Kilby Prison
Montgomery, Alabama
September 14, 1934

Mrs. Ida Norris
My dear Mother:—

I was indeed happy to hear from you. This leave me in the best of spirit and no way discourage.

Very happy to know that you have had good meetings on your tour.

Give all of the workers my warmest regards. tell them my faith and courage is always at its peak. I have the greatest of faith in them that they will continue this mighty fight until we Scottsboro boys are free. With the workers behind me, I have faith that I will be a free man in the near future.

Mother, I trust that you will continue to be in good health, where you can carry on your good work for my liberty.

Many thanks and appreciations to the workers for the pass and the greatest success in the future.

Your loving son,
[signed] Clarence Norris

6.

Molina, Ga.
Sept. 18, 1934

International Labor Defense:
Dear Sir:

Received the ($10.00) ten dollars.
thanking you very much.

Inez Norris,
Molina. Ga.

7.

July 15th, 1936

Mrs. Ida Norris
Molina, Ga.

Dear Mother Norris:

Somehow a letter in which you inform us that you returned to Molena is not at hand and I was under the impression that you were at Atlanta. I expected to see you there, However, when I arrived at Atlanta I found that you were not there. This is too bad, because I had your teeth with me and I had planned to make arrangements in Atlanta for a dentist to see that the teeth were properly fitted for you. Now I really don't know what to do.

It is impossible for you to come to New York at this time but if you can arrange to go to Atlanta and stay there a while with Mrs. Powell, or perhaps someone else we would see that the teeth are sent down and we will also send you the cost for getting them fitted.

In so far as getting any dentist is concerned, Try to see Ben Ronin, his address is 313 Wellborn Street, Atlanta, Ga. and he will see someone who will be able to find a dentist for you.

I am enclosing herewith $10.00 from the Prisoners Relief Department. Please write me as soon as possible what arrangements you are able to make.

Very best wishes from everyone,
Anna Damon, Acting National Secretary
International Labor Defense

AD:EB

8.

November 4, 1936

Clarence Norris,
Birmingham, Ala.

Dear Clarence:

I have just recently had a letter from your mother and you will be glad to know that she is well.

I am enclosing $8.00 for the month.

It is very hard to write to you Clarence, because you never answer my letters. I am sure it is not hard for you to sit down and write a few words telling me how you are. You know I am anxious to hear from you and cannot understand your silence.

May I expect to hear from you soon?

Best Greetings.
Anna Damon
Acting National Secretary

AD:RN
BS&AU
12646

9.

County Jail
Birmingham, Ala.
11-25-36

Miss Anna Damon.
Dear Madame.

I am writing asking a favor. Something which I do not understand. That is about some stamps I have. I am asking you to exchange them for me and to know how much they value. I would like to know very much, and send me the money for them. they were sent to me from some friends of England, their names are Mrs. Edith Odonnell, and husband. I am enclosing a letter with this for you to mail to them for me please. they live, 6 oxford road, southsea Hants, England. and please do this at once. you can send the money for these coupons next week when you send me the money for the month. I'll close wishin you a Happy Thanksgiving.

Sincerely yours
Clarence Norris
County Jail
Birmingham, Ala.

10.

December 2, 1936

Clarence Norris,
Birmingham, Ala.

Dear Clarence;

I have your letter of November 23 on hand and am very glad you are well.

I sent the letter to England as you requested. I am sure it makes you feel good to know that you have friends all over the world that are interested in you and are working to set you free.

I am sending you back the English postage. It is worth very little, and I suggest that you exchange them for American postage at the Prison Post Office.

Enclosed is $8.00 for the month. I hope you will write again soon.

Very best greetings,
Anna Damon

11.

County Jail
Feb. 16, 1937

Dear mother.

I recieve your letter a few days ago. and it found me doing very well—and truly hope when these few lines Reach your hands will find you well and Enjoying the Best of Life. listen mother I need a little money. this food they feeds Dont agree with my Stomack. You Know I suffer with the stomach ache. if you send me a little money I can send out and get me someting to eat. that will agree with my somack. of course the food is All Right. But it just Dont suit my appitipe. So mother I will be looking for it Soon. Send me much as $2.00 are $3.00 any way—I am awfully glad to know the children are still going to School. and tell all of thems I say hello and Be good. I hope to meet yuou all again soon. so I will close.

from your son,
Clarence Norris
County Jail
B'Ham. Ala.
Ans. Soon

12.

July 24, 1937

Dear Rose

it has Been sometime Since I have written You. I am awful sorry I waited so long to write. I was in good hopes of Bein out where I could talk with Each and Every one of my friends face to face. But although I was unsuccessful in my trial. But by chances I may overcome. Listen rose I am in need for [ed. note: unclear word] five dollars to buy me some things. I Realy need, and I would apprecate it. You send me much as five Dollars any way to buy me the things I need. listen rose I hate to ask any one for no more than I can help. But I hate to worry you an any one else. But I am just realy in need. and are at a place where I cant get anything. unless Some one give it to me. So I hope you don't do like the rest. Dispoint me in what I ask for. So I hope to hear from you very soon, So I will close.

Yours Sincerely,
Clarence Norris
County Jail
B'ham Ala.

13.

July 27, 1937

Mr. Clarence Norris
Jefferson County Jail
Birmingham, Alabama

Dear Clarence:

I was very glad to receive your letter. I am enclosing $5.00 as per your request, and hope you will be able to get the things you want for the money.

I am sure, Clarence, that there will be a time in the near future when you will be able to speak to every one of your friends face to face. I hope you realize that the I.L.D., the Scottsboro committee and all your other friends will not give up the fight until you and the other four boys are free. I don't have to tell you how happy we are to have Montgomery, Williams, Roberson and Wright free. We are now celebrating this partial victory and hope to celebrate in the near future the full victory when you and the other boys will be free.

Write to me when you have a chance, and let me know how you are.

Fraternally,
Rose Baron

14.

County Jail
Aug. 3, 1937

Dear Mr. Morris [Shapiro], yours was receive this morning and I certainly enjoyed hearing from you. Your letter found me well. and I hope when these few lines reaches you they will find you the same. Mr. Morris I wish some one would help me out of this miserable place now. Because I am tired of such place.

Mr. Morris I appreciate having friends all over the world. But it seems to me like all of my firneds are working mighty slow. Mr Morris I have Been in jail for over Six in a half years and I am tired of hearing the samething about what my friends are doing I have Been hearing about what peoples are doing trying too do for the whole time that I have been in jail. and it dont seems like they have did anything for me. Because I am still in jail. and also in the some shape that I was in over six years ago. Now I wonder how long do I have to stay in jail now, Mr Morris. do you have any ideas about how long do I haft too stay in jail now. if so tell me where I wont haft to Be all the time studying and wondering about it.

Mr. Morris I am in need for some money and I would appreciate it. if you would send me much as $3.00 out side of the money ordere that I gets every month Because I am in need for some things that I realy need. I have a whole lots of letters to ans and also needs cigarettes and stamps. and statineary to ans thems with and I cant buy all of that out of the little money that I gets every month. Because I needs some more things awaful bad.and I would appreciate it if you would send me the amount of money that I ask for.

So this is all for this time hoping to hear from you soon. telling me about some things I ask you.about my case. So this is all for this time from y ours sincerely.

Clarence Norris

15.

County Jail
Aug. 3, 1937

Dear Rose, yours was receive a few days ago. and I indeed was glad to hear from you. and I also receive the money. and it come in a needed time. rose I wonder what do you all call soon a month ore two are a year are said. I cant understand what some people call Soon. Rose I only call a few days soon. But I wont you to give me some kind of ideas about soon. Because I am anxious to know. Rose Because I am tired of bein in jail suffering for something that I know nothing about. and a crime that I didnt not to commit. and never thought of commiting Such crime because I have no right to commit Such crime. Rose I am hoping to Be out of jail Before xmas. Do you have any ideas about how long do I haft to Be in jail? if so tell me where I can Be satified.

So I guess this is all for this time. I will write more in my next letter. I have a lots of letters to ans now. so that why I am making yours short. so I am looking for a long encourging letter from you soon. telling me about some things that I would like mighty well to hear about. So this is all for this time.

From yours sincerely

Clarence Norris

16.

County Jail
Aug 3, 1937

Dear Anna
I hope when these few lines reaches you they will find you well and enjoying the Best of life.

anna I am wondering how long do I haft to Be in jail. could you give me some kind of ideas about it? Because I am sick of this place. anna what you was telling me in your letter I don't wont to hear nothing about all of the friends that I have on the out side because I have been hearing that Same thing for over six and a half years. and I am tired of hearing that now what peoples are been doing it dont seems like it have did any good Because I am in Jail and also in the same shape that I was in over six years ago.

anna what I wont too know now how long do I haft to stay in this miserable place. I wish you would give me some kind of ideas about what I am asking you. I am not interested in the Dimertration that peoples are giving on the out side. What I am interested in now that is getting out of jail. and then another thing that I cant understand and that is why that Mr. Leibowitz had to repeal my case and Didn't repeal the other Boys. if he had of taken a repeal in the other Boys case it seems like they would of been here in Birmingham instead of Bein in the state penitentiary. that is why I feel so funny about my case. anna I dont guess I haft too Be in jail another xmas. Do I? If I Do I wish you all would tell me. and then probly I could Be patience. anna I am asking you for $2.00 out side of the money that you send every month. Because I am in need for a fews things and I also haft to Buy cigarettes and stamps and statinary. Because I have a lots of letters on hand now. and havent got any stamps and statinary to ans thems with. and I would apprecite it anna if you would send the $2.00. that I ask you for next week when you send my money for the month.

So I guess I will close for this time.hoping to hear from you soon.

from yours sincerely
Clarence Norris

17.

August 12, 1937

Clarence Norris
Jefferson County Jail
Montgomery, Ala.

Dear Clarence:

I am enclosing our regular $8 for you. I have seen the other boys, who are here, several times and I hope that the time will not be to far away when we will see you too. As you know, motions for retrial have been filed in all the cases. these motions and the appeals are necessary to prevent the sentences from being carried out. there is no other way to do it.

The reason that you were separated from the other boys is that under the law, if you were moved to Kilby you would have been put in the death cell, which none of us want.

The Scottsboro Defense Committee is pushing as hard as it can to secure your freedom but the slow process of the courts is what is holding things up.

Hoping to hear from you soon,

Fraternally,
Anna Damon

18.

Birmingham Ala.
Sept. 23, 1937

Dear rose I recieve you letter and also the clippers a few day ago it found me well and I do hope when this letter reaches you it will find you all O.K.

listen rose I am in solitary which I have already told you all I was and you all havent made no kind of effect, to get me out of solitary. rose you all dont know how Bad I am suffering in this miserable place. I am treated odd From any other prison here.

you all know as long as I have Been Bound in jail and you all know how Bad I need Exercise. and rose I wish that you all would make some kind of peparation to get me move From solitary. Because I need some Exercise. You take the whole time that I have Been in jail I have spent the most of the time in solitary and you all know at that rate I will soon be dead. Because half of the time I am so stiff untill I cant hardly walk for my limbs paining and hurting me. and then to this food that they Feed here it is not healthy For any one without Exercise. When I eat it it keeps me in pains all the time. I cant rest day are night in peace, and you all know how miserable I am as many places here that these people can let me get exercise they wont do it.

listen I wish you all will hurry up and do something Far me Because I am in miserable. rose I am writing this letter to you and Anna and all of the rest Far you all to do sometehing Far me. and please lete the rest read it. So this is all

From yours sincerely,
Clarence Norris
County Jail
B,ham Ala.

19.

Birmingham Ala.
Oct. 25, 1937

Dear Mr. Brodsky I am writing you a few lines just to let you know how I am Bein treated here.

Mr. Brodsky I am getting are ill treatment here. I'm not bein treated right. I think that I should Be treated as the rest of the prison here I am placed in solitary in the Back Sided of this jail. I'm not on the side of the jail that I should be on. I have Been placed on the Back side of this jail every since July When I was tried. I am on the side of the jail where they keeps all White prison where I cant get No kind of out let are no Exercise are either see no visitors, and I think I should see peoples who are interested in me in trying to do what they can for me.

listen I had a friend of mine to come down here Sunday to See me From ohio and these Dirty sheriffs Wouldnt let her in to See Me. after spending Money for her rail road fare for over 200 miles. and after all of that she couldn't See me. and after that these old Sheriffs here cursed and doged and abuse her around. and drove her away From the jail. they did that just Because I were a Negro Man and she were a Negro Womon. they dont do these White prisons like that the Colored only have one visiting day. and Every day is visiting day with the White. and nare day is visiting day with me. I am Bein treated worser than any prison here.

listen I am going to enclose the telegram that I rec. I after She was Driven away From the jail. to show you how dirty these No good peoples is. listen I will Be dam Glad When I am out of this No Good State. and I also wish that you all will hurry up and do something For me. if I dont soon Be out of this plce something will happen Badly with me Because I am getting tired of bein treated Worser than a Dog.

listen I wish you would Send me a little money where I can get me a few things that I really Need you promise me some time ago that you would send me the amount of money to help Get the things that I need. But havient heard From you since. So I Guess this is all for this time. hoping to hear From you Soon.

From yours sincerely

Clarence Norris
County Jail
B,ham Ala.

20.

Birmingham Ala.
Oct. 27, 1937

Dear Mr. Morris I read your letter and I also the $5.00 a Few days ago and yur letter did Not find me Getting your along so well.

Mr. Morris I dont think that I am Bein treated right By the Commimittee, and Mr. Leibowitz are either the I.L.D. and I dont think you are Mr. Leibowitz are the committee and the I.L.D. is not are Bit interested in Me Enough to try to regain My Freedom.

Mr. Morris I am innocent of this Crime I amascuse of and dont feel like I will every will Be able to over come this Frame up. Mr. Morris I Believe that I am Bein Framed to the chair are either in prison for the ret of my life. By the committee and Mr. Leibowitz and the I.L.D. Mr. Morris I once have had plenty Faith in the committee and Mr. Leibowitz and also the I.L.D. in regaining My Freedom But now I dont have no faith are either Confidence in None of you all who So call themselves My Friend.

Mr. Morris I Feels like you all have help the State Frame Me out the Best of my life just to Get those four Boys Free who are Free now of course I am glad to see those four Boys go Free. Because they got what they due. and I know I should have the same thing Because I am innocence. Mr. Morris I have Bein asking some of you all to send Some of the Lawyers down. I wont to see Mr.

Leibowitz But I havent seen any one since I was tried in that Kangaroo Court in July.

Mr. Morris its something is going on crooky. that why I cant see any one are either can Get any kind of Detail about my case. Mr. Morris I have known the time that I could see some of you all at most any time But now I cant see any one. Mr. Morris you know as long as I have Been in jail and have Been pending on what Mr. Leibowitz and I.L.D. and the committe and what they all was telling me and nothing they have said have been put to no action and that is Enought to make any one Feel Down hearted and Discourage and lose Faith and confidence.

Of course Mr. Morris I know that none of you all dont care about My Feeling I have be toward you all. of course I cant help how none of you all Feel about what I am saying I am just only telling you about the way I Feel I have lost faith in you all and it cant he helped. Because I always will believe that I am framed until I be Convince. ofcourse if I have been Framed By you all and the state I havent Been treated just. So I hope God will Bless you and I am hoping all of you a good Success in Everything you may do are doing . So this is all.

From Clarence Norris

21.

Birmingham Ala.
Nov. 25, 1937

Mr. Morris Dear Sir I am droping you a few lines to let you hear from me. I am well in health. and I hope when this letter reaches you it will find you O.K.

Mr. Morris when you read this letter I know you will know about how I feel in mind. Listen Mr Morris I wont to know why that I cant get no kind of understanding from none of you all about my case. I think that Mr. Leibowitz is a terribly lawyer. he is the one that I look for to give me Some kind of understanding about what losing on in my case. of course My idea about it I dont think it is nothing going on in my case to benefit me anthing and I think every since I have Been in Jail it is nothing has Been Done By none of you all to Benefit me anything. Evereything have Been Done it was for a out show and for the Benefit of Some one else.

Listen Mr. Morris I wish that you all would send me Leibowitz Down here to see me where I can talk with him my self. and I wont be satified until I see him. Listen Mr. Morris you all know that I dont wont to see any one that dont know nothing concernign my case. Mr. Morris you all just dont know how Bad it is to be confined in jail and cant get no one to tell me anything about what going on in my case.

Listen Mr Morris if my case got to go through the high court I dont think it should lay in Ala. Supreme Court a year are so before bein argue and acted on. if it haft to I know you all dont wont to see me free as Bad as you all pretend. if you all Dont Soon ell me something about what going on in my case if it is where I can have my repeal withdraw I will do so. Because I have been suffering long enought far soemthing that I didnt do, and as quick as I can get this long suffering over with it wont Be none to soon.

I am tired of laying around in prison suffering and bein use by all of these organization. Now Mr. Morris if I dont soon know something concerning my case I will write to the Alabama Supreme Court and ask thems to withdraw my repeal and just takes what come. and the admiration that peoples have been making over me will Be all over with. so this is all.

from Yours sincerely
Clarence Norris.

22.

January 26, 1938

Clarence Norris
Jefferson County Jail
Birmingham, Ala.

Dear Clarence:

I am taking this opportunity of sending you a few words of greetings and hoping that you are well. I just heard from your Mother and was glad to hear that she is getting along nicely. I am sure that you will be glad to hear that the lawyers are getting ready to take your appeal to the State Supreme Court in a very short time and I hope that we will have very good news for your soon.

Why don't you write more often? Have you heard from the other boys? Roy and Olen are coming back to New York tomorrow from their trip across the country. They have done a good job for all of you and have had very good meetings.

I am enclosing you money with very best wishes and warmest regards.

fraternally yours,
Rose Baron

23.

Room 504
112 East 19th Street
New York City
August 10, 1938

Clarence Norris
Kilby Prison
Montgomery, Ala.
Dear Clarence:

We certainly hope next tuesday will prove a very lucky day for you and the rest of the boys, because on that day your petition for complete pardon will be heard by the governor and the Pardon Board. But whatever the outcome, remember that we are always here to do everything that we can to win your freedom.

I hope the enclosed $8 finds you well.
Best greetings from your many friends,
Fraternally,
Rose Baron

24.

June 14, 1939

Clarence Norris
Kilby Prison
Montgomery, Ala.

Dear Clarence:

Again I am enclosing money order for $3 and hope that this finds you well.

We haven't heard from you for a long time and while they say no news is good news, still we like to hear that you are O.K.

Very best greetings from everyone here in the office. Best personal regards from myself.

Very sincerely
Rose Baron

25.

Montgomery, Ala.
Camp Kilby
1-3-40

Mrs. Anna Damon

My Dear Mrs. Damon

I trust the holidays brought you much happiness and the New Year hold much success for you and my many friends.

Listen Mrs. I began to want to see my Mother & baby sister. it have been back in 1934 since I had the chance to talk with her. And I would appreciate it very much if you would fix it some way for them to come down. I am expecting you to be so right. any way it would mean so much to me to see them after so long a time. I am quite sure you all will do so because you all have help the other boy mothers to come an see them. Here is My Mother address, 3017 E. 30th St.[in rear], Cleveland, Ohio.

I am going to write my mother and tell he that I worite you all to help her come to see me.

I will close with many wishes for a succesfully New Year.

Clarence Norris

26.

March 19, 1940

Mr. Clarence Norris
Kilby Prison
Montgomery, Ala.

Dear Clarence:

Everyone in the office was shocked and disappointed at the refusal of the Board to grant you parole. We have not slackened our efforts and will do everything in our power to continue the fight for your freedom.

The Defense committee is also taking steps to find out what can be done in your behalf.

I am enclosing the allowance. Everyone in our office sends greetings to you.

Sincerely,
Hester Huntington

27.

Montgomery Ala.
Camp Kilby
June 3-40

Mrs. Anna Damon
Dear Comrade:

I am sure you will be surprise to hear from me but however I trust you all are been served with the very best of health.

I have not been so well especial in health. My teeth have been causing me much suffering. I have several decaing teeth and I can save them if I start in time. I have already save fifteen dollars $15.00 for that perpose and I need ten more I am writing to Mr. Shapiro asking for a little increase in my month allounce. So I want you to increse your as much as five dollars ($5.00) extra fro that perpose. I want to have them fix just as soon as I get the money.

So I hope you all will not disappoint me. Now I do not want you to send me that amont every month just this month. I would not ask you all for this extra amount if I did not need it. So I will clase expecting to hear from you soon. Respectfully Yours, Clarence Norris

28.

Montgomery Ala.
August 12, 1940

My dear Miss Huntington

I am at a total loss as to why I did not receive my regular allowance at the usual time which was lose Friday, Is it possible that you made a slight mistake and sens an order to one of the others on the date you should have send mine? I noticed that one of them that usually get his aftrer I do, received his the day I should have received mine. Although this has been done before I do not know what to make of it as it is. I was put to a bit of inconvinence and I am badly in need just now.

I have written to my mother several times but she has failed to answer. I wonder whether you have heard from her lately. if so please let me know and I would appreciate it very much if you would write to her and find out why she does not answer my letters. I send my good wishes to you and all. I am as ever

Clarence Norris

29.

Kilby Prison
Montgomery Ala.
March 18, 1941

Miss Huntington

Your letter of last month was received. It found me and also the other two boys that have been good health and doing the best we can.

Miss Huntington I am in debt. I realize its my own fault—I own out more money than I can pay and the fellows that I own think now that we are liable to be released any day now. So they are pressing me daily for their money. So if you can please send me as much as twenty dollars at once and then you can deduct it from my allowance. for I am sure if I dont soon pay the fellows it will be some serious trouble. and I know of no one to turn to except you all. I will expect an answer soon.

Yours Sincerely
Clarence Norris

30.

March 20, 1941

Mr. Clarence Norris
Kilby Prison
Montgomery, Alabama

Dear Clarence:

I am much concerned about your letter which arrived today, having crossed in the mail with one I sent to you yesterday enclosing the usual allowance.

We are not in a position to forward more money to you. We are obliged to share what we have with all of Labor's needy people and all of labor's prisoners. You did not say anything in your letter about receiving a radio that I had sent to you. If you did not receive the radio, please tell me, and I will immediately put a "tracer" on the order from the store where I bought it.

We are all thinking about you, and we all send greetings to you.

Sincerely yours,
Hester G. Huntington

31.

2576 E. 40 St.
Cleveland, Ohio
April 8, 1941

My Dear Friend: Mrs Hester G. Huntington

Your letter found me well and getting alone allright. hope these few lines will find you all likewise. We are having some very nice weather it is getting warm I am sure glad to see it.

Tell me in your next letter what is being done on the Scottsboro Boys case. I would also like for you to find out if possible why Clarence dont write me. I havent had a letter from him in some time. I would like to know if it is that he is or is not allowed to write or if it is his own fault.

I am thinking about the parade you all are going to have there in May. I sure would like to be there. because I know it is going to be wonderful. listen dear, if possible please try to send me as much as #6.00 this time if you can. the baby say please try to send her some dress for the summer. Write and tell me where is angelo and send me his address. and where is Richard B. Moore? give all my friends my Best regards

I remain your truly
Ida Norris

32.

Montgomery, Ala.
Kilby Prison
Nov. 12, 1941

Hello Hester.

I Rec. your letter of the Nov. 12th, i also receive Sweater and Really liked it. it really a Beauty, and i certainly appreciate it and hope some day that i approve to you all just how much i really appreciate the kindness of every one.

hester in speaking of the cap, just for get the Big apple part, *smile.* and get a cap of the very Latest style and your pick is mine. But please let it be of Dark Brown. Size 7. and listen hester, the information i asked you of. here is the name; Mr. George E. Hayner. hester he one time held the same office that Morris Shapiro is holding now. Can you remember how who I am asking of. Then if you don't please ask Morris and he will tell you. Hayner use to be secatary of the Scottsboro committee.

hester Dear i know that you cant put in all of your time writing and doing for me. But honestly i do appreciate every stept and every little turn that you make in my behalf. and I will approve to you some day. how much i really appreciate you. See as it is please give every one in office my very Best Regards. may good such good wishes and happiness cooperte with every one.

Sincerely yours,
Clarence Norris

* Please send two pair of socks

33.

Montgomery Ala.
Camp Kilby
Dec. 28, 1941

Dear Miss Huntington

Dear madam I am writing you on a very urgent matter. I am a bit worry over my mother — it have been over four years since I have sein her and I would like mighty well to see her. if there is any way possible for you all to send her down I would more than appreciate it. I have been under the Doctor care for about a month now. therefore I would like to see her more than ever I tried my hardest to put it off until I hear from my case but my patience have broken And I want you all to send her down as early as you possible can. I hope that I am not asking to much of you all. I will depend on you attending to this little matter which would mean a great deal to me. If you all can not send her down please let me know when I will be expecting her.

I hope that will not be disappointed wishing every one in this struggle for my freedom much success through out the new year.

Sincerely yours
Clarence Norris

p.s. my mother address is 2576 E.40th St. Cleveland, Ohio

34.

INTERNATIONAL LABOR DEFENSE
National Office

112 EAST 19TH STREET NEW YORK CITY
Hon. Vito Marcantonio Anna Damon, Secretary
William L. Patterson, Vice-President Robert W. Dunn, Treasurer

February 25 '42

Mr. Clarence Norris
Kilby Prison
Montgomery, Ala.

Dear Clarence,

All of us at the office were shocked and sorry to hear that parole had again been denied for you. We send you our real sympathy. If you have time will you please write to tell us all about the parole hearing [if you decided to ask for parole, or did someone else suggest to try and ask again?]

We are enclosing an extra two dollars to day so that is possible, you can buy a few comforts.

Sincerely
Hester G. Huntington

35.

Kilby Prison
March 9, 1942

Miss Hester G. Huntington
Dear Miss Hester,

This is to acknowledge your letter of March 2 and the some was much appreciated.

I was much afraid I would be imposing on *good nature* however — I did not mean that you stop the allowance. I was only offering my months allowance for the articles that I have no other way to get. Nevertheless, I am grateful that you will get them. I don't know how to show you just how much I appreciate your kindness. I must confess that I must be a lot of trouble to you, and you seem to have the patience to console us in our present Solitude, you all kindness is a great example to me, and my destination is; to be able to return this same kindness to some one of the same condition that I am in some day.

I am going to have some pictures made — and if you all wish, I will send you some for your D.W. if it is convenience. I do wish you could send the articles this *week end*, that is — if it is possible, and in case that you have forgotten the articles, I will state them here again: a pair of shoes, color: Black. Size, 8 narrow toe, a suit of shorts, Size 34, and some Camel cigarets. two pair of sox. Soap and tooth brush and paste. I did not say anything about a shirt on the first letter, but I need one, if you can — please include a white shirt, size 15 and after I receive these things I will promise to try not to ask for anything out of the ordinary any more. please pass my best whishes to other members and you have my personal best wishes — with luck and success to you.

yours sincerely
Clarence Norris (col.)
Kilby Prison
Montgomery, Ala.

36.

Montgomery, Ala.
Kilby Prison
Aug 2, 1942

Dear Mrs. Huntington,
Once again i am writing to you in all manner of hope that you will help me out of search distress as i am now in. hester I wrote you to day a week ago But for some particular Reason I failed to get any reply to my letters. So I was Forced to write you again. It is not because I can write. But it is because i am in a pretty bad spot now. i am still in the hospital, and when i will be out is unknown.

i had something to grow over my left eye that caused my whole head to worry me. So i was stop off duty for a Doctor examination. and after ward i was told that it would have to cut or stand a chance of losing and eye. So I Did have it cut. So after being in hospital for short period it seems as it every thing is going Bang. Smile.

Listen Mrs. Huntington, the kindness i mention to you in my letter a week ago. please if you can send it along with the monthly advancement. please for i am completely out of cigaretts, in fact i am out of everything Search as i am alowed to have them,[unclear] that is suitable and at nursing to a sick person is not furnished by the state.

hester i grant you understand. We don't get any thing good of course hester i realize that i am a plum worry to you. But you have been so dear and a mother like to me and seems to be the only one that feel my sympathy. you really seems more like a mother than your a friend. So for that reason i put fourth my febly confidence in you and ask you to do all thing for me. *Smile.*

So hester please do your best for me with you please. P.S. I havent heard from the N.A.C.C.P. that one reason i have to call on you: a month have past with out any hering from them.

So I will close hopeing that you will continue to stand by me, as you have allways.

From Sincerely yours
Clarence Norris
Please answer soon

37.

INTERNATIONAL LABOR DEFENSE

112 EAST 19TH STREET NEW YORK CITY

August 6, 1942

Mr. Clarence Norris
Kilby Prison
Montgomery, Ala.

Dear Clarence—

A few days ago I had a letter from you saying you were still sick. I am sorry to hear that you feel badly. This week we have managed to send along an extra dollar. Please let us hear from you if you are somewhat better.

How long do you think you will have to stay in the hospital? Best wishes from all.

Sincerely,
Hester G. Huntington

38.

Montgomery, Ala.
November 23, 1942

Mis Hester G. Huntington

Dear Miss Huntington

I am writing this letter with a [unclear] to good feeling the reason I am not feeling so well is because I am trouble in mind over the debts owe here. So listen I want you to hold up my monthly allowance for this month and send it next month with the other allowance and the extra money witch you all send me for xmas. with that all together I will have that much on the twenty five dollars, $25.00 that I want for xmas and all that it like I want you to make out the rest because I really need it with out fail. If I dont get these debts off of hand they are going to cause me to get in a world of trouble and I dont want to get hurt or hurt any one over a little money. So I hope you all will understand and send the money right away. Now I will depend on you to send if I will not look for anything this month. with my best regards to each one in the office.

Sincerely yours
Clarence Norris

39.

Camp Kilby
Jan 18, 1943

Miss Hester Huntington

I received the Shoes and am very pleased with them. Listen Hester, you said in your letter for me not to ask for anything else soon, but I am forced to ask you to do me this favor and then you can rest assured that I wont ask you for anything else soon. I owe some small debts and I'll have to get my cigarettes out of the check you send. And I need some socks and underwear which I can get here cheap. So I want you to send me two extra dollars which will make my check for this month five dollars.if you do this for me I wont need to ask you for anything soon. So please ans soon.

Respectfully yours
C. Norris

40.

2483 E. 35th
Cleveland, Ohio
Feb. 11, 1943

Mrs. Hester G. Huntington
112 E. 19th Street
New York City
Miss Huntington;

I received your money in the nick of time. I was very happy to see it. I was working on W.P.A. [Works Progress Administration] when I fell and broke my arm. I'll get compensention but it has not started yet. It seems to be taking quite sometime, all the blanks have been filled and sent in.

My arm was broken in the wrist the doctor says it will be a long time before I can work again.

As soon as you can please try and send me $10.00 in this next supply. As I do need it very bad.

Give all my friends my best regards. I am feeling so much better but I go to the doctor every day to get my arm treated.

Write soon
Mrs. Ida Norris

41.

Montgomery, Ala.
Route 2, Box 130

Dear Mrs. Huntington

We have been paroled here in Montgomery and will go to work at Foshee

Lumber Co. of course you know we was pennyless and needs clothes and when we go to work we wont be making no furtune and our Board is $7 per week.

and if possible send us some money at once to buy clothes, shoes and hat. as you know everything is very high Please send cash money and as much as possible. We only asks you all for a start in life and here after I am confidently we can carry on ourselves.

Please send it at once the weather is very-very bad.

Yours Truly
Andy Wright c/o foshee Lumber Co.
Route 2 Box 130

Clarence Norris c/o Foshee Lumber Co.
Route 2 Box 130
Montgomery, Ala.

42.

Montgomery, Ala.
24 Davidson St.
May 1, 1944

Dear Hester

Just a few lines to let you hear from me. I am well at this time & truly hope when these few remarks come to your hand they will find you enjoying the very best of life. Listen Hester I got married on the 27 of April & now I am living at 24 Davidson St. So from now on send all my mail to this address.

Listen I am in need for much as ten dollars. I wont ask you to give it to me but I will ask you to send my little money that I receive monthly-send it for this month & also next month. hester please send it by in time enough where I can receive it Friday. I am sending this letter by air & I hope you will get it in time enough to do this for me. So this is all at this time. Mrs. Dora Lee Norris sending her best regards to you from yours sincerely.

Clarence Norris

43.

2483 E. 35th St.
Cleveland, Ohio
May 23, 1944

Miss Hester Huntington

read your letter and was very glad to hear from you. We all are well and hope you all are the same. I am so sorry Miss Anna Damon pass away. she was a grand person. We all must go some day. her family has our sympathy. she will be miss by all who knew her.

in your next letter please send me Mr. Richard Moore address and I will write him. I had a letter from Clarence he isent so well. had hurt him self on the job. He married now. in your next letter tell me when Clarence will get a proal from the State of Ala. I would have liked to have been there for May day. I know you all had a nice time. send me Mother Wright address. give all my best regards. I will close with lots of love. Sincerely

Ida Norris

44.

Montgomery, Ala.
145 Oak Street
June 15, 1944

Dear Hester

this is to say I am doing fine and working every day & I am so proud of that.

Well hester hope when these few lines caome to you it will find you the best of life. hester hope you dont think I am hurring you but I havent got my money for this month & Andy have been got his. so now otherwise I am fine so far.

Well guess you will notice my address is now change. hester I will be so glad whenI can get where I can do something for myself but I will have to be out of this part. hester you no I cant do much making from 18 to 20 dollars a week & sometime less then that if it rain. Never nothing left after I pay board & buy grocery. I am disgusted but have to wait till my time come. hope that wont be very long. guess I have said enough.

From yours sincerely.

Clarence Norris to a True Friend, Hester GH

Chapter 8

A Philosophy for Survival

Clarence Norris: Andy Wright and I, now thirty and thirty-two years old respectively, were paroled for the first time on January 6, 1944. The war was going on, and everything seemed so different from ten years earlier when we was just young men. It didn't take long before both Andy and myself decided that it was time to jump parole and leave Alabama. I came to New York City and tried to make a go of it. But man, with all of the talk about New York being the "big apple," jobs were hard to find.

I finally got in touch with some people with the NAACP, and they told me that the best thing for me to do would be to get in touch with Alabama and return there as soon as possible. When I did return, I telephoned Jack Lender of the Alabama parole board. I told him that I went to visit my mother who lived in Cleveland, Ohio. He told me that by doing this without the parole board's permission I was breaking an agreement to stay within the state of Alabama.

When I finally did report to the parole board, a woman by the name of Miss Mitchell interviewed me and asked, "Well Clarence, since you come back, what did you go through?" I told her, I went to Ohio to see my mother and came back on my own just like I would've if they had just given me permission to go. I didn't tell her that I also went over to New York City to see the lights and everything but when some friends told me that "if they catch you they're going to put your butt in the army," I realized that it was best to get back. And in fact, when I returned to Alabama, they forced me to register for the army anyway. I had to fill out some questionnaires, but I could read very little and couldn't write past by name. They classified me 4F or something like that but warned me, if needed, I could very easily be reclassified, class A.

In any case, it was decided to send me back out on a job site where I had earlier encountered problems with a racist foreman, to say nothing about the low salary which was insufficient to survive on. They said it didn't matter, I was going back there because I broke parole, and if I didn't like it, they'll send me back to prison. I tried to explain to my parole officer that the foreman wanted to give me all the heavy work while continually harassing me by asking,

"Did you all have those women, ... you must have, 'cause the women said so, etc." I told them, I wasn't going to live my life being pestered by remarks like that.

When they sent me back to the same job site I once again refused to work when it was clear that the foreman was going to give all the heavy work to me while larger and stronger workers stood around and watched.

The final straw occurred one day when I was doing my job just fine and I was suddenly told to stop what I was doing and start moving some heavy green lumber about eighteen and twenty feet long from one spot to another! This lumber weighed so much that it was just like a log. Some great big guy weighing about 200 pounds was doing this work before they assigned me to it. Here I am, just a small person, 130 lbs. at the most, and I'm supposed to lift this heavy wood, no way. The foreman told me, "You just go on and do what I told you." That's when I told him: "The hell with you. Why you trying to hard time me? All I'm looking for is a decent job and to be treated as a human being, but instead you going to give all of this shit."

The field agent walked right off, telephoned the penitentiary, and told them what was happening. Before I knew it, the parole board called him back and said that I should sit there until they decided what to do. Now I knew that was a bunch of nonsense. I figured that it would take them about a half-hour to drive up to this site, because it wasn't but five miles from the prison to Montgomery. So sure enough, they arrived there about thirty minutes later and told me to get off my chair. They slapped some handcuffs on me and said, "Let's go." When I think about it, I probably could have tried to escape within that half-hour rather than just sit there, but then with the police headquarters downstairs in this building I just might have been killed in the attempt.

There's something else you have to know, and this has bothered me for the longest time. Andy Wright and me were released or rather paroled somewhat differently than Eugene Williams, Olen Montgomery, Willie Roberson, and Roy Wright back there in 1937. They were released and pardoned with a lot of fan-fare, celebration, and everything. There were parades and all kinds of people wishing them luck, giving them money, and you know, just treated them as heroes. People were making money off of them right and left, but they were also getting their share of it. I was told that they even appeared at the Apollo Theater in Harlem for about two weeks as well as at Madison Square Garden with the governor of New York State. They even had well-known guardians to advise them and generally look out for their best interest until they could finish school and take care of themselves. For example, middleweight champion Ray Robinson was Eugene Williams' guardian, and the tap dancer Bill Robinson was Roy Wright's guardian.

Now, while the public probably thought this was nice, them boys didn't want that kind of thing because they had more pride about themselves. I wouldn't want it myself. That's how come when I left prison I did it myself. I didn't want nobody every time I left prison saying I couldn't help myself. I always tried to take care of myself on the street. It was because of this attitude it was difficult for me to adjust when released and eventually forced me and Andy Wright back to prison. I spent another two years behind those walls until paroled again in 1946. Andy was paroled a second time in the spring 1947 but returned to prison when his employer discovered that he was one of the Scottsboro boys. He fired Andy causing him to be returned to Kilby Prison.

When I walked out of prison in 1946 on my second parole I knew as I would never return to this place again. They just as might have told me to get on out of Alabama, 'cause that's exactly what I was intending to do until I eventually received my pardon from Governor George Wallace in 1976.

1

In many ways, a new life began for me in the 1950s. This was the time of the civil rights marches, desegregation cases throughout the southern states including Alabama, fighting for integration on buses, and all that mess down there in Selma, Alabama. I remember how brave you had to be in order to get involved in these kind of demonstrations, such as what Martin Luther King, Jr., was continually doing. But while segregation was bad in the South, whites were also trying to keep blacks "in check" right here in New York City. I know for a fact that when King was doing his thing, segregation right here in New York City was very strong. Furthermore, at this very moment whites are trying to keep us down too. I know that because I've been down there and up here. These folks in the North are supposed to be giving blacks rights to everything, like jobs, protection of the courts and everything, but you and I both know that in reality, things are not that way.

In the South, after our people struggled to get just laws passed, our folks just went on about their business. But here in the North, regardless of what the law said, white folks did whatever they felt was necessary to keep power for themselves. You know that yourself.

Things have gotten so bad I've often wondered if black youth today know how to survive without being turned around into something negative against themselves. You take blacks in the South not too many years ago: they knew how to survive when they became teenagers. They knew how to get out and work and make a living regardless of what had to be done. Today, especially in this part of the country, you got so many people who have never worked a day in their lifetime that they can't tell you what it means to do for oneself. Things are so wicked today that their mothers and daddies didn't even do for themselves. So you know if that's the case with the parents, how in pure hell are their children suppose to learn how to survive?

Then you got a bunch of young people whose parents did so much for them that when their kids got up in size, if they couldn't get what they wanted, they would steal. Yeah, you see it going on right now. They don't want to go to school, though they have always had a free opportunity to do so in this part of the country. They're just a bunch of spoiled kids. At least in my time, you first had to work the farm, and then if you were lucky, and there were enough hands to work the land, you might spend a few years in a schoolhouse. Today, that lifestyle is no longer the case. People think about surviving only by killing, murdering, raping, breaking in apartments and attacking old women for their checks. The goings-on in most of the cities in this country is the damnedest thing I ever known, but I believe it's worst here in New York City.

This is why, I'm not surprised that the black family is having problems staying together, especially here in the big cities. There are so many strikes against you. First of all, it's very hard, unless there are two people working, to give children the clothes they need, pay rent, put food on the table, deal with transportation, and have some money left over for other things you must pay for if you want to live nicely. And we haven't even mentioned anything about saving a few dollars. In this kind of environment you shouldn't be surprised if youngsters begin to steal those things they see others with.

When I was coming up, you had to wear nothing but overalls, and maybe every now and then you would get a shirt, a pair of shoes or something. That's the way it was down on those farms. But today, if a kid sees something they want, they'll just go on out and steal it. Now, their parents might ask them where or how they got this new shirt or something like that, but generally they just won't chastise the child in any way. All you hear is, "Stop that, so and so," or "You shouldn't do that, etc." Beyond that there just doesn't seem to be any control or influence over today's youngsters as there was when I was coming up. You have children, and I mean around ten years old, who walk out of the house when they feel like it and return whenever they feel like it. Parental control in these cases is almost nonexistent. It's almost as if the kids are saying, "If you can't give me what I want, I'm not going to pay any attention to you." Furthermore, if parents were able to support their families in a decent manner, and these teenagers around the age of fourteen, fifteen, or sixteen could get some kind of training for a job that will pay them some real money, not minimum-wage nonsense, there would be less thieves prowling about in the streets and more respect by youngsters towards their parents. Maybe then these kids could buy the things they desire without the risk of robbing folks.

You know, the bottom line to all of this is that being poor is going to make you do what you think must be done to be either independent or dependent on someone or something. And man, let me tell you, the rules of the game in either case are not always nice.

In 1946 I jumped parole and quickly realized that I was basically on my own. I couldn't be writing the ILD or NAACP folks all the time for money, because out here my needs were such that a few dollars for cigarettes and stuff like that would not suffice, and my previous supporters were not too happy about my decision to "wheel away." They just couldn't understand that for me, getting a job to make a living and begin enjoying life occupied my mind every single day.

When I arrived in New York City and got my first job I started looking for a few girlfriends here and there. I found a few who weren't too demanding and very soon we would go dancing and all of that and just generally have a good time together. On weekends we would hit all the nightclubs, such as Smalls Paradise, The Baron, Celebrity Club, all of them. Now and then our little excursions would take us downtown to some fancy clubs; however, I soon realized this wasn't for me. I much preferred to go to a house party or see a movie than simply be "hanging out" in club after club. This just wasn't my stick. It wasn't then and it isn't now. I will and do smoke cigarettes and a cigar every now and then, but I ain't never put no dope in my body, no kind of way. Not even a reefer. Now, I've seen plenty a fool do this, and all you had to have was some money to get it, I just never took up with those habits.

Smoking reefers and sniffing coke is bad enough, but the nastiest thing has to be shooting that mess into your veins. Just think it through. Most folks don't like the doctor to give them a blood test, and now you're going to put that needle in yourself! This drug thing is so bad here in Harlem that I lived in buildings where teenagers will be shooting dope, I mean the hard stuff, in their veins with rusty old needles that were laying on the stoop [front steps of a tenement building], in the rain. How could you put that needle in your arm? The most I ever done was to drink some good whiskey, yeah. Now I would do that, and do that right now, as long as it's good quality.

You see the problem is with the values people have today. There are some people, especially in a city such as New York, who just don't give a damn. If you remember, earlier I told you about the South and how it was back there on the farm among us poor folks and to some degree even with the so-called middle-class blacks. People had a good feeling about working, having some pride about oneself, no matter how low your job or class was. But today, there is a real down-and-out type poor person who don't do nothing for a living but will steal and to try and beat the man who is making a decent living.

Let me tell you something else: you can talk all of that stuff about giving anyone a chance and they'll work hard. Maybe so, but there's a dangerous kind out there that I don't give a damn if you put them in a pie factory, they're not going to work. I don't give a damn if the city were to dish out a million jobs tomorrow, you'd find some people catching buses and subways trying to get there and be hired. However, and you'd find others who would never make the attempt, and they ain't got a dime in their pocket. These folks are basically bums. They want to live off the fat of the land and do little or nothing for their earnings. That's why you see all this robbing and stealing going on today. Some folks just do not want to work, but they will take that welfare check.

There was a time when there was no such thing as welfare. You worked at any job you got and forced yourself to live within your means. But today we have a serious problem with drugs and addicts who live off of welfare monies. Whose paying them to live off of drugs? The working-class people, that's who. These folks are taking money out of their checks every month or two weeks to buy drugs, it's a shame. And when they get sick from taking these drugs, they expect welfare again to take care of them. Similarly, you can hardly find a young girl who was raised in the city who is not thinking about screwing and having some babies and getting on welfare. That's what wrong with the system. It encourages people to do these things.

I was even robbed years ago right down the street from where I was staying. I was playing some numbers and had won some money on the night track. I think I had about $200 in my pocket. I stopped in a club called the "Sports Inn," saw a few friends, and ordered a shot of whiskey, which was then about 35¢ or 40¢ a shot. I noticed that there were about four cats shooting dice right by the bar, but I didn't pay any real attention to them. As I was leaving the bar one of them glanced in my direction, we nodded, and that was that. It must have been just a few steps from the bar when I noticed that someone was coming up behind me, but before I could turn around, I was knocked down with a bottle and was almost unconscious. They went through my pockets, took all my money, yet felt somehow that I had some other money stashed away somewhere. I told them that was all I had, but this wasn't good enough. One of them said, "Let's take him up to the roof and throw him off."

Now I'm thinking fast. Here there were about five or six cats who were forcing me up the stairs in this building and all they had, or at least I think all they had, was knives. Should I fight them off and risk getting cut, or maybe they'll change their minds? I decided to not risk it, but I was also certain that no one was going to throw me off a roof without a good fight.

When we got to the roof which was some six or seven flights up, they told me to take off every piece of my clothes. While I was doing this they ripped through each piece looking for some extra cash. I told them I didn't have a money belt or anything like that, but man, these cats were so hungry for money that they kept tearing everything apart. So here I am naked except for my coat, which they let me put over my shoulders, these cats getting mad because they couldn't find any more money and trying to decide if they should throw me off, kill me and leave me up there, or just run off. One guy says: "Let him go. We know who he is. If the police ever start to look for us, we'll come back and kill him." Hearing this I started to put on my clothes. The same guy then tells me, "Look, we're going downstairs, you stay up here for five minutes. If we see you leave the building before then, we'll get you. When you leave, turn right, and go out of the block that way, you understand?" I told him yes. I waited a good ten minutes before slowly leaving the building.

When I got downstairs, instead of turning right, I turned left towards Seventh Avenue and went up to 125th Street. You have to understand that by now I'm a bit nervous, wondering if these guys were watching me because I disobeyed their orders and left the block another way. I told myself they probably thought I was scared shitless, and I was, but then maybe they didn't know how scared I really was. This is really interesting because when I think about that incident, I realize that these cats were uptight and probably new at this. For them to go through all this bother to follow me from a bar, knock me down, take me up to a roof, and then discuss whether they're going to kill me or not is not what you'd expect from someone who makes their living on the street. I think these guys were into drugs, specifically heroin. What they needed was some quick cash. Their little crap game at the bar didn't bring enough in, so I was a target. The more I think about it, during these days, that's all people were talking about, "those damn junkies." Robbing people in their hallways, coming in through the windows when you out working or something, sticking you up in elevators. But then, this was 1948, and Harlem just as other parts of the city were just experiencing the beginning phase of a drug epidemic which today is still very much out of control.

I remember a friend of mind telling me that a few years ago he was in a drugstore on Lenox Avenue and 145th Street buying toothpaste and other toiletries. He noticed this guy standing there next to him who was kind of like looking things over, you know, trying to decide what to purchase. But my friend said he felt something strange about this guy but simply dismissed it. He purchased his items and decided to walk home, some seven long blocks away on Convent Avenue, rather than take a bus.

When he arrived at his apartment building, he unlocked the downstairs entrance door and realized that someone had just come out of the elevator. As he ran to catch the elevator before it went back upstairs, he noticed that someone was behind him, so being nice, he held the elevator door for them without really looking to see who it was. When he got into the elevator he recognized this individual as the same person who was in the drugstore some seven blocks away. This cat takes out a pistol, puts it to my friend's head, and says: "If you want to die, just yell. I want you to live so quietly hand me your wallet, and all your money." He does this.

When the elevator arrives at his floor, the robber pushes the button for the top floor and tells my friend: "When we get off, walk to the staircase which goes to the roof. If you try anything I'll kill you right here." It turns out that the roof door is locked. This probably saved his life, because a gunshot on a roof is not going to cause any concern, whereas a shot on the top floor is going to make a lot of noise and then you have to get all the ways downstairs to escape. In any case, he tells my friend: "If you don't want to get hurt, stay here. Don't leave this building for ten minutes. If you leave before, I'll get you." This mugger then gets back in the elevator and takes it downstairs.

Now the similarities in these robberies are obvious, and they happened in the same time period. I'll bet you, however, these same robberies carried out today would have ended up with someone being killed. No doubt about it. You see, back then people were driven to rob for a lot of reasons, but even in the early stages of the heroin epidemic after the World War Two, people weren't killing neighborhood folk for drug money. They'd knock you over the head, yes, but not kill you with the ruthlessness that you see today for drug money. The fact of the matter is that we were extremely fortunate to have been robbed then and not today.

In any case, when I got to 125th Street, I saw these cops standing there. I told them I was just robbed. When they saw the blood coming down the side of my face, they said: "Look fellow, you better get something done for yourself and go on up to the hospital. There is nothing we could do for you at this moment. Now I knew they were right, because I was bleeding pretty bad at this point, but Harlem Hospital's emergency ward was not where I wanted to be. I've heard all kinds of horror stories about the emergency ward and I didn't want to become part of that scene. When I finally did get up to Harlem Hospital, I laid up there all night long, right up until the morning, when I was carried up to the X-ray room to see if anything was fractured. Nothing was, so they gave me a few stitches and sent me on my way.

Now I don't want to sound like I'm always complaining, but if my injuries would have been more critical, I might have been in serious trouble in that emergency ward. When it comes to us black folk, these hospital emergency wards seem to have a negative attitude about how important our injuries are. For example, years ago I had a badly sprained ankle which I wanted a doctor to look at. So one evening around seven or eight I went to this same hospital's emergency ward. When I arrived there were only four people ahead of me. The group of us sat there for hour after hour after hour waiting for some treatment. So here I am, laying up there with a busted ankle, no medical attention, and a bunch of doctors and nurses walking around feeling each other's buttocks, acting like they're getting ready to make love in the next second!

As the hours passed by I sat there and watched them roll in ten or twelve patients on gurneys, one right behind the other, and no one seemingly giving a good goddamn about these people. The hallways outside the emergency room was lined up with people needing medical help but everything seemed to be moving in slow motion. It was as if us being sick was not really that important, you know, nothing to get excited about. This was the general attitude these white folks and even some of my own people had towards poor black folks right there smack in the middle of Harlem. They didn't seem to really give a damn back then, some forty years ago. You see, the truth of the matter is that they didn't give a damn what happened to you years ago when you was a slave, and they don't really give a damn about you today. We really shouldn't be surprised by this.

Look, the problems we have today in New York and all other urban centers of this country ain't nothing but a situation which we as blacks had very little to do in creating. What we call a problem is really a situation, a political situation which we haven't any control of. All this posturing about getting drugs out of the community sounds good, but it ain't going to do no good until we get enough power to change the situation. Once we do that, those crooks who control our communities will find some other place to do their business.

I'll tell you why I say this. First of all, some things haven't really changed in years. The names have changed, but the situation is still the same. Folks such as the police, who are supposed to give a damn about the city, are in on the take. They get their share in these so-called illegal numbers and gambling joints, and they get their share from these cats who are stealing and peddling dope. They did it when I was in the street in the forties and fifties and they do it now, today. This is why drugs and killing is escalating in our communities. We don't control the situation. We think we do, but shooting and killing your own people shows that you don't control anything. We read it every day in the newspapers: police making hauls of dope for others who control the situation. These police don't turn it all in, but they do turn enough in for you to go to jail. They sell it to us for those who really control the situation, and then get their cut. But it is you and I who eventually end up in jail, strungout, dead, or worse still, going to kill someone over this nonsense. Man, that's a shame.

I know this, because I've seen how this thing works from firsthand experience. It ain't changed. I know times you couldn't even run a card game around here, in Harlem, without paying off the police. I know this for a fact because at one time I was one of the biggest gamblers in Harlem and I had to pay them off. I was running games right here on 123rd Street. And why? Well, If you didn't do that you didn't eat. You know, we hear a lot of talk about how better things got for black people right after World War Two as a result of more jobs and everything. Well, that might have been true for some, but I know a lot of folks, such as myself, who didn't have it that good. The jobs we got were jobs whites considered to be beneath them. The good jobs, even right out here on 125th Street, we had to fight for. That's right. Your best bet was to try and get a government job in the post office or something like that because all these white folks wanted you to do was to clean this or shine that. In fact, part of my hustle from about 1947 on was using my brother's name and personal identification to get me a better-paying job. From then on people referred to me as Willie Norris. But then I never did have too much trouble getting some kind of job.

2

If you recall, back in 1946 I left Alabama in a hurry. My first stop was in Ohio, where I got a job working for a construction company. We were putting down sewer and water lines all over the state. This was a decent job until the winter arrived and the temperature began dropping to zero degrees and then below. In fact, I can recall when on a particular occasion, it went down to five degrees below zero. I didn't realize that Ohio could be that cold. You'd be standing out there in the morning around five o'clock, freezing half to death, just waiting for a pickup truck to get you to work, and then nearly die from frostbite during the day! The only thing that really saved you from freezing to death in the middle of an Ohio cold spell was that when you're working in a tunnel underground, it's actually warmer than above ground. But you know, I couldn't continue working like that, no way. It was just too damn cold.

I eventually got a job working for Apex Aluminum Company, right out there on Grand Avenue in Cleveland. This job wasn't too bad. The pay was decent and I got a chance to work in a factory where aluminum was being used to make all sort of things. This was the very first time I got to see aluminum when it was like water. I mean, hot aluminum pours just like hot steel, but it's not as heavy. In any case, I stayed with this company for about five years. I had never worked for any company this long, and while the money was good, I needed something more. Just working and getting by is satisfying for some people, but I needed to have more control over my life. There was only so much I could do with the money which comes from a nine-to-five job. So I decided to move on.

As you can see, for me, getting a job, some work, was no big deal. The problem was getting enough money to live not just day to day, but comfortably. Everybody wants to do that. So when I finally got to New York City in 1953 with my new identification, I simply knocked around in several kinds of jobs and then eventually got me one of them state jobs, you know, buffing floors and doing general cleaning work.

Now you know, people are something. They always trying to tell you something about how to live your own life. Here I am, no education to talk about, damn near unable to write my own name, trying to make as little waves as possible. Could hardy read a lick, and folks would come up to me and say, "Why you doing that kind of work?" or "Why don't you get a better job?" and all that stupid shit. I wouldn't tell them, I got the job in the first place because I knew the right people to talk to about getting this job in the first place. When you're hustling the way I was, you come in contact with a lot of people doing a whole lot of things. You make these contacts work for yourself. Everybody should know this. Am I right or wrong? I, however, had the sense to know I couldn't tell any of these folks about the details of how I got my state job, because they would simply run their mouths and cause nothing but confusion.

My thing was so together that I was even fingerprinted, photographed, the whole works, and was never "dug" as an escaped parolee from the Scottsboro Case. People working with me every day simply knew me as Willie Norris. I ran my outside hustle as best I could and did my regular nine-to-five as best I could. No hassle, everything smooth.

Out of all of this, I've come to learn one essential thing about life: if you live long enough, you begin to learn about what's going on in the world, and how it operates. That's called experience. If things don't happen to you, you can't learn. It's as simple as that. Yeah.

So once I got established in New York, my thing was to learn how to develop what we called a "second front." A second front was basically a job outside your regular nine-to-five. It helped to take off the strain of trying to make it on one salary. I realized that when people got laid off from work, with nothing to do, they had to have some kind of income or at least chance of an income. I sure did. So me and a lady friend of mine started this gambling house. We'd have a poker game going on, a crap game, selling whiskey, everything. Whiskey was bought by the gallons right from the liquor store, but we would sell it in shot glasses to maximize our profit. I used to have games running from Friday night, all day Saturday, Saturday night, and all day Sunday up until midnight. Sometimes if there was a demand we would extend it until Monday.

Now there was some money to be made, no question about that. Every game that was played, the house would of course get a cut. Since poker and blackjack were very popular games, the house, that's me and my woman, would get 10 percent of every dollar if it was a poker game. You take a poker game that runs all night long, if it's any good, from every pot you're going to get $1, $2, or $3 out of it. Whatever is in that pot on any hand being played, you get 10 percent. Now man, that was some money.

You see, I knew this "second front" was going to work because there were times before I got my state job when I'd be laid off work and have nothing to do. I knew how it felt to have this feeling of being frustrated bottled up inside of you, wanting to explode but somehow you can't. And I'd see other people walking around with this same feeling. I had rent to pay and kids to feed, so we decided to run a gambling game, sell some whiskey, and maybe even have a little food. That's still going on today. For some people, that's all they know how to do. They don't never work anywhere, all they do is run crap games and card games, and do very well by it. And this was money you didn't have to pay no income tax on. But of course, we had to pay the police off, regularly, otherwise they would close you down. Once they were paid, they would in fact watch your back. It made sense because they had to eat, feed their families, and this extra money was something they weren't going to let anybody jeopardize.

3

Life is often strange, unpredictable, sometimes just plain bizarre. When I think about how I left Alabama in 1946 and arrived in Ohio to find a better life for myself as a so-called fugitive from the law, in reality I was simply doing what black folks have been doing for the last two hundred years or more.

Keep this in mind, I escaped from parole in 1944, but after listening to some Negroes, returned to Alabama, was locked up, and had to jump parole again in 1946 to be free! Now if that ain't a lesson about my people's situation

I don't know what is. Slavery, they say, was over in 1865, and while that was a little more than one hundred years ago, back then we was doing the same thing, you know, jumping some jive-ass parole trying to be free. Now I'm not saying everybody has the same values and desires when they get locked up, but I was innocent. All nine of us were innocent. It was my duty to myself to jump parole. How is someone going to give me something which I already have?

After I was in Ohio for some seven years and then came to New York, got married, raised a family right here in this same apartment where I am sitting right now, I still had to be careful. In fact, before Governor George Wallace pardoned me in 1976 for jumping parole, I had actually thought about appealing to those southern crackers about giving me my freedom. I even went back to those same folks who got me to return the first time, the NAACP, and talked to them about returning to see what could be done. They supposedly sent a lawyer down there, but he came back saying that I had to first go back behind the wall and then the Alabama parole would consider my claim! Now have you ever heard such foolishness? I thought about this method because I got to a point where I just wasn't going to run anymore. Psychologically I knew I couldn't and wasn't going to live my life constantly looking over my shoulder. For me it had come down to a kill-or-be-killed situation, if necessary. I wasn't going to run anymore. I was going to have to do just what [Haywood] Patterson did. Now, I don't like to talk about it, but that's the way it was.

I wanted my total freedom so bad that if someone who had known me for many years would have walked up to me and said, "Hi, Clarence, your name is Clarence Norris, isn't it?" they would have been a dead sucker. You see, I lived on an emotional edge out there in the streets for a long time — always looking over my shoulder, not really trusting anyone, never forgetting the years those people in Alabama took away from me or the fact that they was still looking to take some more from me.

I remember one day, when I jumped bail and was staying at my mother's house in Ohio, some folks saying they was the FBI came looking for me. By that time I had my brother's identification, so when they asked me who I was, I lied and told them I was Willie Norris. And every time I got arrested after this incident, sometimes for serious stuff, fingerprinted, and ran through a lineup, as strange as it seems, they never made the connection between me and my brother. Years later I was even arrested for selling liquor without a license in a nightclub, right here in New York City. They sent me to the "tombs," as they called the city jail in downtown Manhattan near Chinatown, but nothing ever happened. I did a couple of weeks and that was that.

In another incident, this guy I knew who was always harassing me about some money he lost in a gambling game decided to take things into his own hands. One evening when I was coming home, right inside this apartment's hallway, he jumps me. I warned him to keep away from me and back off. He didn't. As were arguing, I'm backing up and eventually end up right inside the gate area to my apartment. By now, he's really feeling that this is his chance to kick my ass or something. Well, when he tries to hit me, I just backed up, and shot him. Now you know, I don't let nobody take over where I live at. If I can't protect that, then I just might as well step off and be on my way. The truth is, if I'm not going to let anybody take over me in the streets, how then am I going to let this punk push me right inside my home? He had to be crazy. Now that's the kind of man I am. I ain't going to bother anyone and I don't want anybody bothering me, not after all I went through. I don't interfere in your business, you don't in mine, and I don't care what you're into.

Once in court, I explained to the judge that this guy was a complete stranger to me, and it appeared he was trying to mug me, so I defended myself. In any case, the judge turned me loose because I was in my own apartment and it was self-defense.

After situations like this, I've come to understand that regardless of what the law tells you, if you start knowing, seeing, and telling everything you're into, you ain't going to be around long. There are some things you must keep to yourself rather than trying to impress everyone with your knowledge. Only a fool would give away the only thing he might have to bargain with when things get real tight. Yet many folks do run their mouths and live to regret it. It's all about seeing and not seeing, hearing and not hearing. That's the only way to live and survive in this world.

4

So back there in 1970 when I began thinking about the possibilities of getting my freedom or pardon from them crackers in Alabama I began to consider the ideas these folks in the NAACP suggested. Now, I knew that I would never voluntarily return to Alabama unless it was under conditions guaranteeing my protection. You see, I had actually called down there earlier before contacting the NAACP to see what those folks on the parole board would say if I told them I was tired of running and hiding. Man, what they told me was very plain. This woman told me over the phone, "If we can catch you, you'll be behind those walls again!" Obviously for them, it was as simple as that. This response made me think about contacting the NAACP and see if anything else could be done.

Can you imagine what would have happened if I would have simply gone back to Alabama and asked the parole board in person to reconsider my case? Man, they would still be laughing today.

Sometime back there in 1976, the *New York Times* began publishing articles about my case. I thought this was a good idea because it got everybody used to the idea that I was innocent and if anybody was guilty, it was the state of Alabama.

> *New York Times* (October 19): The National Association for the Advancement of Colored People has begun a drive in Alabama to get the last known surviving "Scottsboro boy" pardoned from a 1946 parole violation.
>
> The effort has included an appeal to Gov. George C. Wallace by Roy Wilkens, the NAACP's executive director. The association's 92 chapters and 14,000 members in Alabama have been mobilized to work for a pardon for 64-year-old Clarence (Willie) Norris, who now lives in Brooklyn....
>
> ... Mr. Norris's supporters, including Alabama's Attorney General, say he should be pardoned immediately. But the chairman of the state's Parole Board insists that he must first surrender to the board and face arrest so the parole violation can be settled before the full pardon can be considered.
>
> Mr. Wilkins has sent a telegram to Governor Wallace saying that "charity, justice and mercy—even though delayed—would be served" by the pardon.
>
> A spokesman for the Governor said Mr. Wallace had no control over the Parole Board. But several people familiar with the case, both black and white, in Montgomery disagreed. They said the Governor's informal influence could be brought to bear on the Parole Board.
>
> The appeal to Governor Wallace was only a part of the NAACP's effort on behalf of Mr. Norris.
>
> Members of the association were asked to work with the Black Political Caucus of Alabama, an organization of more than 100 black elected officials in the state, which is also seeking a pardon for Mr. Norris.
>
> Alvin A. Holmes, the director of the caucus and a State Representative, said he was preparing legislation for the special session of the Alabama legislation in November to pardon "all surviving members" of the Scottsboro group.[1]

The position of Norman F. Ussery, chairman of Alabama's Board of Pardons and Paroles, was of course based on the strictest interpretation of the law. He specifically argued that Norris' legal situation was "just not that simple" but that Norris must first "comply with the law." He added, "As long as he's a fugitive from justice, I'm not going to go into the pardon question." Norris was "a man on the run."[2] None of this made any sense to Norris' attorney or, more important, to the attorney general, who argued that in this particular instance, "no crime was committed in this case ... and that Clarence Norris was an innocent man."[3]

Clarence Norris: Once Wallace was contacted and had enough time to study my case and understand what his political options were, it didn't take him but so long to realize that he could probably make some political points with Alabamian blacks if he would announce that I was pardoned.

There was one telegram which was sent from Roy Wilkins to Wallace which went right on pushing this process along.

> In the name of justice we urge you to use the influence of your high office to spare Clarence Norris the additional humiliation of returning to your jurisdiction before he is granted a pardon.
>
> We ask you to do all you can to convince the Board of Pardons and Paroles to free this man without further delay.
>
> We respectfully state that we do not see how the public interest could be

> served by the Board's insisting upon compliance with the technicality of return. To the contrary, charity, mercy and justice even though delayed would be served by immediately lifting from Clarence Norris and from Alabama's judicial system the burden of making new and unnecessary assessments. My General Counsel, staff and I stand ready to confer with you or any persons you designate.[4]

CLARENCE NORRIS: The attorney general then sent a letter on my behalf in which he chronicled the lengthy and controversial trial and asked that "Norris be pardoned."

> In my opinion, after a thorough review of all aspects of the case of Clarence Norris, ... this individual never should have been charged with any offense against Ruby Bates or Victoria Price, and ... his repeated sentences of death and his 15 years spent incarcerated in Alabama prisons can only be termed tragic.
>
> ... It was indicative of a time in our history when justice in our courts was not equally and impartially meted out. It was a time when men were judged by the color of their skin and not the content of their character.[5]

CLARENCE NORRIS: However, what I wanted to hear was George Wallace saying "Clarence Norris is innocent and I will not make a damn move to try and expedite him back to Alabama." Only with that kind of assurance would I consider returning to Alabama for some kind of official ceremony. I tried to explain to my attorney, Jimmy Myerson of the NAACP, that if I go down there to Alabama without Wallace's guarantee that no harm will come to me, those cats down there might do anything. I figured that essentially nothing had really changed over the years and that I'd be talking or walking on the streets one day, somebody would pass by you, and then, boom-boom, you're dead! I was afraid that those crazy folks down there just might shoot me as I was getting off the plane in Alabama or in the capital while I was talking to the governor. You see, when you've traveled the road I've been on, you think seriously about these things.

Now in reality, Wallace didn't give two shits about me, but politically he had no choice. You see, the attorney general of Alabama had already decided that he was no longer going to continue looking for me with the hope of extradition back to Alabama. He realized that, if I'm going to be out there somewheres, why not undercut Wallace's racist political platform by appealing to injustices done to me over the years and thereby enhance his own political credibility among African Americans by appearing to be someone seeking justice for Clarence Norris! This made sense when you realize that this same attorney general, William J. Baxley, ran against Wallace for governor in the last elections and lost. So with an eye on the next election, he figured a few points could be gained with blacks by letting it be known that it was he who caused Wallace to "see the light." It was like putting political hay in the barn for future use. This was something even racist George Wallace could understand because he too was also forever trying to convince Alabamian blacks that he was really a nice guy.

So with an eye on future elections, it basically came down to the question of how white Alabama politicians could benefit from this situation by using the Scottsboro Case for their own benefit. Man, this had nothing to do with liking anybody, or feeling that we "boys" were taken advantage of years ago. When you get right down to it, it was all about people getting out of a tight spot. For them, it was how to politically survive — for me, how to physically survive.

In any case, a deal was made, Governor Wallace agreed to grant me a pardon, and before I know it, I'm on this plane headed towards Montgomery, Alabama, with Roy Wilkins, of the NAACP, attorneys James Myerson and Nathaniel Jones, and a newspaper reporter, Thomas Johnson of the *New York Times*.

5

When I arrived in Birmingham, Alabama, and saw all of those black reporters, I knew immediately that some things had changed. During the thirties there were no black reporters in Alabama. And if there were, they sure didn't make themselves known to us when we were in the thick of it. I do remember seeing one reporter during the early trials, but he wasn't allowed to sit with the others and he was the only one, and for only one trial. But now, seeing all these black folk, well, I just couldn't get over it. Yes, I was still scared, because life had taught me that people don't change that quickly, especially whites in Alabama. Remembering what Martin Luther King, Jr., had gone through in the sixties indicated to me that many of them were still very much the cracker.

These reporters began asking me all kinds of questions about what I was going to do once my pardon was official. Was I going to sue the state of Alabama? Was I still mad about the false charges of rape? Was I still mad at white people? You name it, they asked it. I told them I didn't know, I had no plans, and I wasn't mad at all white people, etc.

We drove directly to the capital. Once we arrived at the governor's mansion, a very large building sitting up on a little hill, we sat, waiting for Wallace to receive us. Now I didn't know too much about Wallace, except that he was trying to run for the presidency of the United States. However I do remember that when he was in New York City campaigning for the presidency, his entourage had to pass through some black folk who were picketing city hall and construction sites nearby for more jobs. These demonstrations by African-American and Latino construction workers became increasingly hostile as many white construction workers, who were portrayed as being very pro-American and politically conservative in the press, waved American flags and shouted insulting remarks and in some cases threw items at these demonstrators, who they thought were trying to take their jobs by charging discrimination in union

Clarence Norris in 1971 (UPI/Corbis-Bettmann).

hiring policies. It became so disorderly and confusing at these work sites that black and Latino construction workers were often considered to be somehow tainted with radicalism, possibly communism or at least not really patriotic Americans!

So anyway, a reporter asked Wallace what he would do if these picketers tried to block traffic by laying down in front of his motorcade as it passed by city hall. He said, "I wish one of them would be laying in front of my car, he wouldn't be laying long." This is the same man who was running for the presidency, and the same individual who was going to give me my pardon!

In any case, we were finally called into his office and there he was, sitting in his chair. He looked up at me and said, "Clarence Norris, how come black people look so young when they get old?" I didn't say anything. I just looked at him. The silence was probably an embarrassment for some, maybe for Wallace, I don't know, but in any case, one of the fellows who works there in the capital building said, "Well, Governor, we eat collard greens and chicken, and you eat steak." Wallace responded, "I differ with you there: I eat raccoon and cornbread for breakfast!"

Once the ceremony was over, Governor Wallace remarked, "Norris, any time you come back to Alabama, make sure you come up to see me before you go back." I know he probably meant that, but I wasn't going back down there to see nobody. In fact I really wanted to get the hell out of Alabama as quickly as possible. However, one of my attorneys, Nick Jones, and a guy who had some kind of office there in Alabama invited us to go down to Tuskegee, Alabama. I said okay, but man, I was scared because I knew them "dye in the wool" crackers would take a shot at you if given the opportunity. But much to my surprise, once we got there, I saw whites and blacks sitting everywhere together, talking with each other. I mean, I was totally surprised by this. Even after I gave my first speech down there, some of them came up to shake my hand and kiss me on my cheek. All I could say about this was that while the world had certainly changed somewhat in forty years, I still wouldn't want to live down there. I can't forget that people were killed right down there in Montgomery, Alabama, during the civil rights marching and boycotting days. I know what it means to be around these folks when they was down on us, it was pure hell.

When I left Alabama back there in 1976, I knew I would never return. No love lost, no sadness, just memories. At that point in my life all I wanted to do was to return to New York and continue working until I retire. And now that I've retired, you couldn't give me a job, not even in a pie factory where I could sit and eat pies! I just live, stay quiet, and enjoy myself, that's all. In fact, even in this building I seldom see other folks enough to say we're close friends. I mind my business and they mind theirs. That's something I learned years ago about life. When you start being buddy-buddy and friend-friend, you're finished. You're either going to kill or be killed over some nonsense. The one or two friends I do have live over on the other side of the city. We sit down and have a few drinks, sometimes take a ride to a few places, but that's it. I just don't go around making new friends, that's not my style.

Now, I'll make an exception if I'm invited to make a speech or something on that order about my experiences, like when I gave a speech up there in

Boston. Man, them chicks, white and black, were all over me. But you know, I didn't pay too much attention to them. After all, I've been married three times. Some men can't deal with a lot of attention, to say nothing about being surrounded by women wanting your autograph, phone number, and all that.

For example, I often think about Roy Wright and the situation he got himself into after he was released. He was one of the first of us to be freed, and as soon as he got a chance he married and then joined the navy. You would think that his life would now begin to make a turn for the better. But due to his inability to realize that because you marry a woman, you don't own her, he eventually kills her over some other guy she's hanging with when he was away on a cruise. Now from my perspective, when you get weak over a woman with all of these other women out here, and then want to kill somebody over this love, man that's crazy! Let her go. You can always find someone else. But you see, some people are weak. Any woman I ever had was free to go when they were ready and free to come back when they were ready, you know what I mean? If she's running around too much, tell her so. If not, leave her. But Roy took all of this to the extreme, and committed suicide.

My philosophy about these sorts of relationships was quite different than Roy's. I married a girl in Alabama years ago who wasn't my first love, but she was my wife for a time. My first wife and I tried to make it but our differences were such that we just couldn't get along. So when I left Alabama and went to Cleveland, Ohio, I married this chick who had her own home, etc. After a while it got so tight that soon we couldn't get along, so I left her. She begged me to come back but I wanted to make my own money, that's how I am. Though she had some business interest and a couple of houses, I just couldn't be bought off that way. Now you have to understand, though the woman was good to me, she was also very jealous. If I stayed out late, she'd complain about this. If I dropped a piece of clothing on the floor she'd complain about that. In fact, it seemed she was forever complaining about every little thing imaginable. In any case, I should have known this wasn't going to work because she was much older than me and I really didn't love her.

It took me many years to learn that there are some women who can be very independent, and others who want you to do everything for them. You have to know the difference because while you may feel that the relationship is just about money, for her it may really be about love. In any case I've always been careful about these sort of things because some people will just use you for money or fame. You can't keep me like that because I've always been able to just move on, make my own money, and find me another good woman.

But I tell you something that's always on my mind. I got two grown daughters, but my daddy raised nine of us. None of us went to college, but one of my daughters entered into college and was just about to finish but didn't. I hope one day she does finish, because this is something she has to do for her own sense of self-esteem. I often think that if I would have had that opportunity I would have done it, but I didn't. You will never know how I felt being behind those walls in Alabama year after year, wanting to be able to read, write my own letters to my mother and supporters around the world. When you can't read or write, you're trapped and dependent on others telling you about a world you can see and feel but can't explore directly with your own thoughts. My education instead came from behind those walls of the penitentiary. My math classes were learning how to play poker, blackjack, and bid-whist. Hustling inside and outside prison taught me the basics of economics and politics, and I was good at it.

And in the street, I learned early on that you can learn to make a dollar or more simply by using your brain, and I didn't work for it nor did I steal it. I did it by playing cards, gambling, shooting dice, and playing numbers. Hell, not having any schooling, what was I to do? When the time came that I had two little kids and our little bit of money from working a regular job was taking care of the necessities, man, I did what any man would do, I took care of my own. And yes it's true, playing cards and gambling can be dangerous and sometimes you have to take risks and cheat to win, but that's the way it goes.

The important thing here is that I didn't beat anyone over the head for their money, but I did use my mind to win at hustling. Similarly a man with book knowledge, paper, and a pencil can screw you out of your money while you're standing there watching him! He can do this simply because you don't have his knowledge about the process. It's life.

However today it's different. Whereas I could hustle up hundreds of dollars within an hour or two without hurting anyone, kids today want to show they are powerful by hurting someone in the process of making thousands of dollars in an hour or two. Today's youth are basically trying to find themselves off the backs of other peoples. It's no longer simply a question of survival; for them, self-esteem, power, and respect is how many things one can accumulate. That's the main problem, because in a sense they have become dependent on others like crabs in a barrel.

The things we do to each other is really sad but then there are beautiful things about my life which I cannot deny. I'm free. I do what I want to do, go when I get ready, and when I look back I can truthfully say that I've lived pretty good when you consider my entire life. I don't crave a whole lot for things which other people have. I don't crave for a beautiful Cadillac or Lancer, but of course I'd like to have one if I ever get rich enough, ain't nothing wrong with that, but that's not a goal in my life like it is with many other folks.

You see, I've made peace with many aspects of my life. But most important I know that what we Scottsboro boys went through will always be remembered, studied, talked and argued about. I'll never be forgotten, and for that I'm grateful. How many people can say that? And all this happened because we were black kids. Just think, if it had been nine white boys accused of raping two black girls they never would have went to the jailhouse. They never would have went into a courthouse. That's something to think about. Even if those white boys were guilty of raping two black girls, they wouldn't have been arrested, nor would they have seen the inside of a jail or courthouse, no way.

Of course, today it's different. They can't lynch you the same way as in the past without some of them getting sued, hurt, or even killed in the process. Yeah, today they try to be a little sophisticated about it. There are some places right here in New York where you can tell they don't want you in there by the way they serve you. You could be looking like a prince, it don't matter, they will take their own damn time serving you, just like in prison, you know, that sneaky shit.

If I went into a restaurant right now and didn't get served, I'd get up and walk the hell out. The hell with them. You see, in a certain way, it wouldn't bother me. I'm helping you out by patronizing your store, you're not helping me out. But you know, if I had a store and a white man came in, I would serve him like he was one of my own people, because I'm a person that understands what freedom is all about. In fact, I would want people to remember me as a person who spent many years in prison and in the process learned to appreciate freedom and respect for all who respected me. However, this didn't come easily.

Think about it, there were nine of us in this case, and today, I'm the only one left. All the boys in the case with me are now dead, but I'm still living. Some of them didn't have the strength to stand the punishment like the others, but I did. Some didn't really believe that they would one day walk out from behind all that steel. I always believed I would. I now realize that to think the way I did really took nerve, courage, strength, and everything I could hustle up to get through those years. Maybe almighty God looked down upon me, I don't know, because at times I was really helpless. Whatever it was, my belief that I would survive Alabama's prison system helped me to break away from a sense of helplessness while incarcerated and even gave me strength when I eventually did get out.

The problem is that not everyone who spends time in prison can escape this feeling of being incarcerated once they get out. There's many a man who once paroled out of the penitentiary, found work on farms owned by these same old crackers. They again faced hard times from these folks by being kicked around, threatened, shot, and beaten just as they were in prison, and didn't have the sense to get away or to free themselves. And in a sick sense it's understandable. They couldn't, because their minds still belonged to the crackers. I've seen this time and time again.

For me it was different. Once I got from behind those bars in this big wide world where I could walk right on off and didn't need to take anymore of their punishment, I did. You don't have to let that kind of thing happen when you call yourself free and there are no shackles or chains on you. If you don't like what one of these suckers is doing to you, just go on about your business and the hell with everybody. You tell the law and everyone else, you want to be free. That's the way I've seen it, and that's the way I see it today.

Chapter 9

Postscript

On December 11, 1980, Clarence Norris appeared before a group of college students in a South Bronx neighborhood of New York City. Standing erect, dressed in his usual impeccable manner and carrying his ever-present cigar, Norris outlined the events that had made him a part of the infamous Scottsboro Case. He exuded a warmth that seemed always present when he was speaking to an audience in their late teens or early twenties. One can speculate that this might have been due to an identification with a time and period in his own life that was harshly curtailed by the exigencies of racism and economic depression. What was very obvious was that his ability to communicate to this type of audience was both exciting and informative.

In this presentation Norris described the distinctive social and political circumstances that had surrounded those of the southern American populace in the 1920s who were male, black, and the sons of poor Georgia sharecroppers. He made it very clear that if his life had taught him any particular lesson, it was that "a whole lot of us have to sacrifice our lives for freedom." He added: "Sure enough, freedom don't walk up to you like this, ... you got to do something for it. I suffered in jail, got beaten, called names, and then I learned in jail how to fight back, ... and I did fight back in jail."

At the end of his presentation, he agreed to answer a few frank questions about his recollections of imprisonment. In this session he displayed a wit and charm that clearly indicated that behind his rural Georgia personality was an extremely perceptive and intelligent man.

Q: Mr. Norris, how do you feel inside, being that you lived through something that while many of us may be somewhat familiar with having lived in the South, do not really understand, or not to the extent you do?

A: Well I'll tell you, frankly I wanted to kill, but I couldn't. I didn't have anything to kill with but my bare hands. Yes, ... many times. If at any time I could have taken somebody's life, so as to come out from behind those walls, away from those who had the hammer on me, I certainly would have loaded the hammer on them. But I didn't get that chance, that's why they put you behind them walls. You don't understand, some will kill to come out from behind them walls, yeah. And that goes for the black as well as the white prisoner.

But what makes it so bad is when you're in and you haven't done anything. I could see it if you have committed a crime, because then you know why you're being punished. But when they put a man behind a wall and abuse him and scorn him because somebody told a lie on him about some white woman, or some white man, well that's something else.

Q: What is your feeling about black men with white women?

A: Let me tell you something, the white man will try to use his women as a weapon when he gets mad with the black man. These things have happened right there in Alabama. For example, a black sharecropper working for a white farmer quit due to the bad deal he was getting. When he found another farmer who would give him a better deal, the first farmer got so mad that he had his little six-year-old daughter to meet this black man on a highway not too far from his house and then have her claim that he raped her. This black man was quickly sentenced to die and placed on death row. After reviewing the case, the governor commuted his sentence to life in prison and about a year later pardoned him. Now, you know this man was a family man about forty years old. No way was he involved in any so-called rape, but the first farmer was so mad at him for leaving that he set his own little girl on him, knowing full well that a charge of rape on a black man was equal to a death sentence. Even a doctor who testified in this case stated that this little girl was not touched by anyone.

Now the point is that this black man stayed on death row for two years before the governor commuted his sentence, made him a trustee, then gave him a complete pardon! All this simply because he was black. I believe his name was Adam Sanders.

Q: Did you keep in touch with other members of the Scottsboro case after you broke parole in 1944?

A: No, ... no. I didn't want to see anyone I might have known. I certainly didn't want to see anyone I served time with in prison. If I did, I might have been forced to get tough with them because they snitched on me. You see, seeking out individuals you were in the joint [prison] with while you are a parole violator is one of the worse things you could do. If any one of them snitched on you, how would you be able to tell which one said whatever at what time with whom?

Furthermore, If you would have seen and experienced what I saw [thirteen years of imprisonment] you wouldn't want to be reminded of it. However, with that said, I still ran into at least two individuals who were in prison with me when I was out in the street. One was a fellow named Eugene Foster. He had a forty-year sentence but somehow escaped from a highway prison road gang. I saw him at an after-hour spot. He looked at me, and I looked at him. I didn't say anything to him, and he didn't say anything to me. But he continued looking at me. I knew he wanted to say something, but I wouldn't say anything to him. Finally he came over and said, "You know man, you just might as well say something, because I know who you are." And I said, "Yeah, and I know who you are too!" Now, I saw him about twice since then, but recently he just seemed to disappear. But you know, I don't want to see him anyway.

Then there is another guy who lives right here in Harlem. He was wanted in Alabama and had a lifetime sentence over his head. One morning while working at the Federal Machine Company I was surprised to see him working in the same building. I decided to make sure we didn't run into each other since it appeared he was working on the third floor and I was generally on the thirtieth floor. The very next day while I was getting on the trolley I saw him sitting near the rear of the car. I sat in the front. However, I could tell by the way we were seated that he was looking at me, trying to figure some time out. Finally, he came up to me and said, "Man, I know who you is, and you know who I is, ain't no sense in kidding ourselves." I said, "Yeah, I saw you working at the company, but I didn't know you and still don't." He just had to laugh. But you see, if both of us are wanted by the law, why are you going to admit to something foolish.

Now, I'll tell you how things are. This same guy eventually had an accident on a construction company here in New York City. It seems he messed up his back something bad but got a whole lot of money out of it. He bought a brand-new car and started to drive back and forth down to Mississippi to see his mother. I told him, "Man, you keep on running on down there and they gonna' nab you one to these days." Sure enough, he was coming back through one of them southern states and was caught for speeding on the highway. They put him in jail, fingerprinted him, and then let him go. Well, when he returned to New York he just forgot about the whole incident. One night two black detectives came to his apartment, asked his wife if Willie Riggsly lived there. She said yes, and before you know it, he was under arrest and on his way back to those gray walls and steel cells in Alabama.

So you see, in Harlem at that time you would never know whom you might run into. It was very much a mecca for everybody. In fact when I first arrived I stayed at the YMCA on 135th Street. Nobody knew who I was except the manager. He knew because Roy Wilkins of the NAACP told him so. Wilkins also advised me that this would be the place to stay at until everything cooled down and I would not be bothered by anyone.

Q: Did you receive your pardon based upon your innocence or did they give it to you just to be done with the case?

A: You know one thing, you're right, they did just give it to me, but because I was innocent. The attorney general [William J. Baxley] told the world I was innocent. In fact, he said he wouldn't make one move to bring me back to Alabama.

Q: What I mean is that, did the court say that individuals perjured themselves against you?

A: Well, let me tell you something, there were a lot of blacks who wanted to see me free all over the world. But the man who really helped this process was the attorney general of Alabama. Now if he would have said "bring him back," then that would have changed the situation. You see, when I first made an attempt to get folks to work for my freedom [pardon], it was through the office of the NAACP. Wilkins introduced me to attorney James Meyerson, who was able to make contact with the Parole Board in Alabama. After a lot of discussions back and forth, even some suggestions that I be paroled to New York State, etc., it came down to the fact they, the Alabama Parole Board, wanted me first to return to Alabama, serve some time behind the walls, and they would then decide what kind of deal could be worked out! When the lawyers who went down to Alabama to check on this returned, I said, "They ain't talking nothing but junk."

Q: Mr. Norris, did you meet your wife here in New York?

A: Yes, she was born and raised here.

Q: Did you tell her right away that you were an escaped convict from Alabama?

A: No, … I didn't tell her right away.

Q: How did she accept it when you did tell her?
A: She *had* to accept it, because she sleeps in bed with me!

The self-assurance that one associates with the rebel is also indicative of an individual who has experienced a series of crises and has managed to survive when others have fallen. For them, life is a continuum of experiences and risks, which they accept as part of reality. In many such instances there is very little that is conspicuously appealing about this kind of person except what one discovers either from personal interaction or from what others attribute to the person, either correctly or not. In Norris' case, his appeal to those around him was often punctuated by an intuitiveness and level of realism that stripped away annoying pretenses of formality.

During the above college presentation, Norris suddenly grabbed his stomach as if he were in discomfort. Knowing that he was a diabetic, I feared that he was having an attack of sorts. I rushed up to him and with my back to the audience asked him what was wrong. He looked at me with a sort of incredulous smile and said, "My piece is falling." I said, "What, ... what do you mean, your piece?" Not wanting to believe what I heard, I said, "You're not packing, are you?" He said: "My Tre-eight [.38 cal. pistol] was falling. I thought I had it stuck in my waist, but it began to fall. I caught it just in time." He quickly adjusted his weapon in his waist holster, smiled at me, reached for his cigar, and before I could leave the stage was charming his audience with his marvelous rural Georgia personality.

The fact is that Norris lived his reality. He had few if any misconceptions about human nature in the world in which he lived and survived. To be sucker punched was not in his lexicon of experiences. To be elderly, vulnerable, and exposed to the vagaries of the world was antithetical to his philosophy of life. To see and not see, to hear and not hear, were often passwords for his own sense of personal security and survival, a survival premised not on an indifferent world but on a world inclusive of Malcolm Xs, Paul Robesons, James Baldwins, Langston Hughes, and Claude Mckays — a world that reflected a wellspring of African-American experiences, both feared and loved.

Clarence Norris' experiences in Alabama's prison system were largely contextualized by the southern American racial relationships of the 1920s, the 1930s depression era, and the hard-fought battles between the International Labor Defense and the National Association for the Advancement of Colored People. Notwithstanding this, more contemporary reports in American media suggest that Norris' five years on death row, his systematic brutal beatings by guards, and his chain-gang experiences were not simply unfortunate remnants of a past penal philosophy but were a precursor for a present-day penal system based on legalized institutional vengeance.

A contemporary article in the *Atlanta Journal — Atlanta Constitutional* entitled "Back to Hard Labor" reported, "Alabama's belief in punishment means a return to Chain Gangs breaking rocks." This announcement sent shock waves throughout sectors of the legal profession who have for years championed a more liberal approach to the question of prisoners' rights and rehabilitation.[1] Such a shift, many argue, is a harbinger of even more drastic correctional institutional policies in the near future.

For example, nine southern states have adopted harsher institutional policies towards prisoners—policies similar to Alabama's now infamous "electrified fences that deliver a deadly dosage of 5,000 volts to anyone who touches it," some 2,800 volts stronger than the electric chair! Rationals for such a fence, with its increased level of voltage, are indicative of a growing philosophy of punitive justice within American society in general.[2] However, a more compelling question would be, why are state authorities reluctant to support prisoner rehabilitation programs as opposed to punitive measures? Is it that humans have developed a higher toleration for electric voltages and a decreased desire for rehabilitation? Clearly many correctional authorities either do not accept or simply discount Norris' complaint that a major problem when incarcerated is one's powerlessness and the desire for violent retribution. This perception, Norris argued, grew into profound feelings of rage, which were either turned inward, resulting in a variety of self-destructive pathological acts, or were inflicted outward on other inmates. In this environment, institutional violence perpetrated by the guards or other inmates simply heighten the feeling of victimization rather than diminished it.

Marc Mauser, the Assistant Director of the Sentencing Project in Washington, D.C., has noted that research data suggest that the continuing demeaning and dehumanization of people does not work to make them into responsible individuals. "People may feel good in their gut, but when they wake up in the morning they aren't going to be any safer from crime. It's unfortunate that we are creating an illusion that we're doing something about crime."[3]

With disagreements so fundamentally diverse, one can only speculate how Clarence Norris, Haywood Patterson, or Ozie Powell would have faired under the contemporary Alabama prison authority who espoused: "Alabama should consider caning—repeatedly striking the bare buttocks until the skin splits—especially with juvenile offenders. I don't think it will work that well on the adult offender. It might work on these kids. It would be more applicable."[4] What we do know is that the Scottsboro youths would have responded that they were culpable only because their crime was to be black and poor; they were scapegoats for a failing economic and judicial system and, as such, were not supposed to assume or anticipate any rights of protection by the Constitution of the United States. For them, as in 1857, the *Dred Scott v. Sanford* decision was very much in force.

In a manner, Clarence Norris' life was a litmus test for what many human rights advocates assert is the sanctity of life, that is, the honor and spirit of humanity. There are few lasting values that we can place on the altar of human life other than the expectation to live a life without shame. Yet, in Norris' life, we see the weakness, fear, and utter emptiness of others who, with emblazoned emblems of rank, class, status, and race, exercise satanic gratification from the depths of an eternal abyss. Little do they weigh as they sink from sight, but sink they must if the human spirit of resistance is to be raised and honored.

On January 23, 1989, Clarence Norris, at the age of seventy-six, died in New York City. He was the last surviving member of the infamous Scottsboro Case. He carried the torch of freedom well.

Appendix A

Hoboes: Wandering in America, 1870–1940

By Richard Wormser (Walker and Company, 1994), pp. 107–114

You wonder why I'm a hobo and sleep in a ditch
Well, it's not because I'm lazy, I just don't want to be rich ...
Now I could be a banker if I wanted to be.
But the thought of an iron cage is too suggestive to me.
Now I could be a broker without the slightest excuse.
But look at 1929 and tell me what's the use?
—traditional hobo verse

In 1921, a hobo by the name of Bill Quirke applied for a job at a packinghouse in Yakima, Washington, a job he was confident of getting. He was told that while there were jobs, the foreman had been ordered not to hire "floaters"—hoboes. They had been replaced by "the home guard"—local people, many of whom could drive to and from work in their own cars.

The 1920s saw the rise of the "rubber tramp," the migrant worker who owned his own car. The Pacific Rural Press had commented as early as 1923: "The automobile has created a new class of fruit workers." Henry Ford had made automobiles cheap enough for most people to buy, and a man who could scrape up $50 or so and knew something about mechanics could get a used "tin Lizzie," as cars were called in those days. In it he could pack all his cooking and camping gear.

As the automobile replaced the railroad as the major means of transportation, machines replaced manual labor. By the 1920s, new equipment made it possible for employers to hire far fewer men than before. Three men with a machine could now do the work once done by fifteen. A hobo in Chicago in 1922, looking at the jobs offered by the "slave markets," wondered why there were so few jobs in many areas that traditionally needed workers. Hoboes who looked for jobs in lumber camps and wheat fields saw that they were far fewer than before World War I. Many began to take jobs they had once despised, like dishwashing or ditchdigging, because there was little else available. Other hoboes began to gravitate toward cities where, during the boom period of the 1920s, certain industries had a great need for labor.

There were other signs of the end of the hobo era as well. Prohibition had become the law of the land and the "Main Stem" of Chicago had changed dramatically. The saloons and the barrelhouse were gone. Speakeasies, where illegal liquor was served, didn't admit tramps and hoboes. The flophouses and the cheap restaurants, secondhand clothing stores, and missions survived, but everything else was changing. Many of the old-timers were aware that their way of life was over.

The final blow to the hobo world was the Great Depression. Until 1929, there were still some jobs for hoboes even though the number of men on the road seemed to be decreasing. When the depression struck, the jobs vanished, but suddenly millions of unemployed men and women took to the road. Businessmen and factory workers, lawyers and college students, farmers and teachers joined the ranks of the hobo world. By 1933, over 16 million men and women — almost a third of the labor force — were out of work. Just as in previous depressions, millions of men and a smaller number of women and teenagers took to the road in search of work....

[An] estimated 200,000 teenage hoboes wandered across America. They came together in boxcars or jails, mission houses or "jungles," and banded together for protection and friendship.

Like the hoboes of earlier generations, the road kids took to the trains. Thousands of them were killed or injured trying to do so. For one railroad alone, the Missouri Pacific, the overall statistics for death and injuries during the first four years of the Depression were grim: In 1929, 103 killed, 156 injured; in 1930, 114 killed, 221 injured; in 1931, 125 killed and 247 injured; in 1932, 91 killed and 214 injured. Overall, 433 people were killed and 838 injured.

The road kids of the 1930s had left nothing behind them and had little to look forward to. Their one concern was survival. They were poorly clothed and underfed; they lived by their wits. Most of their time was spent carrying the banner on the Main Stem for food, money, and alcohol. When they couldn't get anything, they stole — milk from doorsteps, groceries from vegetable trucks, purses from ladies, fruit from grocery stores. They admired big-time gangsters, but they themselves were, at best, petty thieves. They would walk as much as twenty miles in a day for food. Many turned to the mission houses, where they often had to sleep on the floor and eat peanut butter sandwiches, beef stew without the beef, and stale bread and doughnuts, washed down with dark water called coffee. Older men would grab food off young people's plates if they weren't careful, and many teenagers had to teach these men a lesson by beating them up or jabbing their wrist with a knife.

One major change that took place during the Great Depression was in the number of women on the road. Before 1929, there were very few women on the road. One study concluded that there was approximately one woman to every 200 hoboes and tramps before the Depression and one woman to twenty men after. Male hoboes generally did not think very highly of them. William Aspinwall, who spent most of his life wandering, recalled: "I have seen several women on the tramp but generally very low down creatures. The boys call them Bags, Old Bags." This was a limited view. There were women who lived genuine hobo existence and were considered "road sisters." Some were extremely resourceful and made excellent hoboes. They "decked" trains [riding on top of a car] and rode the blinds [space between the engine and the mail or baggage car], rods [space underneath the box car], or reefers [riding in refrigerated cars] like any other hobo. When they needed money, they put on their one good dress, went into town and got a job-as a typist, file clerk, or house cleaner. One woman worker was a nurse. It wasn't easy. Another woman who worked as a housekeeper found herself exploited, spending sixteen hours a day cooking, cleaning, sewing, washing, ironing, and taking care of ungrateful children. It was not surprising that many quit after they earned enough money to move on to the next location.

Many women on the road usually wore flannel shirts and coveralls to protect themselves from men. Sometimes, men's clothes served to disguise a woman as a young man. One woman dressed as a man worked her way across the Atlantic on a cattle ship. She smoked, drank, and chewed tobacco, and she cursed all the time. Only when she told her story to a newspaper after the voyage did the crew know that the young man was a woman.

However, many teenage girls had no skills other than domestic ones. They had left home for many of the same reasons as the boys: There were too many mouths to feed, bad relations with their parents, and the need to find work. Life in the road was more difficult for girls unless they had the protection of a boyfriend or a gang. Girls were under constant sexual pressure. Some exchanged sex with a brakeman for a ride on a train, or with a hobo for money or food. Another major problem was that the police and courts were much tougher on girls than on boys. A judge would tell a boy to get out of town, but put a girl in jail or send her to a reform school, usually charging her with being promiscuous. Sometimes a girl could persuade a policeman to let her go in exchange for sex.

Some road girls preferred to hitchhike rather than ride freights. They felt that men who owned cars were generally a better class of people than tramps that rode trains. It was fairly easy for a young girl to get a ride. It was also easier to control the situation. A man who had to keep his hands on the wheel of a car going forty miles an hour was far more manageable than a man or group of men sitting in a boxcar on a train and set on having sexual relations.

Appendix B

"Killing, Rioting, and Race War"

Published in the *Literary Digest*, August 1, 1931

These triplets of evil are the latest progeny of "the now notorious Scottsboro case."

A Negro is killed and five others are wounded. A sheriff and another white man also are shot. A Negro church is burned. Thirty-four Negroes are jailed as scores of others flee in terror.

All this happened at or near Camp Hill, Alabama, on July 17. But the outburst served to clamp world attention upon Scottsboro, another little Alabama town. For it was there that eight Negro boys, the oldest twenty, were sentenced to die in the electric chair for alleged assault upon two white girl "hoboes." With their case the violence at Camp Hill is said to have a direct link — news dispatches tell us that the trouble broke out when Communist agitators tried to organize a protest meeting in behalf of the eight youths.

Around the globe has gone the story of Scottsboro. And back to Alabama have come protest and denunciations.

For months the Communists have been making capital out of the case. Liberals here and in other countries are raising their voices against "a miscarriage of justice." In behalf of these obscure, nondescript youths, the great Albert Einstein, in Berlin, sends a protest to the President of the United States. So does Thomas Mann, German novelist and Nobel prize-winner, we are told by the *New York Evening Post.* Conspicuous among American liberals who have jumped in to the fight is Theodore Dreiser, novelist. He calls it "a national emergency in justice." Other protesters speak of "wholesale slaughter," "mass electrocution," "legal massacre," "legal lynching." To all these charges Alabama enters an emphatic denial.

But this world agitation over their fate seems to mean little, if anything, to the eight boys who face the electric chair. Dorothy Van Doren, writing in *The Nation*, gives us a glimpse of them in Kilby Prison, near Montgomery:

> No picture in recent annals of lawbreaking is more touching than that of these eight very black boys in the death cells in Alabama. They are kept two in a cell; they gratefully receive gifts of candy and cigarettes.
>
> With the irrepressible gaiety of their race, they can laugh and joke in the shadow of the electric chair. Yet they are in essence bewildered. "We don't know the rights of it all, Boss, or who ought to help us; we just want to get out of here." This is about all they can say, about as far as they can think.

Now a respite has been granted them, we read, an appeal to the Alabama Supreme Court automatically suspending the death sentences. The court will convene late this month, but the question of a new trial may not be decided before January. Also in doubt is the fate of a ninth Negro, a boy of fourteen, seized with the others, and for whom the prosecutor asked life imprisonment. In his case a mistrial was declared.

Readers can refresh their memory of the major developments in the Scottsboro case by this Association Press summary:

> Interracial tension, which flared up in a raid on a meeting of Negro radicals at Camp Hill, Alabama, and the arrest of thirty-four of them, has been smoldering in that State since March 24, when nine Negro hoboes from Tennessee and Georgia were taken off a freight-train at Stevenson and charged with attacks upon two white girls "bumming" their way after an unsuccessful hunt for work in Chattanooga.
>
> Eight of the Negroes are under sentence of death, imposed in the court-house at Scottsboro, while a crowd of local citizens and mountaineers surrounded the place and armed National Guardsmen set a watch about the prisoners.
>
> Radical groups in all parts of the United States and Russia have taken up the case, and the angry temper of whites and Negroes in Alabama several times has threatened an outbreak similar to that of July 17.
>
> According to the State's evidence at the trial of the nine Negro hoboes, the men boarded a freight-train in which the two white girls were riding with seven white youths.
>
> Two of the white boys were knocked unconscious, according to the testimony for the prosecution, and the others were thrown from the train. The Negroes held the girls, it was charged, until the freight-train reached Paint Rock, where railroad policemen came aboard and arrested them.
>
> Until the trial began, in April, the prisoners were kept in Gadsen, but their arrival in Scottsboro was the signal for the gathering of a mob which menaced the court-house and the jail during the trial and after the imposition of the death sentence.

Then began the agitation by Communists, the National Association for the Advancement of Colored People, and the liberals generally, to save the boys from execution.

Jumping ahead again, we come to James P. Russell's account of the Camp Hill outbreak, wired from Dadeville, Alabama, to the *Birmingham News*. The cause, he says, was a communist demonstration among the Negroes protesting the Scottsboro verdict. Sheriff Young was shot when he sought to disarm a Negro sentry guarding a meeting in a lonely cabin.

Return fire wounded the Negro, and he was killed later in an attack by officers upon a barricaded cabin. Reading on:

> During the night, the constant crackle of rifle and shotgun fire on the wooden slopes near Mary, Alabama, recalled nights in No Man's Land.
>
> Several thousand rounds of ammunition were fired by Negroes and officers seeking to break up the demonstration.
>
> The trouble began when two Negroes from another town came here and began a Communist meeting. It was ultimately forgotten until it was learned that the Negroes, estimated at 500 strong, had gathered in the woods and hills, and that the leaders were in conference in a lonely cabin, while armed Negroes patrolled all approaches.
>
> It was on a mission to break up this meeting that Sheriff Young and Deputy Thompson were wounded.
>
> Chief Deputy Wilson said he had learned that in the course of the meetings governor Miller had been threatened by the Communists.
>
> "Radical literature confiscated from the meeting," adds Mr. Russell in another dispatch, "urged the Negroes to demand social equality, and to take what they wanted if they didn't get it otherwise."

But that version is challenged immediately. Up goes a storm of protest. Adding to the confusion, however, the protesters seem to disagree among themselves. For instance, the *New York Herald Tribune* tells us that while the National Association for the Advancement of Colored People condemned Communists as having stirred up the outbreak, the International Labor Defense, a Communist organization conspicuous in the Scottsboro defense, denies any responsibility.

But there is agreement here, apparently, that the first aim of the Negro "share croppers," or tenant farmers, near Camp Hill was to form a union to better their condition, and only secondarily to protest the Scottsboro verdict.

Although denying that the International Labor Defense was organizing the share croppers, its secretary, J. Louis Engdahl, did say, according to *The Herald Tribune,* that "the poor tenant farmers were kept in a state of peonage through being held perpetually in debt to the planter, who advances them credit and supplies." Quoting Mr. Engdahl direct:

> On Wednesday night 150 Negro share croppers met to formulate their demands and protest the Scottsboro verdict. The police invaded the meeting and attacked the assembled croppers.
>
> Thursday night the share croppers called a meeting in a church, but 200 police and deputies dispersed the crowd, burning the church to the ground.

Bitter words bubble up in editorial comment upon the Scottsboro case and the Camp Hill outbreak. Harsh criticism is aimed at Alabama from many quarters. But the State not only has defenders outside its borders, but its own editors are striking back at critics. Typical of the criticism is the comment of the *New York World Telegram*:

> In the interest of calm justice there should be a new trial for these Negroes.
> It should be held in a new place, where local passions can not seethe around the court-house. Change the venue.
> Nowhere in the United States should any man's life, least of all a Negro's, have to depend upon a verdict reached within, or almost within, earshot of an angry mob that has already condemned him to death.

"Mr. Dreiser is right," declares the *Philadelphia Record*, "when he says the case constitutes a national emergency in justice. The fact that the boys are negroes is incidental. The country can't stand for eight boys all under age being sent to a mass electrocution because of an alleged frame-up."

But Alabama editors insist that the eight boys had a fair trial; they resent the agitation as an improper interference with the State's judicial procedure.

"The race trouble in Tallapoosa County," asserts the *Mobile Register*, "resulting in the killing of one person and the injury of others, is due immediately to outside meddling with the judicial machinery of this State." Then:

> Public officials of Alabama can not be expected to pay attention to noisy agitators, white or black, who threaten to assassinate the Governor unless they are permitted to impose their will upon the judiciary of this State.
> These preachers of violence are playing with fire when they come into Alabama, or any other Southern State, to stir up racial antagonisms and to precipitate clashes between the races....
> These worthless types [the condemned boys] as a result of stupid agitation have attracted national and international note, and finally have been the cause of a race conflict. They are not worth it, nor is there anything in the record of their trial and conviction to justify it.

"The Einsteins and the Manns," declares the *Montgomery Advertiser*, "were misled by liars"—

> Fortunately, the common sense of the masses of the American people does not seem to have forsaken them. They do not seem to be much imprest by the manufactured maledictions which are being hurled at Alabama by Communist scoundrels on the one hand and misguided humanitarians on the other.

And from the town where the trial was held comes the asseveration of the *Scottsboro Progressive Age*, in reply to our telegraphic inquiry for comment, that "no section ever suffered such unfair criticism as this county." And—

> Since the conviction of the eight Negroes and the pronouncement of the death penalty for one of the most atrocious and repulsive crimes ever committed since the Civil War, our section has been the subject of unjust criticism.
> We will welcome the most rigid investigation. We believe they will find that no man or set of men were ever given a fairer trial. Every safeguard our constitution gives to any defendant was given these Negroes.
> There was no room for doubt as to the guilt of the nine defendants. Had the defendants been white men, they would have received the death penalty. It was a crime too revolting to let [ ] with less than the death penalty, regardless of the section of the country.

Appendix C

"The Scottsboro Case"

Felix Frankfurter on the Supreme Court: Extra Judicial Essay on the Court and the Constitution (1932), ed. Philip B. Kurland (Cambridge, Mass.: Harvard University Press, 1970), pp. 280–285

The rags and tags of cases that excite public interest usually draw the headlines. But even the lay comment upon the *Scottsboro* decision was alive to a significance that went beyond a respite from death for seven illiterate Negro boys. In truth, the Supreme Court last Monday wrote a notable chapter in the history of liberty, emphasized perhaps in importance because it was conveyed through the sober language of a judicial opinion.[1]

The evolution of our constitutional law is the work of the initiate. But its ultimate sway depends upon its acceptance by the thought of the nation. The meaning of Supreme Court decisions ought not therefore to be shrouded in esoteric mystery. It ought to be possible to make clear to lay understanding the exact scope of constitutional doctrines that underlie decisions like the *Scottsboro* case.

The seven vagrant negro youths involved in the *Scottsboro* case were convicted of the crime most abhorrent of all others to the community in which they found themselves. The conviction was sustained by the Supreme court of Alabama, but over the vigorous dissent of the chief justice of the State. Thereafter leave was asked and granted for a review of the case by the Supreme court of the United States. There the denial by the Alabama courts of fundamental rights under the federal Constitution was urged.

Specifically, it was claimed that: "(1) they were not given a fair, impartial and deliberate trial; (2) they were denied the right of counsel, and the accustomed incidents of consultation and opportunity of preparation for trial; and (3) they were tried before juries from which qualified members of their own race were systematically excluded."[2] The court, through Mr. Justice Sutherland without considering the first and third claims, sustained the second, reversed the judgment of the Alabama court, and ordered a new trial in which the denied safeguard would have to be assured.

A rapid summary of the circumstances of the trial, as given by Mr. Justice Sutherland, is a necessary preliminary to the discussion of the legal issues. The defendants were nonresidents of Alabama, riding through the State in an open freight car on which were also several white boys and two white girls. A fight ensued in which the white boys were thrown off the train. Upon the complaint of these boys the train was stopped at a station down the line. There the girls accused the Negroes of assault. They were arrested and taken to Scottsboro, the county seat, where a large crowd had already gathered. Six days later indictments were returned. In six days more — the defendants, without families or friends in the State, having meanwhile been closely confined under military guard — the trial began.

"No one answered for the defendants or appeared to represent or defend them."[3] The trial judge stated that he had designated generally the entire local bar for the purpose of arraigning the defendants, "and then, of course, I anticipated them to continue to help them if no counsel appears."[4] A Tennessee lawyer, acting at the suggestion of unnamed "persons interested" but not in their employ, addressed the court; he stated that he had not had opportunity to prepare the case and was unfamiliar with local practice, but offered to appear with such local counsel as the court might appoint. An attorney expressed his willingness to serve under those conditions: "I will go ahead and help, do anything I can do." The Court: "All right."[5]

"And in this casual fashion," writes Mr. Justice Sutherland, "the matter of counsel in a capital case was disposed of."[6] "The defendants, young, ignorant, illiterate, surrounded by hostile sentiment, haled back and forth under guard of soldiers, charged with an atrocious crime regarded with especial horror in the community where they were to be tried, were thus put in peril of their lives within a few moments after counsel for the first time charged with any degree of responsibility began to represent them."[7] "We think the failure of the trial court to give them reasonable time and opportunity to secure counsel was a clear denial of due process ... we are of opinion that ... the necessity of counsel was so vital and imperative that the failure of the trial court to make an effective appointment of counsel was likewise a denial of due process within the meaning of the Fourteenth Amendment."[8]

From this conclusion only Mr. Justice Butler and Mr. Justice McReynolds dissented.

The stock offenses of American criminal law, it must be remembered — murder, arson, rape, theft — are violations of State law and prosecuted solely through the State courts. As a generality, these are matters wholly outside the concern of the federal judiciary. Understanding of this division of function as to criminal matters between the state and the nation is essential to an appreciation of the *Scottsboro* decision. It is no part of the Supreme Court's duty to protect errors inevitable to every administration of criminal justice. Erroneous applications of law, the admission of prejudicial evidence, disregard of the conventional niceties of procedure — all these infringements of common rights, if they are to be remedied in the highest courts of the States. The *Scottsboro* decision works no impairment of these fundamental assumptions of our constitutional system.

But upon the freedom of all State action the federal constitution imposes a broad limitation, applicable to criminal as well as to civil proceedings, to judicial as well as to legislative acts. This is accomplished by the Fourteenth Amendment, which provides that no State shall "deprive any person of life, liberty, or property without due process of law." The assertion of that limitation is a duty of the federal judiciary, and a right of defendants under the federal Constitution. In its application of this prohibition in the review of the conduct of a State criminal trial, the significance of the *Scottsboro* decision resides.

The words of the amendment are words of "convenient vagueness,"[9] definable only by the cumulative process of judicial inclusion and exclusion. In matters affecting property rights, and notably the regulation of economic enterprise, they have come to be the foundation of a large body of doctrine often interposing irksome barriers to restrictive legislation. Only last Term they served Mr. Justice Sutherland in the famous Oklahoma ice case[10] as a touchstone for the invalidity of a statute which authorized the State Corporation commission to deny to any person the right to enter the business of manufacturing ice in a community where in its opinion the existing facilities made such entrance injurious to the public.

Now, in the hands of the same Justice, they return to their more immediate purpose of protecting black men from oppressive and unequal treatment by whites.

In the illuminating phrase of Judge Learned Hand, due process "represents a mood rather than a command."[11] The mood of the Supreme Court in subjecting the conduct of State criminal trials to the measure of the Fourteenth Amendment has been insistently cautious. Properly so, for the amendment is not the basis of a uniform code of criminal procedure federally imposed. Alternative modes of arriving at truth are not — they must not be — forever frozen. There is room for growth and vitality, for adaptation to shifting necessities, for wide differences of reasonable convenience in method.

Thus it was long ago settled that proceedings in State criminal actions need not be initiated by indictment of a grand jury, albeit the common law so required. Trial by a jury of twelve is not imperative in state courts. The administration of local justice knows no such rigid federal fetters. Here, too, freedom must be left for new, perhaps improved, methods "in the insulated chambers afforded by the several States."[12]

But — and this is of the essence — certain things are basic to the integrity of the judicial process. One of them is a proper tribunal, impartial and uncoerced.

In the memorable case of *Moore v. Dempsey,*[13] concerning, like the *Scottsboro* case, the trial of a Negro in a Southern community inflamed by racial hysteria, it was held that a court surrounded by a howling mob threatening vengeance if a conviction were not returned was no court at all, and the case was remanded for retrial under conditions more likely to conduce to the substantial ends of justice. Until the *Scottsboro* case, this decision stood virtually alone. Counsel for the Scottsboro defendants sought to bring their case within its authority. But the Court, instead of reviewing the circumstances of the trial and finding that in substance there was no trial because reason was barred, seized upon a different aspect of the case and enunciated another fundamental requisite of the judicial process.

Not only must there be a court free from coercion, but the accused must be furnished with means of presenting his defense. For this the assistance of counsel is essential. Time for investigation and for the production of evidence is imperative. Especially is this true in a capital case. The more heinous the charge the more important the safeguards which the experience of centuries has shown to be essential to the ascertainment of even fallible truth. Never is it more so than in a case of rape, turning heavily upon the testimony of the alleged victim and requiring to be defended largely by evidence of circumstance and character.

The *Scottsboro* case announces the doctrine that to every defendant must be assured the minimum conditions for an ordered and reasoned investigation of the charges against him — a proper and a heartening guarantee of fundamental law. The history of liberty, Mr. Justice Brandeis has reminded us, cannot be dissociated from the history of procedural observances. In no sense is the Supreme Court a general tribunal for the correction of criminal errors, such as the Court of Criminal Appeal in England. On a continent peopled by 120,000,000 that would be an impossible task; in a federal system it would be a function debilitating to the responsibility of State and local agencies. But the Court, though it will continue to act with hesitation, will not suffer, in its own scathing phrase, "judicial murder."[14] Here lies perhaps the deepest significance of the case.

Thus the judgment of the Court transcends the fate of the seven pitiful defendants concerned. It leaves the fate ultimately untouched. Upon the question of guilt or innocence it bears not even remotely. That question remains to be determined in normal course by the constituted tribunals of Alabama. The Supreme Court has declared only that the determination must be made with due observance of the decencies of civilized procedure.

Appendix D

"What Negro Newspapers of Georgia Say About Some Social Problems, 1933"

By Rollin Chambliss, A.B.; published in *Bulletin of the University of Georgia* 35, no. 2 (November 1934), Phelps-Stokes Fellowship Studies, no. 13

Communism

Communism has not made much headway among Negroes. That is obvious to anyone who reads Negro newspapers. And it is not that the Communists have made no effort to win Negro support, for, "taking advantage of the trying times during the past four years, they have redoubled their efforts to win converts to their cause. How many Negroes they have won it is difficult to estimate. If one lives in the shadow of Washington Park in Chicago, or Union Square in New York, one is likely to conclude that 'der Tag' is just around the corner. If however, the observer moves about other parts of the country, he is forced to conclude that Communism has not gained any real hold on most Negroes."[1]

The International Labor Defense, "hand-maiden of the Communist party,"[2] has made itself quite active in Negro affairs in the South during the past years. In the Scottsboro case this organization succeeded in driving the powerful N.A.A.C.P. from the field and taking over entirely the case for the defendants.

The success of the I.L.D. in the Scottsboro case, as well as in the Crawford case, has undoubtedly won many Negroes to its ranks, and it is possible that "membership of the I.L.D. will stretch into millions. The young Negro is not going to submit or condone injustice any longer. He is going to find a way to fight. He is going to line up with the organization that fights with brains and whatever else is necessary to win. Right now it appears that the I.L.D. is not short on either of these."[3]

The revival of the Ku Klux Klan in Alabama brought the editorial comment: "We have been opposed to the principles of Communism, because we think it as wicked as Klanism, in some respects; but if the Ku Klux Klan renews its unjust and inhuman practices against Negroes, we see no good reason why the Communist should not make heavy gains in securing new converts in the South."[4]

But the program of the Communist leads to a class rather than to a race struggle, and Negroes and poor whites cannot get together for any cause. The Negro may suffer more under the capitalist system than do white people of the lower class, but the Negro is far closer to white people of the higher class than to those of the lower. This is a condition for which the Communist program makes no provision in its appeal to the Negro. Nothing is more obvious, at least here in the South, and it is here that most Negroes still reside, than the fact that it is among the uneducated and poverty-stricken white people that race prejudice is strongest.

Negroes recognize full well that their cause is defended by the Communist only because it furnishes good material for propaganda. The race problem is only a small concern of the Communist; in this country it is an enigma peculiar to the Negro, and consequently his first interest. Even in particular cases where the Communist have aided the Negro, as in the Scottsboro case, it is recognized that "Scottsboro boys alive or Scottsboro boys dead are equally good propaganda."[5] And not propaganda for a racial adjustment, but for a class adjustment.

"While the Communist have acquainted other dis-advantaged people with the nature of the American race problem and perhaps orientated world public opinion towards the future development of that problem, yet their very connection with the Scottsboro case and their methods of procedure have greatly periled, if they have not utterly destroyed, the chances of the nine defendants for ever again knowing life and liberty."[6]

In a talk made at Livingston College, Salisbury, N.C., Congressman DePriest "next turned his attention to the Communists and attacked them furiously. He scored them for exploiting the Scottsboro case, while, however, admitting that they had done some good. Communism, he said, is a controversion of the fundamentals of American life and the principles of the Christian religion, in which the Negro is a strong believer."[7]

The attitude of the Negro is often militant, but he is not willing to go to the extreme often advocated by the Communist. "We seriously doubt that our connection with such radical organizations as the Communists, or I.L.D., will make conditions any better. When all our social, political, industrial, and other inter-racial problems are settled rightly, if they are ever fully settled, they must be adjusted by the conservative element of both groups. There are many men and women of high standing in the white race who are working unceasingly to improve our plight; and if we line up with them, we can secure better results than by affiliating with some irresponsible body displaying a red flag. We need courageous leadership, but let us use common sense."[8]

The fight between the I.L.D. and the N.A.A.C.P. is evidence of a feeling that exists. For while it may be, as William L. Patterson, Executive Secretary of the I.L.D., says, that the N.A.A.C.P. has interested itself only in the upper tenth and not in the mass of Negroes; and while it may be true, as Mr. Patterson also says, that "an analysis of the financial history of the N.A.A.C.P., quoting its own figures, will show that without authorization from any responsible source, it collected more than $7,000 for the Scottsboro defense, before the re-trial of Haywood Patterson, but that only $1,000 ever found its way to the accomplishment of such a purpose;"[9] yet the confidence of the great majority of Negroes in the N.A.A.C.P. is based on a long experience with this organization and is not easily shaken.

"Any intelligent individual who knows Dixie and has watched the I.L.D.'s scatter-brained tactics since entering the Scottsboro case knows it would be suicidal for the N.A.A.C.P. to support the I.L.D. program without reservations. The Association has conducted its legal cases without the ballyhoo of schoolboy threats and demands. It has spent its monies wisely and well, and in a way calculated to obtain the best returns. It is interested primarily in seeing justice done."[10]

The Communist send out through their news agencies a great deal of propaganda, some of which finds its way into Negro newspapers. Most of these papers use some of the news stories; but a great deal of the material sent out is consigned to the waste basket after a hasty perusal of its contents. The Negro wants no revolution, and he certainly has no intention of giving up his church. It is his understanding that Communism involves both.

Appendix E

"The Scottsboro Case: Opinions of Judge James E. Horton of the Alabama Circuit Court Granting a Motion for a New Trial in the Scottsboro Case on the Ground That the Conviction Was Against the Weight of the Evidence"

Published by the Scottsboro Defense Committee (January 1936), composed of representatives of the National Association for the Advancement of Colored People, the Methodist Federation for Social Service, the American Civil Liberties Union, the League for Industrial Democracy, the International Labor Defense, and the Church League for Industrial Democracy (Episcopal)

[Editor's note: Headings and some punctuation have been added in Judge Horton's opinion to make it more clearly readable.]

Judge Horton's Decision in the Scottsboro Case

The defendant in this case has been tried and convicted for the crime of rape with the death penalty inflicted. He is one of nine charged with a similar crime at the same time.

The case is now submitted for hearing on a motion of a new trial. As human life is at stake, not only of this defendant, but of eight others, the Court does and should approach a consideration of this motion with a feeling of deep responsibility, and shall endeavor to give it that thought and study it deserves.

Social order is based on law, and its perpetuity on its fair and impartial administration. Deliberate injustice is more fatal to the one who imposes than to the one on whom it is imposed. The victim may die quickly and his suffering cease, but the teachings of Christianity and the uniform lessons of all history illustrate without exception that its perpetrators not only pay the penalty themselves, but their children through endless generations. To those who deserve punishment who have outraged society and its laws — on such, an impartial justice inflicts the penalties for the violated laws of society, even to the tabling of life itself; but to those who are guiltless the law withholds its heavy hand.

The Court will decide this motion upon the sole consideration of what is its duty under the law. The court must be faithful in the exercise of the powers which it believes it possesses as it must be careful to abstain from the assumption of those and not within its proper sphere. It has endeavored with diligence to enlighten itself with the wisdom declared in the cases adjudged by the most pure and enlightened judges who have ornamented the Courts of its own state, as well as the distinguished jurists of this country and its Mother England. It has been unstinted in the study of the facts presented in the case at bar.

The law wisely recognizes the passions, prejudices and sympathies that such cases as these naturally arouse but sternly requires of its ministers freedom from such actuating impulses.

The Court will now proceed to consider this case on the law and evidence only making such observations and conclusions as may appear necessary to explain and illustrate the same.

There are a number of grounds for the motion. The Court has decided that no good purpose may be subserved in considering a number of these; without deciding whether these grounds are well based or not, the Court sees no need of their being considered. These omitted grounds are such as probably would not re-occur in another trial, and if they did they would certainly be under a different form. The vital ground of this motion, as the Court sees it, is whether or not the verdict of the jury is contrary to the evidence. Is there sufficient credible evidence upon which to base a verdict?

[The judge then cites the authorities for granting a new trial and for considering the evidence in doing so. They are omitted here as of interest only to lawyers but can be supplied on request.]

The Facts of the Alleged Crime

With the law so written, let us now turn to the facts of the case. The Court will of necessity consider in detail the evidence of the chief prosecutrix, Victoria Price, to determine if her evidence is reliable, or whether it is corroborated or contradicted by the other evidence in the case. In order to convict this defendant, Victoria Price must have sworn truly to the fact of her being raped. No matter how reliable the testimony of the defendant and his witnesses, unless the State can make out a case upon the whole evidence a conviction cannot stand.

The claim of the State is that this defendant raped Victoria Price; that is the charge. The circumstances under which the crime was claimed to have been committed appear as follows:

On March 25th, 1931, the prosecutrix, Victoria Price, and Ruby Bates, her companion, boarded a freight train at Chattanooga, Tennessee, for the purpose of going to Huntsville, Alabama. On the same train were seven white boys, and twelve negroes, who it appears participated or are charged with participating in the occurrences on such train. All were tramps or "hoboing" their way upon this same freight train.

About Stevenson, Alabama, a fight occurred between the negroes and the white boys and all the white boys, except one named Gilley, got off the train, or were thrown off the train, a short time after the train left Stevenson, Alabama. The distance from Stevenson to Paint Rock is thirty-eight miles. The train was travelling between twenty-five and thirty-five miles an hour. Some of the white boys who were thrown off the train returned to Stevenson, Alabama, and the operator telegraphed to Paint Rock, a place down the line, reporting the fight, causing a posse and a large crowd to form at Paint Rock, and they surrounded the train as it pulled into Paint Rock and took therefrom nine negroes, one of whom was this defendant, the two white girls, and their white companion, Gilley. The negroes were arrested and lodged in the Scottsboro jail as well as the two women and the seven white boys. The two women were forthwith carried to the office of a physician in Scottsboro, arriving there from one hour to one and one-half hours after they claimed a rape was committed upon them, and were examined by two skilled physicians, Drs. Bridges and Lynch. It was while the train was travelling between Stevenson and Paint Rock between shortly after noon and three o'clock that the alleged rape was committed.

There have been two trials of this case; one at Scottsboro and the other the recent trial at Decatur. The trial at Scottsboro was reversed by the Supreme Court of the United States, who declared the defendants did not have the assistance of counsel. The motion in this case is upon the result of the trial at Decatur. The evidence at the trial at Decatur was vastly more extensive and differed in many important respects from the evidence at Scottsboro.

Much of the evidence at Scottsboro was introduced at the trial at Decatur, and the Court will consider the entire evidence submitted as it may appear necessary in considering this motion. The Court shall endeavor in quoting the evidence to quote it substantially, and sometimes literally as given, only stating its substance when requisite to make its meaning clear.

As stated, the State relies on the evidence of the prosecutrix, Victoria Price, as to the fact of the crime itself, necessarily claiming that her relation is true. The defense insists that her evidence is a fabrication — fabricated for the purpose of saving herself from a prosecution for vagrancy or some other charge.

The Court will therefore first set out the substantial facts testified to by Victoria Price and test it as the law requires as to its reliability or probability, and as to whether it is contradicted by the other evidence.

The Testimony of Victoria Price

She states that on March 25, 1931, she was on a freight train travelling through Jackson County from Stevenson to Paint Rock; that Ruby Bates was with her on the train; that she had boarded the train at Chattanooga, Tennessee; that when she first boarded the train she got on an oil-tank car. That at Stevenson, she and Ruby Bates walked down the train and got on a gondola car — a car without a top. That the car was filled with chert, lacking about one and one-half to two feet of being full; that the chert was sharp, broken rock with jagged ends.

That as the train proceeded from Stevenson seven white boys got in the car with them and that they all sat down in one end of the car, next to a box car; that in about five or ten minutes twelve colored boys jumped from the box car into the gondola, jumping over their heads. That the defendant was one of them. That the colored boys had seven knives and two pistols; that they engaged in a fight with the white boys, ejecting all from the train except one, Orville Gilley; that this white boy stayed on the gondola, remained there and was still on the car when Paint Rock was reached, and saw the whole thing that thereafter occurred on this car.

That one of the negroes picked her up by the legs and held her over the gondola, and said he was going to throw her off; that she was pulled back in the car and one of the negroes hit her on the side of the head with a pistol causing her head to bleed; that the negroes then pulled off the overalls she was wearing and tore her step-ins apart. That they then threw her down on the chert and with some of the negroes holding her legs and with a knife at her throat, six negroes raped her, one of whom was the defendant; that she lay there for almost an hour on that jagged rock, with the negroes lying on top of her, some of whom were pretty heavy; that the last one finished just five minutes before reaching Paint Rock and that her overalls had just been pulled on when the train stopped at Paint Rock with the posse surrounding it.

That she got up and climbed over the side of the gondola and as she alighted she became unconscious for a while, and that she didn't remember anything until she came to herself in a grocery store and she was then taken to Scottsboro, as the evidence shows, in an automobile and that in about an hour or an hour and one-half Dr. Bridges and Dr. Lynch made an examination of her person.

This witness further testified that she was wet on her private parts; that each negro wetted her more and more; that her private parts were bleeding; that the blood was on her clothes; that her coat had semen on it; that when Dr. Bridges and Dr. Lynch examined her they saw her coat and it was spattered over with semen; that her dresses had blood and semen on them; that she had them on when the doctors examined her; that the coat was cleaned and that she washed the dresses in the jail before the trial. The evidence further shown without dispute that all nine negroes were taken in charge by the officers and carried to the Scottsboro jail.

The Judge's Comment on Victoria Price's Story

With seven boys present at the beginning of this trouble, with one seeing the entire affair, with some fifty or sixty persons meeting them at Paint Rock and taking the women, the white boy Gilley, and the nine negroes in charge, with two physicians examining the women within one to one and one-half hours, according to the tendency of all the evidence, after the occurrence of the alleged rape, and with the acts charged committed in broad daylight, we should expect from all this cloud of witnesses or from the mute but telling physical condition of the women or their clothes some one fact in corroboration of this story.

Let us consider the rich field from which such corroboration may be gleaned.

1. Seven boys on the gondola at the beginning of the fight, and Orville Gilley, the white boy, who remained on the train, and who saw the whole performance.

2. The wound inflicted on the side of Victoria Price's head by the butt-end of a pistol from which the blood did flow.

3. The lacerated and bleeding back of the body, a part of which was stripped of clothing and lay on jagged sharp rock, which body two physicians carefully examined for injuries shortly after the occurrence.

4. Semen in the vagina and its drying and starchy appearance in the pubic hair and surrounding parts.

5. Two doctors who could testify that they saw her coat all spattered over with semen; who could testify to the blood and semen on her clothes, and to the bleeding vagina.

6. Two doctors who could testify to the wretched condition of the women, their wild eyes, dilated pupils, fast breathing, and rapid pulse.

7. The semen which must have eventually appeared with increasing evidence on the pants of the rapists as each wallowed in its spreading ooze. The prosecutrix testified semen was being emitted by her rapists, and common sense tells us six discharges is a considerable quantity.

8. Live spermatozoa, the active principle of semen, would be expected in the vagina of the female from so recent discharges.

9. The washing before the first trial by Victoria Price of the very clothes which she claimed were stained with semen and blood.

The Court will now present the evidence which will show: that none of the seven white boys, or Orville Gilley, who remained on the train, were put on the stand, except Lester Carter;

that neither Dr. Bridges nor Dr. Lynch saw the wound inflicted on the head by the pistol, the lacerated or bleeding back which lay on jagged rocks;

that the semen they found in the vagina of Victoria Price was of small amount;

that the spermatozoa were non-motile, or dead;

that there was no blood flowing from the vagina;

that they did not testify as to seeing the semen all spattered over the coat, or blood and semen on the clothes; any torn garments or clothes;

that these doctors testified that when brought to the office that day neither woman was hysterical or nervous about it at all, and that their respiration and pulse were normal;

and that the prosecutrix washed the clothes evidencing the blood and semen.

Taking up these points in order, what does the record show? None of the seven white boys were put on the stand, except Lester Carter, and he contradicted her.

Next, was Victoria Price hit in the head with a pistol?

For this we must turn to Dr. Bridges. It was agreed in open court that Dr. Lynch who in company with Dr. Bridges at Scottsboro examined the two girls, would testify in all substantial particulars as Dr. Bridges, and Dr. Lynch was excused with that understanding when Dr. Bridges completed his examination. In considering Dr. Bridges' testimony we observe he was a witness placed on the stand by the State. His intelligence, his fair testimony, his honesty, and his high professional attainments impressed the Court and certainly all that heard him. He was frank and unevasive in his answers. The Court's opinion is that he should be given full faith and credit. In further considering his testimony it was shown that he was examining these women with the most particular care to find evidence of a rape upon them, and that the women were accusing the negroes, and were being required to cooperate and exhibit whatever indicated they had been abused.

Returning to the pistol lick on the head, the doctor testifies: "I did not sew up any wound on this girl's head; I did not see any blood on her scalp. I don't remember my attention being called to any blood on the scalp." And this was the blow that the woman claimed helped force her into submission.

Next, was she thrown and abused, as she states she was, upon the chert—the sharp, jagged rock?

Dr. Bridges states as to physical hurts:—we found some small scratches on the back part of the wrist; she had some blue places in the small of the back, low down in the soft part, three or four bruises about like the joint of your thumb, small as a pecan, and then on the shoulders a blue place about the same size—and we put them on the table, and an examination showed no lacerations.

The evidence of other witnesses as well as the prosecutrix will show that the women had travelled from Huntsville (Alabama) to Chattanooga (Tennessee) and were on the way back. There is other evidence tending to show they had spent the night in a hobo dive; that they were having intercourse with men shortly before that time. These few blue spots and this scratch would be the natural consequence of such living; vastly greater physical signs would have been expected from the forcible intercourse of six men under such circumstances.

Victoria Price testified that as the negroes had repeated intercourse with her she became wetter and wetter around her private parts; that they finished just as they entered Paint Rock, and that she was taken in an automobile immediately to the doctors' office. There Dr. Bridges and Dr. Lynch, as has been shown, examined her. They looked for semen around her private parts; they found on the inside of her thighs some dirty places. The dirty places were hardly dry, and were infiltrated with dust, about what one would get from riding trains. It was dark dirt or dust. While the doctor did not know what this drying fluid was, his opinion was that it was semen, but whatever it was, it was covered with heavy dust and dirt.

He next examined the vagina to see whether or not any semen was in the vagina. In order to do this he takes a cotton map and with the aid of a speculum and headlight inserts the cotton map into the woman's vagina and swabs around the cervix, which is the mouth of uterus or womb. He extracts from this vagina the substance adhering to the cotton after he has swabbed around the cervix, and places this substance under the microscope. He examines this substance to see if spermatozoa are to be found, and what is the condition of the spermatozoa. Upon the examination under the microscope he finds that there are spermatozoa in the vagina. This spermatozoa he ascertains to be non-motile. He says to the best of his judgment that non-motile means the spermatozoa were dead.

For any fluid escaping from the vagina to become infiltrated with coal dust and dirt, this dirt under the circumstances in this case must have gradually sifted upon the drying fluid, and necessarily a considerable period of time would be required for such an infiltration. The fresh semen emitted by so many negroes would have had a tendency rather to wash off any dirty places around the vagina, and it must have remained there for a considerable period for it to become thus infiltrated with dust and coal dust. Around the cervix the spermatozoa live under the most favorable conditions. While the life of the spermatozoa may be variable, still it appears from the evidence that in such a place as this it would have taken at least several hours for the spermatozoa to have become non-motile or dead.

When we consider, as the facts hereafter detailed will show, that this woman had slept side by side with a man the night before in Chattanooga, and had intercourse at Huntsville with Tiller on the night before she went to Chattanooga; when we further take into consideration that the semen being emitted, if her testimony were true, was covering the area surrounding the private parts, the conclusion becomes clearer and clearer that this woman was not forced into intercourse with all of these negroes upon that train, but that her condition was clearly due to the intercourse that she had on the nights previous to this time.

Was there any evidence of semen on the clothes of any of the negroes?

In the case of State vs. Cowing, 99 Minn. 123, 9 Am. & En. Ann. cases, 566, the Court said the physicians who testified stated that the semen would have remained on the clothes and could have been found after the expiration of several days. And this is probably a well known fact. Though these negroes were arrested just after the alleged acts, and though their clothes and pants were examined or looked over by the officers, not a witness testified as to seeing any semen or even any wet or damp spots on their clothes.

What of the coat of the woman spattered with semen, and the blood and semen on the clothes and the bleeding vagina?

Dr. Bridges says he did not see any blood coming from her vagina; that Mrs. Price had on step-ins, but did not state that they were torn or had blood or semen on them. Not a word from this doctor of the blood and semen on the dress; not a word of the semen all spattered over the coat. And this was a doctor so conscientious and thorough in his examination as to make the woman undress and to examine with care every part of her body; a doctor who in his search for semen went to the extent of swabbing out the vagina and of examining its contents under the microscope.

What of the physical appearance of these two women when the doctors saw them?

Dr. Bridges says that when these two women were brought to his office neither was hysterical, or nervous about it at all. He noticed nothing unusual about their respiration and their pulse was normal.

Such a normal physical condition is not the natural accompaniment or result of so horrible an experience, especially when the woman testified she fainted from the injuries she had received.

The fact that the women were unchaste might tend to mitigate the marked effect upon their sensibilities, but such hardness would also lessen the probability of either of them fainting. If the faint was feigned then her credibility must suffer from such feigned actions. And this witness' anger and protest when the doctors insisted on an examination of her person was not compatible with the depression of spirit likely to be caused by the treatment she said she had received.

Lastly, before leaving Dr. Bridges let us quote his summation of all that he observed:

> Q. In other words the best you can say about the whole case is that both of these women showed they had had intercourse?
> A. Yes, sir.

Is there corroboration in this? We think not, especially as the evidence points strongly to Victoria Price having intercourse with one Tiller on several occasions just before leaving Huntsville. That she slept in a hobo jungle in Chattanooga, side by side with a man. The dead spermatozoa and the dry dirty spots would be expected from those earlier acts.

Victoria Price testified that she washed her clothes, which were stained with semen and blood, before even the trial at Scottsboro.

The Supreme Court of Minnesota in the case of State vs. Cowing, 99 Minn. 123, 9 Am. cases, 566, in setting aside a conviction of rape laid great stress and largely based its action upon such conduct of the prosecuting witness.

This Court said:

> While not without some corroboration, the testimony of prosecutrix is aided most largely by that of her sister; but that corroboration is to be weighed in connection with the fact that she and her sister, by washing the skirt, which if her testimony were true, would probably have borne evidence of blood and semen, effectually destroyed the best possible evidence under the circumstances.

Court's Comment on Other Witnesses

Is there any other corroboration? There was a large crowd at Paint Rock when the freight arrived there. While they differed in many details as to the make-up of the train and the exact car from which the different persons were taken, all of which is apparently unimportant, all agreed upon the main fact that the nine negroes, the two women, and the white boy were all taken from the train. This undisputed fact constitutes about the whole extent of their evidence except a statement by Ruby Bates that she had been raped, which experience the said Ruby Bates now repudiates.

This statement by Ruby Bates appears to have been made under the following circumstances. There were three witnesses who testified to having seen the women at Paint Rock. One of the witnesses first saw them after they had gotten off the car and were both standing. Another witness did not see them for some time, he having first rounded up all the negroes. The third witness saw them as they were getting off the car. He states they first started to run toward the engine and as they approached a crowd of men they turned and ran back in the opposite direction, and met a part of the posse who stopped them. Mr. Hill, the station agent, then came up to the women and asked them if the negroes had bothered them. Thereupon Ruby Bates stated that they had been raped. The facts appearing that the women instead of seeking the protection of the white men they saw were at first frightened, and the question propounded was in itself suggestive of an answer. Mr. Hill also states that the negroes were in a coal car; that he saw the heads of the negroes over the top of the car and they were trying to climb over the sides, were pulling themselves up, trying to get off. This clearly indicates that the negroes were not in the car filled with chert, as the prosecutrix claims.

For any other corroboration in the evidence we now return to the freight train as it passes along the track just after leaving Stevenson. The witness, Lee Adams, at a point about one quarter of a mile from the train, sees a fight between a number of white and colored boys; this is an admitted fact in the case.

The evidence of Ory Dobbins was admitted in corroboration of Victoria Price. When his evidence is studied it is found it does not corroborate her, or if so very slightly. The good faith of this witness need not be the slightest questioned, only the lack of correspondence of his testimony with hers. He stated that he lived three miles from Stevenson near the railroad as it ran toward Scottsboro; that as he walked to his barn he saw a freight train; that as it passed his house he saw a white woman sitting on the side of a gondola and a negro put his arm around her waist and throw her back in the car; that he saw the car as it passed; that it was in his line of vision for a few feet, pointing out a door in the court room as the distance. His reason for stating it was a woman is as follows:

> Q. You know it was a woman don't you?
> A. She had on women's clothes.
> COURT: She had on women's clothes?
> Q. What kind of clothes, overalls?
> A. No sir, dress.

The very basis of this statement that she was a woman because she had on a dress does not apply to the women in this case, who were dressed in overalls.

He said it was in a coal car and there were five or six people in the car. Victoria Price says when they took hold of her that it occurred in a car almost filled with chert, and there were fifteen people in the car. The witness Dobbins said the gondola was between two box cars, while the evidence shows the gondola in which the woman was, was the fifth of a string of eight gondolas.

The witness further stated that the car upon which he saw this occurrence was back toward the caboose. On the other hand the official make-up of the train shows the freight train consisted of forty cars; that the women were in the eleventh or twelfth car from the engine and there were twenty-eight or twenty-nine cars between this car and the caboose. In view of the fact that it was along this vicinity that the fight was occurring between the negroes and the white boys, and as his reason for saying it was a woman was on account of the dress, and all agree these women had on overalls, this can at its best be only slight corroboration.

The Court's Comment on the State's Case

This is the State's evidence. It corroborates Victoria Price slightly, if at all, and her evidence is so contradictory to the evidence of the doctors who examined her that it has been impossible for the Court to reconcile their evidence with hers.

Next, was the evidence of Victoria Price reasonable or probable? Were the facts stated reasonable? This is one of the tests the law applies.

Rape is a crime usually committed in secrecy. A secluded place or a place where one ordinarily would not be observed is the natural selection for the scene of such a crime. The time and place and stage of this alleged act are such to make one wonder and question did such an act occur under such circumstances. The day is a sunshiny day the latter part in March; the time of day is shortly after the noon hour. The place is upon a gondola or car without a top. This gondola according to the evidence of Mr. Turner, the conductor, was filled to within six inches to twelve or fourteen inches of the top with chert, and according to Victoria Price up to one and one-half feet or two feet of the top. The whole performance necessarily being in plain view of any one observing the train as it passed. Open gondolas on each side.

On top of this chert twelve negroes rape two white women; they undress them while they are standing up on this chert; the prosecuting witness is then thrown down and with one negro continuously kneeling over her with a knife at her throat, and one or more holding her legs, six negroes successively have intercourse with her on top of that chert; as one arises off of her person, another lies down upon her; those not engaged are standing or sitting around; this continues without intermission although that freight train travels for some forty miles through the heart of Jackson County; through Fackler, Hollywood, Scottsboro, Larkinsville, Lin Rock, and Woodville, slowing up at several of these places until it is halted at Paint Rock; Gilley, a white boy, pulled back on the train by the negroes, and sitting off, according to Victoria Price, in one end of the gondola, a witness to the whole scene; yet he stays on the train, and he does not attempt to get off of the car at any of the places where it slows up to call for help; he does not go back to the caboose to report to the conductor or to the engineer in the engine, although no compulsion is being exercised upon him, and instead of there being any threat of danger to him from the negroes, they themselves have pulled him back on the train to prevent his being injured from jumping off the train after it had increased its speed; and in the end by a fortuitous circumstance just before the train pulls into Paint Rock, the rapists cease and just in the nick of time the overalls are drawn up and fastened and the women appear clothed as the posse sight them. **The natural inclination of the mind is to doubt and to seek further search.**

Her manner of testifying and demeanor on the stand militate against her. Her testimony was contradictory, often evasive, and time and again she refused to answer pertinent questions. The gravity of the offense and the importance of her testimony demanded candor and sincerity. In addition to this the proof tends strongly to show that she knowingly testified falsely in many material aspects of the case. All this requires the more careful scrutiny of her evidence.

The Court has heretofore devoted itself particularly to the State's evidence; this evidence fails to corroborate Victoria Price in those physical facts; the condition of the woman raped necessarily speaking more powerfully than any witness can speak who did not view the performance itself.

Comment on the Credibility of Victoria Price

The Court will next consider her credibility, and in doing so, some of the evidence offered for the defendant will also come in for consideration. In considering any evidence for the defendant which would tend to show that Victoria Price swore falsely the Court will exclude the evidence of witnesses for the defendant, who themselves appear unworthy of credit, unless the facts and circumstances so strongly corroborate that evidence that it appears true.

Lester Carter was a witness for the defendant; he was one of the white boys ejected from the train below Stevenson. Whether or not he is entitled to entire credit is certainly a question of great doubt; but where the facts and circumstances corroborate him, and where the failure of the State to disprove his testimony with witnesses on hand to disprove it, the Court sees no reason to capriciously reject all he said.

Victoria Price denied she knew him until she arrived at Scottsboro. It became a question to be considered as to whether Lester Carter knew her at Huntsville and saw her committing adultery on several occasions with one Tiller just before leaving for Chattanooga, and returning on the freight the next day. The facts he testified to might easily account for the dead spermatozoa in her vagina. He says he met Victoria Price and Tiller in jail at Huntsville; that all three were inmates of the jail at the same time; that Ruby Bates visited

Tiller and Victoria Price while they were in jail, and he, Carter, met her at the jail; that after all had gotten out, and he had finished his sentence, he stayed in the home of Tiller and his wife, and he and Tiller would go out and be with these girls; that they all planned the Chattanooga trip together, and that just before the trip, or the night before, all four were engaged in adulterous intercourse.

Victoria Price stated on the stand that Tiller, the married man, was her boy friend and was in her home the night before she left for Chattanooga; that he had a right there, and he was corresponding with her. Tiller was in the State's witness-room then and identified by Lester Carter when he was brought out of the witness-room by the Court's order. Tiller, though there in court, was not put on the stand to deny what Carter said. There is no reason to doubt Carter was telling the truth then. Next, Carter said that when he and Ruby Bates and Victoria Price arrived in Chattanooga about eight-o'clock at night, all went to what is known as the "Hoboes Jungle," a place where tramps of all descriptions spent the night in the open. There are numerous witnesses who corroborate him in this statement; that they met the boy Gilley and all four slept side by side, he by the side of Ruby Bates, and Victoria Price by the side of Gilley.

Victoria Price said that she and Ruby Bates went to Chattanooga seeking work; that they went alone and spent the night at Mrs. Callie Brochie's, a friend of hers formerly living in Huntsville, but who had moved to Chattanooga. Was this true? The Chattanooga directory was introduced in evidence; residents of Chattanooga, both white and colored, took the stand stating that no such woman as Callie Brochie lived in Chattanooga and had not ever lived there so far as they knew. Though Victoria Price first made this statement more than two years ago at Scottsboro, no witness was offered either from Chattanooga or Huntsville showing any such woman had ever lived in either such place.

Victoria Price said the negroes jumped off a box-car over their heads into the gondola, where she, Ruby Bates and the seven white boys were riding, with seven knives and two pistols and engaged in a fight with the white boys. The conductor of the train who had the official make-up of the train stated there were eight gondola cars together on the train; that the women were in one of the middle cars, and that there were three gondola cars between the car in which they were riding and the nearest box car. Lester Carter stated that he was one of the seven boys engaged in the fight with the negroes; that he did not see a single knife or pistol in the hands of the negroes. And although these seven white boys were kept in jail at Scottsboro until after the first trial no one testified to any knife or pistol wounds on any of them.

Further there was evidence of trouble between Victoria Price and the white boys in the jail at Scottsboro because one or more of them refused to go on the witness-stand and testify as she did concerning the rape; that Victoria Price indicated that by so doing they would all get off lighter.

The defendant and five of the other negroes charged with participating in this crime at the same time went on the stand and denied any participation in the rape; denied that they knew anything about it, and denied that they saw any white women on the train. Four of them did state that they took part in the fight with the white boys which occurred on the train. Two of them testified that they knew nothing of the fight nor of the girls and were on an entirely different part of the train. Each of these two testified as to physical infirmities. One testified he was so diseased he could hardly walk, and he was examined at Scottsboro according to the evidence and was found to be diseased. The other testified that one eye was entirely out and that he could only see sufficiently out of the other to walk unattended. The physical condition of this prisoner indicates apparently great defect of vision. He testified, and the testimony so shows, that he was in the same condition at Scottsboro and at the time of the rape. He further testified that he was on an oil-tank near the rear of the train, about the seventh car from the rear; that he stayed on this oil-tank all the time and that he was taken from off of this oil-tank. The evidence of one of the trainmen tends to show that one of the negroes was taken off of an oil-tank toward the rear of the train. **This near-blind negro was among those whom Victoria Price testified was in the fight and in the party which raped her and Ruby Bates. The facts strongly contradict any such statement.**

Conclusion

History, sacred and profane, and the common experience of mankind teach us that women of the character shown in this case are prone for selfish reasons to make false accusations both of rape and of insult upon the slightest provocation, or even without provocation for ulterior purposes, these women are shown, by the great weight of the evidence, on this very day before Chattanooga, to have falsely accused two negroes of insulting them, and of almost precipitating a fight between one of the white boys they were in company with and these two negroes. This tendency on the part of the women shows that they are pre-disposed to make false accusations upon any occasion whereby their selfish ends may be gained

The Court will not pursue the evidence any further. As heretofore stated the law declares that a defendant should not be convicted without corroboration where the testimony of the prosecutrix bears on its face indications of unreliability of improbability and particularly when it is contradicted by other evidence.

The testimony of the prosecutrix in this case is not only uncorroborated, but it also bears on its face indications of improbability and is contradicted by other evidence, and in addition thereto the evidence greatly preponderates in favor of the defendant. It therefore becomes the duty of the Court under the law to grant the motion made in this case.

It is therefore ordered and adjudged by the Court that the motion be granted; that the verdict of the jury in this case and the judgment of the Court sentencing this defendant to death be and the same is hereby set aside and that a new trial be and the same is hereby ordered.

Appendix F

"Attorneys for Scottsboro Boys Issue Statement"

Published in *The Southern Worker*, February 1936

BIRMINGHAM, Ala. Jan. 26—
The following statement was issued today by Samuel S. Leibowitz and Clarence L. Watts, attorneys for the defendants in the Scottsboro case.

On hearing the news of the shooting of one of our clients, Ozie Powell, we hurried to Birmingham, arriving there at 12:30 p.m. We proceeded immediately to the Jefferson County Jail, where the defendants are held. Chief Deputy Charles E. McCombs informed us that the Governor had forbidden any interviews with the prisoners. Mr. McCombs called both Governor Bibb Graves and Walter K. McAdory, Chief of the State Highway Patrol, on long distance, but we were denied permission to see them. Mr. McCombs then called Judge W.W. Callahan at Decatur. Turning from the telephone he told us that Judge Callahan had said: He "didn't see what in hell he wanted to talk to those niggers about." And he hung up.

Mr. Liebowitz mentioned a writ of Habeas Corpus whereupon Mr. McCombs made another telephone call, after which we were granted permission to see the prisoners. They all stoutly denied that they knew that Ozie Powell had knives on the trip. In the Birmingham jail, Roy Wright was in a cell next to that of Clarence Norris in a tier apart from the other Negroes. As we talked to him the deputies remained within easy hearing distance.

Mr. Leibowitz had no note paper on which to record Wright's statement, but one of the deputies handed him an official bail bond form on the back of which Mr. Leibowitz recorded the statements made by Wright in the presence of Mr. Watts. He asked Roy Wright to tell what the real trouble was between the Negroes and the Morgan County officials. Wright said:

Wright's Statement

"We were taken to Decatur from Birmingham by train on the day we were to be arraigned before Judge Callahan. One of the deputies who took us to Decatur was a man named Waldrop (or Waldron). He said to us:

"When you get up to the court in Decatur, tell the judge that you don't want Mr. Watts or Mr. Leibowitz as your lawyers. The only thing these lawyers can do is to make more trouble for you, and if you say that you don't want them, the judge would then appoint a lawyer for you; and if that happens, then Mr. Knight will drop out of the case and it will not go so hard with you.'

"We went to court but we never told the judge anything of the kind. On the return trip they carried us by automobile. Waldron (or Waldrop) was driving the car with Sheriff Sandlin at his side. Haywood Patterson and Ozie Powell were in the car with me. Waldron (or Waldrop) said to us, after the car left Decatur:

"Why didn't you niggers do as I asked you? You're going to fool around and stay in jail five more years. All the lawyers want to do is to a make a big hurrah, to raise more money for their own benefit. Leibowitz has brought Mr. Watts into the case to draw more money. The lawyers will profit a million dollars on you and then drop you. I don't blame you for not doing as I said before today because you boys didn't realize what the lawyers had been up to, up to now. But you have been told two or three times what to do, and you wouldn't take my advice and from now on I will not have any more mercy on you than on a snake.'"

Satisfied with Lawyers

"I told the deputy that I was satisfied with my lawyers and that if Mr. Leibowitz cared to hire Mr. Watts, who is a southern lawyer, it was up to him."

At this point Mr. Leibowitz had no more space but he found a personal letter in his pocket and on the back of this he noted the rest of Wright's statement as accurately and as quickly as he could.

Wright proceeded as follows, telling of the trip in the course of which a deputy was cut and Powell was shot:

"On Friday, (Jan. 24) we left the jail in Decatur. In the automobile ahead were Olen Montgomery and two of the others. Then in the car with me were Clarence Norris to my right, and whose left hand was handcuffed to my right [editor's note: Ozie Powell's left hand was handcuffed to Clarence's right].

"There were three other boys in the automobile following us. At the wheel of our car was the high Sheriff of Decatur and beside him was the deputy who was cut. After a while this deputy said, 'Waldron has been talking to you; if you had done what he wanted, you-all would have been tried and let off with a light sentence — not more than ten years.'

Sheriff Speaks Menacingly

"The High Sheriff said, 'I told you niggers that you wouldn't get a trial and I'll bet ten to one that you'll not be tried in ten years. If I had my way I'd drive all these lawyers out of town.' Ozie said, 'Oh, ______, I'd rather have those lawyers than any I've ever seen,' and turned to me. He said 'damn what they're talking about.'

"The fellow that got cut was sort of turned around in his seat with his back to the window and his left-hand nearest to Powell. He slapped Ozie and Ozie got out his knife and slashed at him." (He indicated with a gesture how Powell had cut the deputy). "As he leaned forward to slash the deputy he pulled Clarence with him because Clarence was handcuffed to Ozie Powell. Clarence yanked Ozie back and I said:

"Sit down and give up that knife.'

"With that Ozie dropped the knife to the floor of the car. The High Sheriff started blowing his siren and put his foot on the brake and stopped the car. We all threw our hands up as the car stopped. The High Sheriff got out of the car on the left hand side and walked toward the front of the car. Then as though he had changed his mind he started back. He pulled out his gun and pulled open the door a little bit and pointed the gun inside the car and said:

"I'm going to get rid of all you sons of bitches.'

"He fired one shot at Powell. Soon afterwards Mr. Knight and Mr. Lawson rolled up on the other side."

Threatens Boys

"After he fired the shot (this was before Knight and Lawson came up) the High Sheriff put the gun up to my head. I begged him not to shoot us. I begged for my life and so did Clarence. He said: 'Who was it got you the knife — it must have been those bastards of lawyers, Leibowitz or Watts, that smuggled the knife into the courthouse.'

"I said: 'No, Powell got the knife on a little roof over the cell which we could reach if we climbed up on the door of the cells. He found a magazine there too.'

"The High Sheriff then said: 'I know who you got that knife from. You got it from that boy from the drug store that used to come to the jail.'

"I said, 'No, he did not.'

"He pointed the gun in my face and said, 'God damn you, nigger, do you mean to dispute my word? He brought it in.'

"And I said, 'All right, he brought it in.' I was afraid he'd kill me if I didn't agree with him.

"The deputy who was cut was then taken out of the car and the High Sheriff driving the car with the High Sheriff from Cullman [Alabama] beside him started off with us to Birmingham. On the way the Cullman Sheriff said to the Decatur Sheriff that if it had been him he wouldn't have quit shooting until he'd killed us all, and the Decatur Sheriff said:

"We'll Run Him Out"

"I'd like to take a shot at those God-damned lawyers. That man Leibowitz is a God-damned son of a bitch, and Watts has been associating with him and now he thinks he is so smart, we'll run him out too.'

"We then arrived in Birmingham.

"I forgot to tell you that the High Sheriff from Decatur said that Ozie had switched the knife to him and then he said that I had a knife. I had no knife at anytime in that automobile."

When Roy Wright told us about the alleged statement of Waldrop's about changing lawyers, Mr. Leibowitz called the three deputies in the corridor to come to Wright's cell and he asked Roy Wright to repeat in their presence what he had told us. He did so.

We then asked Norris, who during the interview with Wright had listened to the conversation, if he had heard all that had been said. He said he had, and that everything Roy had told us was the truth.

Among other things Roy told us, but on which we did not make notes, were the following: That at no time did he have a knife, nor that at any time did Sheriff Sandlin grapple with him. He also told us about Clarence Norris who was in the middle, pulling back Ozie Powell with all his strength, with the handcuffs which attached them when Ozie leaned forward and cut the deputy sheriff. There are two deep cuts on Norris' right wrist where apparently the handcuffs cut him when he pulled Powell back.

Visits Wounded Lad

We then left the jail and obtained from the chief deputy a pass to visit Ozie Powell in the Hillman Hospital. No one was with us in the room with Powell.

When we got to the head of Powell's bed, he was lying on his left side with his eyes closed and breathing in a labored way. Mr. Leibowitz called him by name. Ozie moaned. Again Mr. Leibowitz said, "Ozie."

The boy slowly opened his eyes and turned his face slightly upward. Mr. Leibowitz asked:

"Do you know who this is?"

He said, "That's Mr. Chamlee," and rambled unintelligibly. Mr. Leibowitz then asked:

"What happened, Ozie?" And he said:

"The boys put me out in front and I almost got killed."

After some more questions which were not answered, Mr. Leibowitz asked him where he got the knife, and he said:

"Bought in Decatur," or possibly, "Boy in Decatur."

Thereupon Mr. Leibowitz said: "This boy is in no condition to make a coherent statement."

Powell was in severe pain. His eyes were glassy, so we turned and left. We were in the room about two or three minutes.

Appendix G

"Report of Neuro-psychiatric Examination"

Completed January 10, 1937

NAME . . . . NORRIS, Clarence.
ADDRESS . . . . Jefferson County Jail, Birmingham, Alabama.
PRESENT AGE—24 . . . .
AGE AT TIME OF INCARCERATION—18 . . . .
EXAMINER . . . . G.C. BRANCHE, M.D.

Family History

Paternal grandfather and grandmother dead; cause of death unknown. Maternal grandfather and grandmother dead; cause of death unknown. Does not know of any history of insanity or nervous "spells" on either side. All aunts are dead; cause of death unknown. One aunt suffered with heart trouble "but I don't know if that caused her death; I never seen any of them."

Mother: Living and well as far as he knows. Says that she came to see him about a year ago. "She was in good health when I left home."

Father: Father died at the age of 47 in 1926; cause of death unknown.

Siblings: Six sisters and two brothers living and all in good health except one sister who is subject to "sick spells" which she has had since the age of seven, she is now fourteen. "She doesn't have anything to say and acts funny at times." One sister and one brother died in infancy; cause of death unknown.

Personal History

Informant born in 1912 at Warm Springs, Georgia. Birth and early development normal so far as could be ascertained from subject. He does not know when he began walking and talking or when dentition took place. Was bottle-fed. States that he was bow-legged (suggesting rickets) in his early childhood. Sucked his tongue in early life and at times does so now when he is not thinking. Did not suck his thumb or bite nails. Talked in his sleep a great deal and talks in his sleep at times now. Has always been subject to night dreams which he states are more frequent since he has been in trouble. There is no history of fainting spells, convulsions or nervous breakdown. He got along well with his mother and father; was obedient. Preferred to play with girls. "The reason I didn't want to play with boys was 'cause I was always afraid I would get hurt; didn't like rough games. I like to see them but I don't like to play them."

Illnesses & Accidents in Early Childhood & Young Adult Life: Admits having had the measles and whooping cough but no other childhood diseases. No serious illness up to the present time. No surgical operation, gastro-intestinal or cardio-vascular disease. Fell and sprained his left knee joint when he was about twelve or thirteen years of age.

Schooling: "I started to school when I was about seven or eight years old. I went to the second grade. I went to school in Warm Springs, Ga., for awhile and Molina, Ga. My father stopped me from school and started me to working. I like school whilst going but I wasn't interested in learning anything. I wasn't interested in learning I wanted to play. I made no effort to go back to school after my father died."

Industrial & Social History: began working when about thirteen years old. Worked on a farm with his father and mother — they rented the farm. He next worked with a construction gang in Atlanta, Ga., earning $18.00 to $20.00 per week. "I left home in Molina, Ga., in the early teens because I just got to the place where I didn't like my father. He was telling me things that was right and I figured he was wrong and now since I have growed up I realize he was right. I stayed away from him for about two years before going back. I remained home about three months then I went back to Atlanta and stayed a little more than six years. I left Atlanta in 1931 and went to Chattanooga, hoboed, and stayed one day. I was hoboing my way to Memphis looking for a job. I had a job in Atlanta working at the slaughter pen and they cut me off and I started pushing the mail wagons at the terminal station and they cut me off from there and that is when I started hoboing." States that this is the first time he has been incarcerated.

Habits: Smokes cigarettes and will take a "sociable drink" but does not care for whiskey.

Psycho-sexual Life: Does not recall when he had his first heterosexual experience; never cared much for a "regular girl." Masturbated until sixteen years of age. He is single although he states that he was engaged at one time but did not think the girl would make him a "good wife."

Informant's statement concerning physical complaints: "I have indigestion all the time since being in this place. I'm hungry because the food they cook I can't eat it, especially in the morning. I have lost weight, never feel good because of no fresh air or sunshine."

Personal Examination

General Observation: General appearance is that of an individual 5' 11" tall and weighing about 160 pounds, fairly well developed and nourished. Physical habitus corresponds to the asthenic type.

Head: Normal in size and contour.

Eyes, Ears, Nose, Throat & Mouth: Essentially negative.

Neck: Negative.

Chest: round and symmetrical. Bilateral expansion free and equal. Lungs negative to palpation, percussion and auscultation.

Heart: Negative to inspection, auscultation and palpation. Blood pressure 125/80.

Spine: Negative.

Abdomen: Negative.

Genito-urinary system: Negative. No history of venereal disease or scar.

Neurological Examination

Station and gait: Normal.

Cranial Nerves: Pupils are round, regular in outline and respond normally to light and in accommodation. Ophthalmoscopy negative. There is no evidence of any cranial nerve involvement.

Coordination: Coordination test well performed.

Reflexes: Deep and superficial reflexes negative thruout.

Sensory Apparatus: All modalities of sensation are present and intact.

Motor Apparatus: Musculature negative.

Vegetative Nervous System: There is no apparent involvement of the vegetative nervous system.

Mental Examination

He is neat in his general appearance and presents a rather even temperament; was composed thruout the examination.

Speech: There are no mannerism of speech or attitude. Stream of talk is relevant and coherent; answers questions promptly and to the point. Offers the normal amount of spontaneous speech.

Mood: "I feel sad and depressed most of the time."

Content of Thought: "I just think and worry about being in this place. I feel and hope that I will get out. Sometimes I feel down-hearted and sometimes I feel a little up-lifted. Can't say just how long I've been in this Birmingham jail. I stayed here nine months and then they taken me to Kilby Prison in 1933, down there to the death house. They brought me back here in June 1935. I've spent the biggest part of my time in Kilby Prison — three years and nine months. I was given the *death sentence* at the Morgan County Court and then they held it up. These people here treat you a whole lot better than those down in the Kilby Prison. My health would be better I think if I could get some fresh air and not be in solitary confinement. They have kept us in solitary confinement since they brought us here from Decatur last January. I'm in jail about something I've never done and know nothing about." No actual delusions or hallucinations elicited.

Memory: Quite well preserved thruout.

Calculation and General Knowledge: While meager, is within the limits of his educational and contact advantages and environment. He names the three largest cities as New York, Chicago and Philadelphia. Special calculation tests were not done because of educational handicaps.

Insight and Judgment: Insight, reasoning and judgment appear to be within normal limits considering his general experience and contact advantages.

Summary

Informant has been confined approximately six years having been given a death sentence on one occasion and in solitary confinement for approximately one year. Seems that these factors have influenced his personality make-up to a large extent. He feels that he has been unjustly retained but still has hopes of being released. As to his plans for the future in case he is released, he states, "I would like to go back to school and learn something. If I had realized the need for education when my mother was trying to school me I'd be more than I am now."

Impression

1- No Neuropsychiatric disability.
2- Mental Age 12, I.Q., 85 plus.

Notes

Chapter 1

1. There would be a meeting between the farm owner and the tenant sharecropper. This meeting, called a "settlement," occurred at the end of each year's harvest.

> The specific percentages and details of the contract vary with the men involved, but always the percentage is so high that the cropper remains poor. It involves an owner-servant relationship that the whites [tenants] inwardly resist and they tend to move on, even when they must sign up with another man for equivalent terms: hope for better luck, somehow. At the same time, the initiative for shifting [moving to another farm] often lay with an employer, and not with the people who actually engaged in the practice. O.B. Stevens, the agricultural commissioner of Georgia, put the balance of interest in perspective: "Sometimes you have a tenant on the place, and he finds he can do a little better somewhere else, and he moves off and goes to the next place. Sometimes, the landlord finds that he can get a better tenant than the one he has. He lets this fellow go and gets the other fellow. They are continually moving around from place to place." Thus at times workers were forced off a plantation by an employer eager to import hands more to his liking; but in other cases the separate histories of blacks and whites converged (that is, their common desire to distance themselves from a recent slave past.)
>
> In 1912 agricultural economist Lewis Gray noted that the plantation system of worker subordination relied on both more and less than a whip or pistol: "the present methods of coercion are more subtle and more difficult of conviction." For blacks in debt to their employer and "so densely ignorant that they know little of their rights under the law … It is easy to impose … a practically coerced service. The mere moral prestige of the white and the fear of physical violence, rarely employed, but always a potentiality, are often sufficient." For Ned Cobb, "a practically coerced service" came in the form of signing a "note" with an employer; for others, a merchant's refusal to accept a debt payment at all, with the disclaimer that "he did not care whether his good customers paid [up] or not, just so they kept on paying." Despite the formal end to debt peonage in 1911 (as a result of the Supreme Court's Alonzo Bailey decision), black and white croppers throughout the South continued to believe that they risked bodily harm to themselves if they left a place over the objections of its owner; and they were right. (Jacqueline Jones, *The Dispossessed* [New York: Basic Books 1992], pp. 112, 113.)

2. Henri Florette, *Black Migration: 1900–1920* (New York: Anchor Books/Doubleday, 1975).

3. Mr. William Lacy of Birmingham, Alabama, stated to the author that a cure for any cold ailment can be derived from burning the hoofs of a hog in a pan until there is burnt crust. You then boil the crust into a syrup-like potion which, when cooled, you drink.

Chapter 2

1. The definition and etymology of the term *hobo* is somewhat vague. *The Random House Dictionary of the English Language* (unabridged edition, 1966) states: "1—a tramp or vagrant. 2—a migratory worker." *A Dictionary of Slang: An Unconventional English*, edited by Paul Beale, states: "1—A tramp; esp. in C.20, one who works. Orig. (—1891, Flynt), U.S.; Anglicized Ca. 1905. The v. has not 'caught on' in England, Americanism rarely heard in English prisons (Tempest, 1950). 2—Hence, a useless fellow; military; from ca. 1910. 3—In NZ and Aus., in Post WW I days, it is often applied to a rough and ready fellow. The Etym. remains a puzzle; See esp. Irwin, who quotes a tramp's c.20 distinction: 'Bums, loafs and sits. Tramps loafs and walks. But a Hobo moves and walks, and he's clean." *The New Dictionary of American Slang*, edited by Robert L. Chapman, states: "N. Fr. late 1800's A person who wanders from place to place, typically by riding on freight trains, and who may occasionally work but more often cadgers sustenance. The Hobo is sometimes distinguished from bums and tramps by the fact the he works [origin unknown; perhaps fr. the call 'Ho Boy,' used on late 19th century western railroads by mail carriers, then altered and transferred to vagrants; perhaps putative 'Hoe-Boy,' a migrant farm worker in the west, who became a Hobo after the harvest season]."

2. Kenneth Allsop, *Hard Travellin': The Hobo and His History* (New York: New American Library, 1967), pp. 283–86.

3. Ibid.

4. Ibid.

5. Ibid.

6. Ibid.

7. Ibid.

Chapter 3

1. Chicago Defender, November 14, 1931, p. 3.

2. Ibid., p. 1.

3. *Chicago Defender*, April 18, 1931, p. 3.

4. *New York Times*, March 26, 1931, p. 21.

5. *Chicago Defender*, April 11, 1931, p. 4.

6. Scottsboro Defense Committee [Fact Sheet], 1936, p. 11.

7. *New York Times*, April 11, 1931, p. 40.

8. *New York Daily Worker*, April 13, 14, 15, 1931.

9. *Phylon*, 28 (1967), pp. 267–87; *New York Times*, April 24, 1931.

10. *Phylon*, 28 (1967), pp. 278–79; *New York Daily Worker*, April 25, 1931.

11. *Harper's Magazine* 164 (December 1931), p.64.

12. *Powell v. State of Alabama*, 237 U.S. 50 (19'2). See Appendix C for Felix Frankfurter's analysis of Supreme Court decision.

13. *Chicago Defender*, May 2, 1931, pp. 1–2.

14. *Chicago Defender*, May 9, 1931, p. 1.
15. *Chicago Defender*, June 20, 1931, p. 1.
16. *New York Times*, June 21, 1931, sec.3, p. 5.
17. *New York Times*, May 24, 1931, sec.2, p. 2.
18. *New York Times*, July 4, 1931, p. 16.
19. *Birmingham Post*, May 3, 1933.
20. *New York Times*, July 1, 1931, p. 9.
21. *New York Times*, July 8, 1931, p. 9.
22. *New York Times*, July 12, 1931, p. 9.
23. *Harper's Magazine*, December 1931, pp. 62–72.
24. Papers of the International Labor Defense Case, *Scottsboro Case* (folder c53), Clarence Norris #000080.

Chapter 4

1. Papers of the International Labor Defense, *Scottsboro Case* (folder c53), Clarence Norris #000088.
2. *Birmingham News*, April 29, 1933.
3. "Benjamin Davis Report," Papers of the International Labor Defense Box 4, #000240-241, April 1934.
4. "Report on Interview with Scottsboro Boys in Birmingham, Alabama, by Benjamin J. Davis," May 13, 1933.
5. To put someone in "the dozens" is to verbally degrade him or a family member. This is done in a rhyming manner. The one who can respond to another's rhyming with more imaginative rhymes is the winner.
6. Haywood Patterson and Earl Conrad, *Scottsboro Boy* (New York: Doubleday, 1950), pp. 216–17.
7. Ibid., pp. 232–34.
8. *Birmingham News*, July 20, 1948.

Chapter 5

1. Testimony given to author by a prison guard, fall 1970.
2. Alabama Department of Archives and History.
3. *New York Times*, March 8, 1933.
4. Kelly Covin, *Hear That Train Blow* (New York: Delacorte Press, 1971, p. 219).
5. Blaine Owen, "Scottsboro Country," *New Masses*, Papers of the International Labor Defense, Box 12, #000829, February 4, 1936.
6. Papers of the International Labor Defense, Box 4, #000263, May 17, 1933.
7. Papers of the International Labor Defense, January 5, 1932, Box 4, #000216.
8. *New York Times*, March 31, 1993.
9. *New York Times*, March 8, 1993.
10. *Afro-American*, April 10, 1933.
11. *State of Alabama (Morgan County) vs. Clarence Norris*, pp. 2, 52–56, December 1, 1933.
12. Ibid., pp. 137, 139–43.
13. *New York Times*, April 7, 1933.
14. Alabama Circuit Court, *The Scottsboro Case: Opinions of Judge James E. Horton* (reprinted by the Scottsboro Defense Committee, January 1936), pp. 7–26.

15. Ibid.
16. Ibid.
17. Ibid. For full text, see Appendix E.
18. Ruby Bates, *World Telegram*, May 3, 1933.

Chapter 6

1. *Daily Worker*, September 15, 1933.
2. NAACP Papers, *Scottsboro Case*, 1931–1950, Reel 9, #00079; Conrad, 1950, p.304.
3. Charles Spurgeon Johnson, *Statistical Atlas of Southern Counties, Listing and Analysis of Socio-Economic Indices of 1,104 Southern Counties* (Chapel Hill: University of North Carolina Press, 1941), p. 53; Dan T. Carter, *Scottsboro: A Tragedy of the American South* (Baton Rouge: Louisiana State University Press, 1979), p. 123.
4. *Pittsburgh Courier*, April 22, 1933.
5. *Chattanooga Daily News*, May 1, 1933.
6. *Jackson City Sentinel*, March 23, 1933.
7. Ibid.
8. "Scottsboro: The Shame of America," Scottsboro Defense Committee, February 1926, p. 18.
9. Ibid, p. 18.
10. *New York Times*, January 21, 1936.
11. *New York Times*, January 26, 1936.
12. *Scottsboro Defense Committee*, February 1936, p. 21.
13. Ibid.
14. *Montgomery Advertiser*, January 26, 1936.
15. *Montgomery Advertiser*, January 25, 1936.
16. *Birmingham News*, August 22, 1938.
17. Papers of the National Association for the Advancement of Colored People, Reel #15, Part 6, #0843, the *Scottsboro Case*, February 3, 1936.
18. Ibid. # 0840.
19. Carleton Beals, "Scottsboro Interview," *The Nation* 142, no. 3684, February 12, 1936, p. 178.
20. Ibid., p. 179.

Chapter 7

1. All documents found in the *Papers of the National Association for the Advancement of Colored People* and the *Papers of the International Labor Defense.*

Chapter 8

1. *New York Times*, October 19, 1976.
2. *Washington Post*, October 13, 1976.
3. Ibid.
4. *The Crisis*, November 1976, p. 311.
5. *New York Times*, October 9, 1976.

Chapter 9

1. Rhonda Cook, "Back to Hard Labor," *Atlanta Journal— Atlanta Constitutional*, August 20, 1995, p. D4.
2. Ibid.
3. Ibid.
4. Ibid.

Appendix C

1. *Powell v. Alabama*, 287 U.S. 45 (1932).
2. Id. at 50.
3. Id. at 53.
4. Ibid.
5. Id. at 56.
6. Ibid.
7. Id. at 57–58.
8. Id. at 71.
9. Hough, "Due Process of Law-Today," 32 Harv. L. Rev. 218 (1919).
10. *New State Ice Co. v. Liebmann*, 285 U.S. 262 (1932).
11. *Daniel Reeves, Inc. v. Anderson*, 43 F. 2d 679, 682 (2d Cir. 1930).
12. *Truax v. Corrigan*, 257 U.S. 312, 344 (1921) (Holmes, J., dissenting).
13. 261 U.S. 86 (1923).
14. 287 U.S. at 72.

Appendix D

1. Rayford W. Logan, *Atlanta World*, July 5, 1933.
2. Frank Marshall Davis, *Atlanta World*, July 9, 1933.
3. Editorial, *Atlanta World*, March 12, 1933.
4. Editorial, *Savannah Journal*, May 10, 1933.
5. Editorial, *Atlanta World*, June 25, 1933.
6. William Pickens, A.N.P., *Atlanta World*, May 23, 1933.
7. *Atlanta World*, June 5, 1933.
8. Editorial, *Savannah Journal*, September 6, 1933.
9. *Atlanta World*, July 9, 1933.
10. Editorial, Ibid., June 25, 1933.

Index